THE KU KLUX KLAN IN MINNESOTA

THE KU KLUX KLAN IN MINNESOTA

ELIZABETH DORSEY HATLE

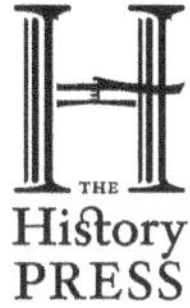

Published by The History Press
Charleston, SC 29403
www.historypress.net

Cover image taken by Kevin Bradford Hatle, with special thanks to the Freeborn County Historical Society in Albert Lea, Minnesota.

First published 2013

Manufactured in the United States

ISBN 978.1.62619.189.1

Library of Congress CIP data applied for.

To Kevin Bradford Hatle.
Love now and forever.

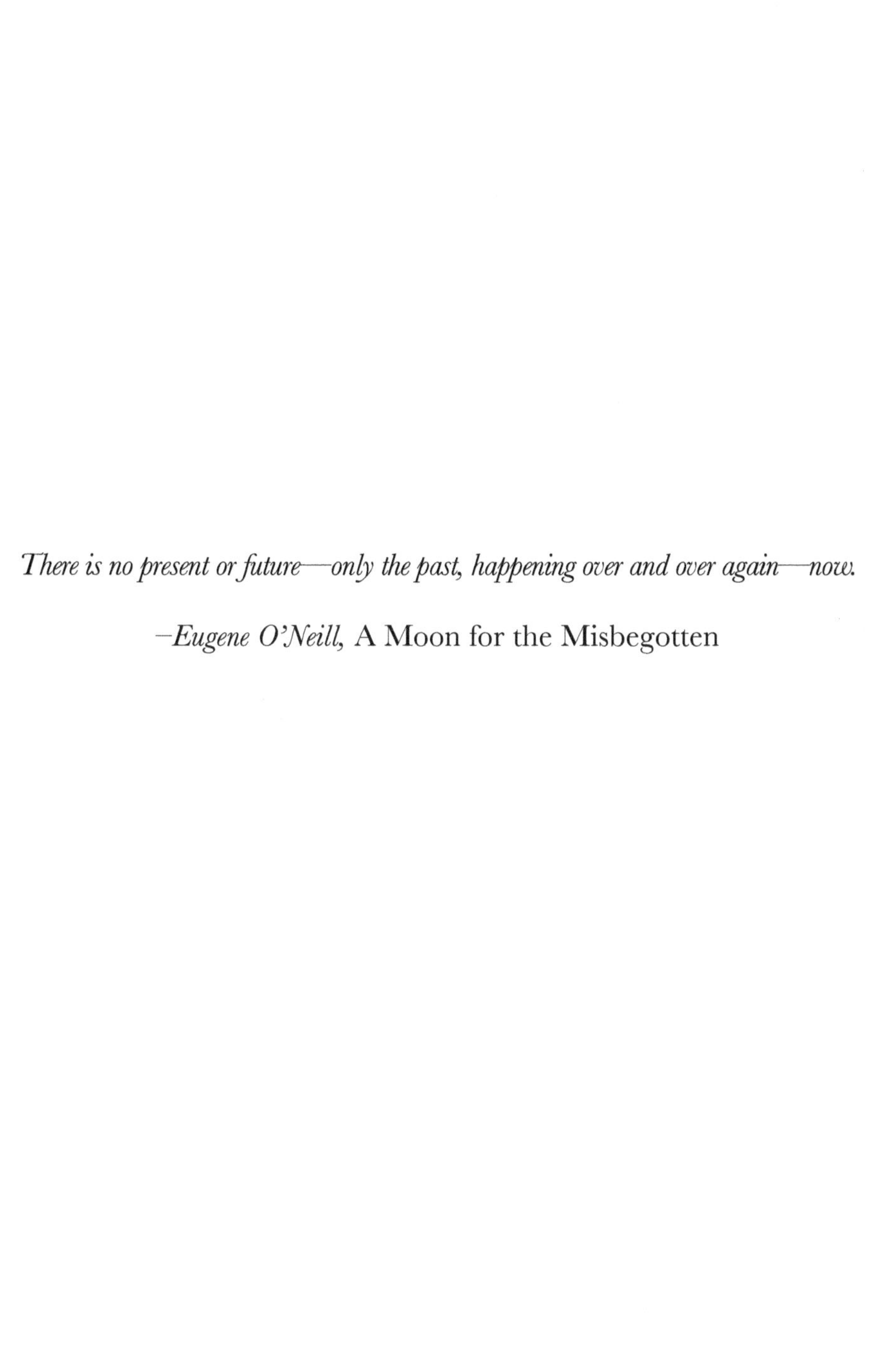

There is no present or future—only the past, happening over and over again—now.

—Eugene O'Neill, A Moon for the Misbegotten

Contents

Acknowledgements

County historical societies are invaluable resources that collect and preserve information that you cannot find elsewhere. I cannot sufficiently thank the people who work at Minnesota County historical societies for the help they provided me in writing this book. I would also like to thank just some of the people who helped me: Matthew Anderson, Vicky Anderson, Carol Blackburn, Kathleen Blee, Maria Brandt, Nancy Breems, David E. Crawford, Steve Granger, Dr. Daniel Harden, Rodney Hatle, Brendan Henehan, Professor David Horowitz, Spencer Howard, Professor Richard Hudelson, Anne Kaplan, Jan Louwagie, James Marushin, Professor Rory McVeigh, Debbie Miller, Professor Leonard Moore, Barbara Nelson, Mark Piehl, Linda Rau, Joli Shamblott, Kathryn Short, Jackie Sveikovsky, Toby Thompson, Eckard Toy, Lenny Tvedten, Jon Willard, Professor Mary Wingerd and Hannah Zabriskie, as well as anyone else I may have forgotten to list. I cannot thank everyone enough for the insight, patience and help you provided me while writing this. Two others who I'm grateful to have in my life are our two sons, Andrew Dorsey Hatle and Matthew Dorsey Hatle. Your father and I are extremely proud of you two and of the wonderful men you're growing up to be.

Introduction

The overt whiteness of Minnesota in the 1920s makes the Ku Klux Klan finding a home in the state incomprehensible to residents today. Selective amnesia does not erase the Ku Klux Klan's presence in Minnesota. The history of the Ku Klux Klan in Minnesota is like working a jigsaw puzzle, with each piece telling us something about the whole picture, enabling us to see additional relationships that Minnesota Klan members had with others in the state. In 1920, Minnesota was lacking in racial diversity, and African Americans constituted not even 1 percent of the state's population, with the Republican Party dominating Minnesota state politics at the time. In Minnesota, there was a lack of understanding between immigrants and nonimmigrants, Protestants and Catholics, agricultural and urban issues and industrialists and emerging labor leaders. The "weaknesses" that the Ku Klux Klan exploited in Minnesota during the 1920s were divisions along ethnic, religious, labor and class lines.

Minnesota was fertile ground for Klan organizers by 1920. During the 1920s, Minnesota's second-largest city, Duluth, had an active Ku Klux Klan chapter, and a second look is needed regarding the Duluth lynchings to examine more closely who else may have been involved and whether there was a cover-up afterward. Minnesota's governor during the 1920s, Theodore Christianson, had open correspondence with a Ku Klux Klan leader. There is strong evidence of state officeholders being Klansmen. A National American Legion vice-commander and Minnesota's longest elected state auditor preserved his KKK membership card in his personal papers. Also, the American Legion had within it a discriminatory white's-only group. There were financial "irregularities" with Klan involvement in the Minnesota Highway Department, as well as the suspicious deaths of prominent Minnesotans—one a judge who had his oath of office administered to him by a Duluth Klan member.

The majority of men who joined the Klan in the 1920s were trying to preserve the values of an older, simpler and less urban nation that had already all but vanished. For the most part, politics had been the domain of white men whose personal and business affairs allowed them alone to deal with the affairs of their communities. Being a "true patriot" was an honor the Ku Klux Klan used frequently to validate their actions. The 1920s Ku Klux Klan expected and urged its followers into a path of blind acceptance, carefully protecting their own interests and those of their class at the expense of others who also called Minnesota home. Saying that it's all in the past—let's just forget about it—just gives us another hood to wear. The only way to make concrete changes in society is to talk openly and honestly about how we treated one another in the past.

Klan involvement in Minnesota life and politics occurred throughout the state. There was not a county in Minnesota that wasn't affected by Klan activities. The Minnesota Ku Klux Klan was politically motivated in its actions and its ambitions. The 1920s Klan used the dynamics of right-wing mobilization to keep power at any cost. When the 1920s Ku Klux Klan lost popularity and members toward the end of the decade, Minnesota was one of the last states in the Midwest to give up on the Klan. Members of the Minnesota KKK did not physically leave Minnesota after the Klan's decline, and neither did their mindset. Closer examination of what occurred in Minnesota is long overdue regarding the Ku Klux Klan and the damage it did to communities here, even destroying some individuals' lives in the process. Compared to other states, why did it take so long for Minnesota to give up on the Klan?

CHAPTER 1

World War I and Its Effects on Minnesota Residents

In October 1917, the first possible indication of the Ku Klux Klan being in Minnesota may have been in Lester Prairie, Minnesota. William Esse testified to the chief of police of Duluth to an event that occurred in Lester Prairie at the Klatts Hotel. Several men and possibly some Lester Prairie police officers were involved, including Dr. E.A. Daggett. This group of men organized themselves before going over to the Klatts Hotel wearing masks. The Klatts Hotel may have been a place where vice-related events were taking place, thus the reason for the attack, according to the newspaper. William Esse stated that he ran early from the attack when gunshots were fired. "Then I went to bed, and the next morning, Mr. Lentz, who is the policeman at Lester Prairie and with whom I lived, told me that they had cleaned out the Klatts the night before and said I had better keep quiet about the affair."

The German-born Klatt family was severely "mauled," and rotten eggs were thrown at them; the local newspaper reported that it seemed to be a well-planned plot, as all the electric lights of the village were extinguished just as the assault began. Hugo Klatt was viciously attacked and beaten, and his brother, Max, was roughly handled. His sisters were struck with rotten eggs, and hotel windows were broken with stones. Hugo had noticed a gang of men gathering a short distance from the hotel at 11:00 p.m. just as he was about to close up. He approached the men and said that he was viciously attacked. His brothers and sisters heard his pleas for help and rushed to his aid in their nightclothes. The Klatts testified to there being white cloth masks over the heads of their assailants.[1]

The state tried to prosecute those involved but did not receive any help from the community. One local newspaper noted:

> *The press had set the Klatts before the people as a family who had bought liberty bonds, subscribed to the Red Cross and talking loyalty. Nobody ever heard of such a thing here. The Klatts did not buy liberty bonds, they did not subscribe to the Red Cross and their talk of loyalty has never been heard, nothing of this kind is true about them as far as local conditions are concerned. On the contrary some of the members of the family have lived in this country for thirty-five years and have not even taken out citizenship papers. They are all alien enemies except Max, the oldest boy, who is a citizen.*

None of this was true. Both Hugo and Max Klatt registered for World War I when the United States entered the war.[2]

Swan Johan Turnblad, whose home is now the American Swedish Institute in Minneapolis, came to the United States from Sweden. Turnblad had left Sweden when he was eight years old, obtaining all his education and work experience in the United States, thus making Turnblad more American than Swedish. The *Svenska Amerikanska Posten* was a Swedish newspaper for which Turnblad originally started working as a business manager, later becoming the newspaper's owner, resulting in great personal wealth. Turnblad was a strong supporter of Governor J.A.A. Burnquist, a fellow Swede. Burnquist was the son of Swedish immigrants and had been born in Iowa. In 1918, when Minnesotans went to the polls to elect a governor, the incumbent governor, J.A.A Burnquist, was challenged by former congressman Charles Lindbergh.

Two major issues disrupted the 1918 election: Americanism and World War I. Turnblad's paper consistently questioned Lindbergh's American loyalties. Lindbergh was Swedish-born and had emigrated with his parents. Compared to Lindbergh, Burnquist was loyal, patriotic and American, according to the newspaper. Lindbergh argued that the war was not about making the world safe for democracy but rather was a way for special interests to make money. Lindbergh also had become involved with the Nonpartisan League. The *Posten* was severe in its criticisms of the Nonpartisan League and attacked Lindbergh, accusing the league of having close contacts with Industrial Workers of the World (IWW) members and socialists. Burnquist won the governor's elections with 54 percent of the vote versus Lindbergh's 41 percent. Lindbergh had his strongest support in Minnesota counties that were dominated by immigrants or native-born citizens with immigrant parents.

On July 25, 1917, ten thousand spectators came to New Ulm to hear speeches that opposed sending American troops to Europe. New Ulm had been settled by German immigrants four years before Minnesota became a state. William Pfaender, president of the Turner Settlement Society of Cincinnati, returned to Chicago, which quickly resulted in the purchase of land in New Ulm. The Turner Settlement Association (or Society) was founded with a socialistic purpose that promoted a socialism that concentrated on the rights and freedoms of the individual. William Pfaender's brother, Karl Pfaender, lived in London, where William Pfaender met Karl Marx and Friedrich Engels. Karl Pfaender belonged to a number of communist organizations.[3]

The Turners, a leading social force in New Ulm, helped lead the rally in New Ulm protesting America's involvement in the World War I. None of the rally organizers attempted to mask the general unpopularity of the draft or of sending draftees overseas during the rally. It was a peaceful rally, and all the speakers expressed loyalty and pledged to defend the nation from aggression or invasion. The mayor of New Ulm, Minnesota, Dr. L.A. Fritsche warned against draft resistance and counseled the audience to obey the draft law. Dr. Fritsche also urged the large audience to work for legislation to limit overseas service to volunteers. City Attorney Albert Pfaender, son of William Pfaender, also delivered a speech that day, along with Captain Albert Steinhauser, publisher of several German-language newspapers in Minnesota.

To agents of the Minnesota Commission of Public Safety, the rally in New Ulm that day was seen as treason, and speakers at the rally were called before the commission on August 1, 1917. It was recommended to Governor Burnquist that the mayor, the city/county attorney and the Brown County auditor be removed from office. These removals were justified on the grounds that the officials had been disloyal and un-American and had encouraged anti-draft sentiment. To ensure compliance elsewhere, the governor and the commission encouraged local communities to form monitoring councils—actually, community vigilante groups—to ban future rallies like the one in New Ulm. Governor Burnquist issued an executive order closing the state to anti-draft meetings. Judge John F. McGee of the Commission of Public Safety said to Albert Pfaender, "You're a traitor and ought to be stood up against a wall and shot."

The *Princeton Union* editor Robert C. Dunn wrote, "Is it any wonder, that there are those who regret the Sioux did not do a better job at New Ulm fifty-five years ago?" In a letter written to Mayor L.A. Fritsche by Dr. A.D. Hard from Marshall, Minnesota, Dr. Hard said, "I despise a traitor. It seems almost beyond belief that you, a man of education and good judgment should subscribe to the disgraceful ideas concerning upholding the honor and future welfare of this our grand old land of opportunities." Mayor L.A. Fritsche died on June 25, 1931, never fully recovering his previous reputation or professional medical standing within Minnesota. Dr. Fritsche was American-born, of immigrant German parents, and he is credited as one of the organizers of the Minnesota Farmer-Labor political movement.

Albert Pfaender of New Ulm was brought up for disbarment by the Minnesota Bar Association for his speech given at the "protest" meeting in New Ulm. Dr. Downs, Albert Pfaender's daughter, said that her father, having a family to support, decided to recant and formally apologized for his statements during World War I. Albert Pfaender was not disbarred. A legal article about Pfaender, written in 1999, revived the story of Pfaender's "disloyalty" without noting all the facts, according to Dr. Downs. The article referred to the remarks that Pfaender made at the protest meeting as disloyal and seditious, which was not the case, according to his daughter. Dr. Downs pointed out that at the end of Pfaender's speech in New Ulm, her father made a point of counseling men of draft age to register and accept induction when ordered to do so.

Princeton, Minnesota resident Christian Neumann was arrested for violation of the Espionage Act on May 16, 1919, by handing out antiwar literature in the city. Neumann was accused of distributing a pamphlet entitled *Shanghaied into War*. Christian was a veterinarian and was born in Germany in 1864. Dr. Neumann had relatives who lived in New Ulm, including his brother, Nicholas Neumann. Dr. Neumann was taken before United States commissioner Abbott of St. Paul the same day he was arrested, waived an examination and gave bonds to await the action of the next United States Grand Jury. In July 18, 1919, Chris Neumann was found guilty, notice of an appeal to the circuit court was given and a stay of forty-two days was granted.

There was a large array of witnesses for the prosecution, and practically the only witness for the defense was Dr. Neumann himself. Christian Neumann admitted giving away two copies of the booklet. The American Legion Post No. 216 in Princeton (William H. Walker, commanding) did not approve of what happened to Dr. Neumann, being released early, and made a public statement that Neumann got off because he was a man of wealth and influence. It was further suggested by American Legion Post No. 216 that the two trials were held away from any possible local bias and prejudice, and the since the second trial was held nearly a year after the signing of the armistice, by which time the feeling engendered by the war had subsided, there was some "leniency" granted to him.[4]

Another major dissident case from the state was *Gilbert v. the State of Minnesota*, after World War I. In 1920, Joseph Gilbert was convicted of violating a Minnesota statute making it unlawful to interfere with or discourage the enlistment of men in the military or naval service of the United States. Joseph Gilbert was charged with "speaking by Word of Mouth against Enlistment Unlawful." Gilbert was the manager of the organization department of the Nonpartisan League. The Nonpartisan League charged that Gilbert's trial was politically motivated and part of a larger conspiracy to destroy the league. *The Leader*, the Nonpartisan League's newspaper, published evidence that should have been admitted to the Gilbert trial, correspondence that showed that the prosecuting attorney in the Gilbert case, E.H. Nicholas, had helped to distribute an anti-league tract financed by Charles S. Patterson, a wholesale shoe dealer and municipal lighting contractor. Charles Patterson was also the editor behind the publication *On the Square*.

Lamberton, Minnesota, during World War I had become an armed camp within its city. People of English and Irish descent accused the German-Americans in the area of being un-American and unpatriotic. Germans were forced to "ride the rail" and kiss the flag in the Lamberton public square. Emil Steinhauser of Lamberton always carried a revolver, and the German class textbooks at the Lamberton high school were burned.[5] The *Westbrook Sentinel* in 1920 noted, "A few of the Westbrook ex-service men attended the American Legion celebration at Lamberton Saturday afternoon. They report that German appeared to be the predominating language on the streets and in places of business where there were gathered any number of people."

Martin Kuhar was Lamberton's baker, and he verbally denounced World War I and did not want America to be brought into it. A government agent came to Lamberton, and Martin Kuhar was jailed. At the end of the war, Kuhar was released with the help of a lawyer from New Ulm. His release was not the end of the anti-immigrant issue for Kuhar or the town of Lamberton.[6]

Lamberton newspaper editor W.E. Schei printed in his newspaper that conscientious objectors should have their citizenship rights removed. According to Schei, they had no right to ask and never should receive the privilege of helping to make the laws or select the men whose duty it is to enforce them for the government of the men who have offered their lives in defense of America.

Naturalization papers (citizenship documentation) were a major issue in Minnesota with World War I veterans, especially at the American Legion posts. Some Minnesota citizens, in particular those of German ancestry, gave up their naturalization papers in order not to fight in

World War I. Minnesota newspapers would out those who gave up their naturalization papers by publishing their names. The American Legion publication for Legion posts in northern Minnesota was proud of itself for publishing the names of the slackers from the area in that section of the state. The American Legion publication went on to state that those who find the people whose names were on the list should notify their nearest post of the American Legion.[7]

Dr. J.J. Eklund of Duluth, Minnesota, was shot three times in the head by John Magnuson, who committed suicide after killing the doctor. Dr. Eklund was the head of the draft board in Duluth in 1918. A.C. Weiss, a good friend of Eklund's and a member of the Minnesota Commission of Public Safety, used his influence to have Dr. Eklund appointed examiner on the draft board. Magnuson's half-brother, Andrew Erickson of Superior, Wisconsin, denied the rumor that Magnuson was a draft evader; John Magnuson did have a World War I draft registration card, but he had never been called. Duluth police were confused as to why Magnuson would have made a medical appointment and then become so violently insane during his appointment that he murdered Dr. Eklund. Local newspapers reported that Dr. Eklund was well known as one of the leading Republicans in Minnesota.[8]

The Federal Alien Registration Act of 1918 led to Governor J.A.A Burnquist's creation of the Commission of Public Safety. The registration act required all aliens to register, to declare their holdings and to explain to the state why they had not become citizens. A bill was introduced to the Minnesota House and Senate on March 31, 1917, that called for an appropriation of $2 million to fund a Commission of Public Safety. The Minnesota Commission of Public Safety was completely free from legislative or judicial oversight. The commission soon gained a reputation for repressing German-Americans, pacifists and radicals, including members of unions, the Nonpartisan League and the Industrial Workers of the World. The Minnesota Commission of Public Safety was composed of seven men who were vested with virtually unlimited authority during the duration of World War I.

Members of the Commission of Public Safety seemed to view the commission as an opportunity to control the social fabric of Minnesota. The commission's operations were shrouded in secrecy at every level, the commission being well aware that few of its political activities could bear public scrutiny. The Minnesota Commission of Public Safety's operations built a "machinery to do things after the war."[9] The 1920 Minnesota election had resulted in a Republican landslide. "Even though Burnquist retained the power to reactivate the MCPS, he did not do so—despite the anti-Red hysteria gripping Minnesota and the nation in 1919. Protectors of the state's power structures were becoming acutely aware of the political vulnerability of the state administration and were relying on other agencies, some public, others private, to guard their vital interests."[10] The Minnesota Commission of Public Safety laid an excellent foundation for the 1920s Minnesota Klan to use and capitalize on; from here, it could recruit for its own purposes later.

When communists came into power in Russia, it had social and political effects on the United States. In this highly charged atmosphere, politicians could ill afford to appear supportive by not violently condemning communism. Minnesota senator Knute Nelson reasoned that government investigations were a legitimate attempt to "smoke out the disloyal elements and the Bolsheviki," and in a matter of time, government agents were paraded before the committee, vividly describing Nonpartisan League activities in misrepresentative detail. Nonpartisan League members' patriotism was questioned, their reputations were slandered and its leaders were judged guilty by association with socialists and communists. American business owners routinely denounced all unions as "communistic" and "subversive."

With the arrival of the automobile, there was a migration of the elite out of the urban area to what were to become the Twin Cities surrounding suburbs. By the 1920s, most of the families of the city founders had abandoned Minneapolis altogether. The wealthy Earle Brown, living on his "farm" outside the city, was just one example of this type of early "white flight." By removing themselves from the area where their employees worked and lived, it also removed social contact between employers and workers. The power, though, remained tightly in the hands of the leading families of Minneapolis, and this privileged group would use whatever it took to maintain that power politically and economically.

The Nonpartisan League was established by Arthur C. Townley in North Dakota in 1915. The league's goals were to give farmers a basic education in politics, the fundamentals of governmental economic policy and the value of organization in gaining redress of farmers' economic troubles. Since the league's program echoed prevailing criticism of the business practices that had plagued farmers for decades, it quickly won support from Minnesota farmers. The Nonpartisan League's platform called for state-owned terminal elevators, flour mills, packinghouses and storage plants; for state inspection of grain-grading houses and storage plants; for state inspection of grain-grading practices; for exemption of farm improvements from taxation; for state hail insurance; and for rural credit banks.

A report from Republican county attorney E.H. Nicholas was made to the members of the Minnesota Commission of Public Safety. Nicholas sent to the commission the pamphlets that Townley was circulating. In the report, the attorney told the Commission of Public Safety that "the doctrine and aim of the Nonpartisan League is to divide the American people upon class lines, to engender class hatred and suspicion and to disrupt the unity of our people, a procedure which, if pursued and its natural consequences accomplished, would soon bring American to the same pitiable condition in which Russia now finds itself." Nicholas believed that the Commission of Public Safety would find everything that he has sent to it about Townley "illuminating."[11]

When Townley was put on trial in Jackson County, Minnesota, he wanted to exercise his own constitutional right to present his own case to the jury, and Judge Ezra Dean denied him that, appointing him a lawyer of Dean's choosing. Judge Dean felt a need to defend his judgment in the Townley case and wrote a ten-page pamphlet, *Did Townley Have a Fair Trial?* Judge Dean characterized various reports on the case as being written by "several writers of known Socialist connections." He accused the *Madelia News* of being a Nonpartisan League paper, dishonest in its reporting of the trial. Judge Dean went on to say that the jury wasn't "hand picked." Throughout his pamphlet, the judge defended himself against the criticisms of the trial but never denied that these problems didn't take place. Judge Dean also used his pamphlet to criticize the Nonpartisan League. In his own words, the Republican judge stated that the trial wasn't just about Townley; it was about "putting the Non-Partisan League on trial too."[12]

Kuhar, Lamberton's baker, was not the only person newspaper editor W.E. Schei relentlessly attacked; there was also Albert Pfaender from New Ulm. Pfaender, who was placed under arrest in 1918 by the Minnesota Commission of Public Safety, brought libel charges against Schei. Pfaender wanted Schei to retract his public accusations and statements about him. For one example, Schei had written in his newspaper that Pfaender was "one of the most notorious characters of the disloyal type to be found in the state of Minnesota."[13] The charges of criminal libel were also based on comments made in Schei's newspaper, the *Lamberton Star*, which defended the actions of the American Legion post of Redwood Falls when the post passed resolutions against Pfaender. In March 1921, Schei was arrested several times but was released each time.

The warrant for his arrest came out of the "German capital" of Minnesota, New Ulm, according to Schei. He accused Pfaender of having connections in Lamberton—hence the hostility directed at Schei there. Schei wrote that he was the only one making it impossible for the "Hun belt of southern Minnesota, extending from New Ulm to Lamberton, [to] ever again to operate with any degree of success." The five libel suits that Pfaender brought against Schei were all thrown out. Besides the conflict between Schei and Pfaender, it was reported in the *Redwood Gazette* on September 13, 1922, that City Attorney Albert Pfaender was charged with striking Justice George Hogen. Justice Hogen said that the city attorney had hit him three times, once under the chin and twice in the back of the head. Mr. Hogen told the newspaper that "he could not understand Pfaender's actions in always being on the side of a certain bunch, and that he was going down, down, further all the time."[14]

Although a less militant and vicious view of poor Albert Pfaender than that from the editor of the *Lamberton Star*, the *Redwood Gazette*'s attitude wasn't any more favorable to Pfaender. Although not publishing anything that showed agreement with Schei, the *Redwood Gazette* made sure that every detail of the cases being thrown out was listed in its newspaper. "Thus the five cases have gone to pot and the great flash in the pan, which caused the sheriff's deputy to travel to and fro to Lamberton every day or so for a time, has resulted in nothing but an added expense to the taxpayers of Brown County." Pfaender's act of speaking out against World War I was not forgotten or forgiven in Redwood Falls. That same month, in September 1922, during the Schei/Pfaender conflict, a building in New Ulm was painted yellow; it was the new parish house for St. Mary's church. If a Klan chapter couldn't be started in New Ulm, it didn't stop Klan chapters from the surrounding counties from coming into Brown County and making things unpleasant.[15]

Events in New Ulm during the World War I "protest meeting," combined with the ethnic and religious population makeup of Brown County, made it difficult for the Ku Klux Klan to gain a foothold or set up a chapter in Brown County. There is but one Klan-related report in New Ulm's newspapers. The New Ulm newspapers also did not come out against the Klan. Possibly New Ulm's reactions toward Klan chapters being set up in counties right next to it was to keep its head down after what occurred to New Ulm during World War I. The *St. James Independent* of December 17, 1925, noted, "A Klan meeting is said to have been held in New Ulm one evening recently. There were but few present and it is intimated there is little hope of securing much of a membership here. It will be remembered that a year ago a small gathering was addressed by a representative of the Klan. There is but little Klan sentiment in New Ulm."

Klan language was used by newspaper editor Schei in the *Lamberton Star*, and the *Steinhauser Review* of New Ulm insinuated in 1922 that there were other "ultra-patriotic editors not a hundred miles distant from New Ulm" who are destined to "creep to the cross." The Ku Klux Klan may have been in western Minnesota as early as 1920. Editor Schei said that he was not responding to the call of "Kamerad," but other articles using Klan wordage are also seen in his newspaper. On September 2, 1920, the *Lamberton Star* noted, "Lamberton extends royal and cultured welcome to those of Questionable Americanism and sets forth not one effort to hold good Americans who are leaving the field for want of decent American atmosphere." Editor Schei went on in 1921 to report how he appreciated the power of "Kultur" in America in helping him in his defense against the attacks on him by Pfaender and the "sons of Herman monument in New Ulm." Schei and the *Star* eventually went bankrupt, and in 1923, the *Northern Light* began publishing in Lamberton as the town's new newspaper.

It wasn't just the Nonpartisan League that Schei railed against; he also went after the immigrants in the community relentlessly. As stated on the front page of his newspaper's banner in every issue, "America First. A good way to talk and there's no better way to live." Schei could not leave poor Martin Kuhar alone either. Kuhar was a regular front-page feature for Schei to use in his hatred of immigrants. Schei attacked the Lamberton community for buying bread from the bakery of "one Martin Kuhar...Russian German [though he was actually Austrian] and an alien enemy." Kuhar—who, according to Schei, was forced to spend seven weeks in the Ramsey County Jail for disloyal utterances during the late war—had every business house in Lamberton handling only Kuhar bread, and there is no other bread to be had in Lamberton, again according to Schei.

Schei was upset that an American World War I veteran, H.A. Tuttle, had attempted to open a bakery in Lamberton and no one would buy bread from him. Schei could not understand how the community could welcome back Kuhar let alone patronize his bakery due to his "activity against the interest of the United States during its war against Germany." Schei continued his relentless attacks against Kuhar in his newspaper. In 1922, the *Lamberton Star* reported, "Kuhar Citizenship Will Come Up in St. Paul Monday." Schei ridiculed Kuhar's application for naturalization, sarcastically calling Kuhar the "popular baker of Lamberton." Kuhar still did not possess the makings of a good American citizen, according to Schei.[16]

There is a man named H.A. Tuttle written about as a Klan organizer who came to speak to the *St. James Independent* editor. In the article, the St. James

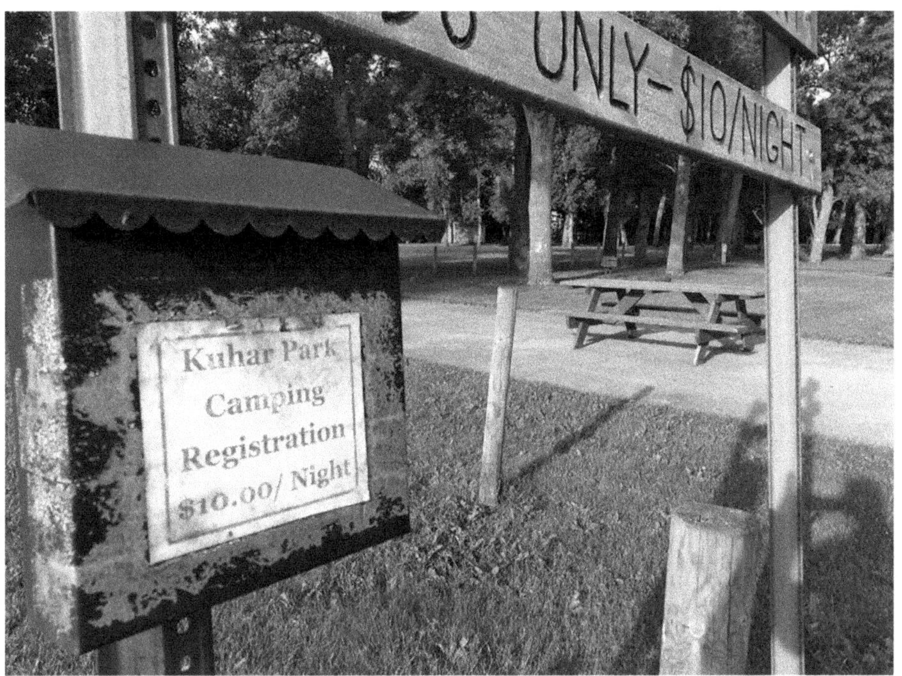

Kuhar Park. Named after Martin Kuhar in his honor by the citizens of Lamberton, Minnesota. *Courtesy of Jonathan Kuehl.*

editor gave Tuttle's initials and where he was from. Harvey A. Tuttle, born in 1897, has his residence on his death certificate as Albert Lea. Harvey Tuttle was single and a World War I veteran, and his parents were from Iowa. Tuttle died in 1970. He is most likely the Klan representative who spoke to the editor of the *St. James Independent*. St. James is not far from Lamberton. It is also likely that H.A. Tuttle was the same baker who was a veteran and tried to establish himself as a baker in Lamberton—the same Tuttle who was defeated by the "evil" Kuhar and his friends in 1920.[17]

In a September 9, 1926 article, "Ten Thousand at K.K.K. Picnic Here," the *Northfield Independent* reported that the Ku Klux Klan homecoming and picnic on Monday brought another tremendous crowd of people to Northfield. The picnic was held on the R.C. Hollis farm south of town, and the place was reported to have been covered with automobiles and people. Local Klansmen estimated that there were 4,500 people on the grounds in the afternoon and easily twice that many in the evening. The newspaper article lists a speaker from Duluth, Mrs. Mabel Crowley, as well as Pat Malone, who spoke in the evening on "The Mexican Situation as It Is

Today." The entertainment was the typical Klan fare: band concert, athletic contests and fireworks. There was parade later that evening in Northfield—the downtown section and Division Street south. The "homecoming" was arranged entirely by the local Klan.[18]

R.C. Hollis celebrated his sixteenth wedding anniversary with his wife in 1928; the couple also announced that they would be moving from the Northfield area that year to Iowa. In R.C. Hollis's anniversary announcement, it was also said that the *On the Square* farmers' group would be celebrating the anniversary with the Hollis couple. *On the Square* was a magazine that was put out before World War I. The magazine was founded to fight socialism and the Nonpartisan League, the "real enemies" of the nation and its institutions, according to the magazine. The periodical was aimed at farmers who supported Burnquist, Minnesota's "fearless-loyal-patriotic Governor of Minnesota."[19]

H.M. Van Hoesene was the publisher of *On the Square*, and as the *Nonpartisan Leader* noted about the magazine, it was set up by a "committee representative of certain interests, to put out a weekly paper, to be circulated among Minnesota farmers, to attack the Nonpartisan League." Located within the *On the Square* corporate records is a list of all the Minnesota counties that had German and Austro-Hungarian populations and the percentages of those ethnic groups that either registered or did not register for military service. The Minnesota editor of the magazine noted in a letter that the magazine would be directed against the "Socialist propaganda which is so strong in the State."

Patterson was the editor of *On the Square* and *Political Prairie Fire*, and those associated with the magazine were identified as an imposing array of prominent bankers and heads of commercial and industrial interests. The most active leaders and those known to the Nonpartisan League from the inception of the magazine included F.A. Carpenter, a wealthy lumberman; Charles S. Patterson, a wholesale shoe dealer and municipal lighting contractor; and Rome G. Brown, an attorney and lobbyist for several large corporations. Carpenter was also identified in Arthur Jacobs's shocking book *The Tinhorn* as being involved with usage of the Minnesota Klan chapters to break the Nonpartisan League and further Minnesota Republican party objectives.[20]

At the same time that the first American Legion National Convention was taking place in Minneapolis, several things happened in Centralia, Washington around November 11, 1919. Four American Legionnaires were left dead, and one IWW member was lynched from a bridge over the

Chehalis River. Elmer Smith, a native Minnesotan, was the attorney who defended the IWW members who were jailed after the American Legion members were killed. The citizens of Centralia, Washington, had gathered to watch the Armistice Day parade on November 11, 1919, and when the participants in the parade marched past the meeting hall of the Industrial Workers of the World, a group of World War I veterans charged the hall and was met by gunfire. Four of the marchers, World War I veterans, were shot dead, and an IWW member was lynched later over the side of a bridge by angry American Legion men in response. Attorney Elmer Smith, a graduate of Macalester College in Minnesota, began a lifelong struggle to free the men who were charged with murdering the Centralia marchers.

Telegrams from the Centralia American Legion post were read aloud to the veterans attending the 1919 Minneapolis American Legion convention as fast as the information came in. Every Legion post in Hennepin County sent messages of sympathy to the Centralia American Legion post. A number of the posts, believing that the deliberate murder of the returned soldiers at Centralia was but a forerunner of other acts equally as malicious or even more dastardly, drew up resolutions demanding that city, state and nation be purged of all "Bolshevists, Communists, I.W.W.'s and all of other followers of the red flag"—those dangerous to the maintenance of the American government, institutions and ideals. "The Centralia, Washington massacre was a somber note injected into the convention late Tuesday." Stirred by the crimes, the Legion convention "blazed out in a demonstration of grief and indignation."[21]

In the latter part of November, an American Legion committee in conference with a committee of Minneapolis ministers unanimously adopted the following resolution: "We recommend that on Sunday, December 7th, the churches of Minneapolis be informed concerning the dangerous teachings and practices of red radicalism evidence by the Centralia outbreak, with a view to constituted legal authorities."[22] An official Legion button was adopted (its slogan, "One Hundred Percent Americanism") at the Minneapolis convention. That emblem, designed at the convention, was reported in the Duluth American Legion's March 1924 publication of *David's Sling* (vol. 2, no. 1), published by Duluth David Wisted Post No. 28, "That little button is something that makes enemies among us cringe when it flashes before their eyes, and makes weak-kneed Americans stronger for your presence. With that emblem in your lapel you can make agitators shut their mouths and be afraid to utter a word against this government within your hearing. If half the people had the right and wore the button proudly and prominently there would be no 'internal menace.'"

It was further stated at the 1919 American Legion National Convention in Minneapolis, "The Legion, the resolution continued, stood 'ready to fight the enemies of the Republic within our gates as we did to face the foes with out.' Not only was it necessary to 'talk Americanism,' but it was necessary to act. And the action called for was for Legion posts not only 'to tender and volunteer their services to maintain law and order in time of public crisis,' but to 'make preparatory plans for such instances of service.'" The Motor Transport Corps was formed during World War I to have enlisted men recruited from the pool of skilled tradesmen who worked for automotive manufacturers during peacetime. They were the men in charge of repairing military vehicles and such, and the Corps was dissolved in 1920. The Corps, having no legal basis, was forced to disband, but the Minneapolis Civilian Auxiliary's postwar campaign for a state constabulary had just begun. As the *Commercial West* pointed out, unless vigorous action was taken against "Reds," the "American Legion Boys may be forced to organize another Ku Klux Klan."[23]

CHAPTER 2

Race, Religion and Rum

To be a member of the Ku Klux Klan, one had to have parents born in the United States; typically, though, most Minnesotans had immigrant parents. Minnesota had an estimated 70 percent of the population that was either foreign-born or the children of foreign-born parents in the 1920s. KKK naturalization services were a way to work around this and increase Klan membership numbers. New members not of native stock could join the "Invisible Empire" at ten dollars per head, plus expenses for costumes, monthly dues and Klan literature. Robert Lyons was a national KKK organizer and Klan official based out of Indiana who came up with the plan of inducting new members into the organization who had immigrant parents.

Lyons was a member of the American Legion and was seen as the power behind the scenes of the Republican Party in Indiana. For some, being the child of foreign-born parents and having the "opportunity" to join an organization like the Ku Klux Klan may have been seen as an opportunity to elevate their social status in their communities. Robert Lyons was the KKK organizer who came into Minnesota to provide naturalization rites. Half of Duluth Klan chapter members were children of foreign-born parents, and naturalizing was how the Klan got over that little hurdle, inducting Duluth citizens into the KKK. The *Indianapolis News* reported, "In the course of work with the Klan Robert Lyons canvassed Minnesota and Wisconsin and reported back that he had found thousands of Klan prospects who could not join because of foreign birth. He created new organization as an adjunct to the Klan and it is said to have profited well by the idea."[24]

The Minneapolis Ku Klux North Star Klan No. 2 meetings advertised that naturalization services in the *Masonic Observer* were available at their meetings. In August 1923, "Hundreds of Klansmen from the Twin Cities and surrounding towns witnessed the naturalization of the largest class of candidates in the history of North Star Klan, No. 2." Naturalization services were a regular feature of Minnesota Klan chapter meetings. In June 1924, the *Masonic Observer* reported that the Klan naturalized one hundred people at Fergus Falls, Minnesota. The district Klan meeting was for the counties of Otter Tail, Wilkin, Becker, Clay, Grant, Douglas, Todd and Wadena. Thousands attended, with the initiation of the one hundred taking place late in the evening.[25]

The Democrat convention in 1924 was put simply, a political mess. Republicans had managed to avoid the head-on collision over the Klan issue during their Republican convention that year, nominating Coolidge. Democrats, however, with clashing southern and northeastern elements, had a long fight for a specific denunciation of the Ku Klux Klan, and this set the stage for an interminable nomination contest. Iowa, right to the bitter end, continued nominating Klan-backed candidate McAdoo as its choice for president up to the 103rd nomination ballot vote. The nation's first radio audience for a presidential convention was treated to a futile, 103-ballot Democrat disaster. Democratic Minnesotans like Z.L. Begin, who attended the 1924 presidential Democratic convention, came back to the state angry.

Letters from Democrat Minnesota World War I veterans were written to American Legion adjutant Stafford King after the convention, asking King if he was a Klansman and noting just how disturbed they would be if that were true after what had occurred at the Democrat National Convention. King received a letter from a veteran who did not want the St. Cloud, Minnesota American Legion Convention to be like the Democratic convention. As the letter writer stated to King, veterans didn't want the Klan to "be a concern in Minnesota." American Legion members did join the Ku Klux Klan, including the Republican King, Minnesota's future state auditor. American Legion members who supported the Klan or belonged to the Klan worked around anti-Klan sentiment in the American Legion by establishing another group within the American Legion called the 40 & 8, which only allowed Protestant veterans to join.[26]

The 1920s Klan could be whatever a community needed to address its concerns. Every county in Minnesota had a different worry. It may have been that the Catholic population was increasing in their county. Or the German immigrant numbers were increasing in some towns. Although Minnesota had very few African Americans, even having one African American reside in a community would have caused a sense of panic. The Minnesota *Wabasha County Herald* reported on June 24, 1920, how white men defending the flag lost their lives at the hands of "Chicago Negroes." News of racial unrest like this frightened people in Minnesota. In the Klan territory of the Midwest, an important reason for the organization's success was the exploitation of hostility toward the Roman Catholic Church. Minnesotans were asked to believe that the Knights of Columbus was an organization pledged to exterminate Protestants and that Catholic churches were arsenals, with Catholics being responsible for the assassination of all presidents. Klansmen did not believe that they opposed Catholics because of their religion directly, but because control from Rome prevented Catholics from becoming true American citizens.

In 1913, when Leo Frank, a New York Jew, was charged with the rape and murder of a young female employee and convicted, Georgia residents were outraged when the governor of the state overturned his death penalty and made it life imprisonment instead. The self-styled Knights of Mary Phagan lynched Frank in August 1915. When William Simmons started the Klan back up, some of those same Leo Frank lynchers joined Simmons's second revival of the KKK in 1915. Jews were specifically excluded from Klan membership. In the 1920 U.S. Census, Minnesota's Jewish population was not kept track of separately. In the U.S. Census of Religious Bodies for Minnesota, numbers are available for Jewish congregations. In 1916, Minnesota had only six Jewish congregations reporting, with 4,686 members. In 1926, the U.S. Census of Religious Bodies reported thirty-three congregations, with 39,925 members.

The Minnesota Jewish Council was created in the late 1930s possibly due to people like Ray P. Chase, former Republican state auditor and one-term congressman, who wrote the campaign book *Are They Communists or Cat's-paws?* Because of this work, Abe Harris (general editor of the *Minnesota Leader* in the 1930s) later filed a libel lawsuit against Chase. Anti-Semitism in the state was a factor in the 1920s. Minnesota Jews had long been excluded from all sorts of businesses, employment and organizations and were not always welcomed in more affluent neighborhoods. Minneapolis was one of the few American cities in the country that allowed the barring of Jews from service clubs such as the Kiwanis, Rotary and Lions' Clubs, as well as other civic welfare organizations in the 1920s.

Lynchings are defined as murders carried out in public, with the knowledge of the entire community. In two cases in Minnesota, African American men were immediately removed to secure jails for their protection. In Duluth, this was not the case. Lynching is a very public act; the hanging of the three African American men in Duluth from a downtown lamppost in Duluth couldn't have been more public. Displaying the bodies like that, even for a few hours, meant that whites were letting African Americans know that white supremacy would be protected in Duluth. The twenty-five police officers on duty on June 15, 1920, at the Duluth jail could not identify one person there that night who broke into the jail and lynched the three young black men.

Elias Clayton, Elmer Jackson and Isaac McGhie were arrested on June 15, 1920, by Duluth police, accused of raping a white woman. It was the John Robinson Circus that brought these young men to Duluth, Minnesota. The night before the young men were lynched, Irene Tusken, age nineteen, and James Sullivan, eighteen, went to the circus in Duluth. In the early morning of June 15, 1920, Duluth police chief John Murphy received a call from James Sullivan's father saying that the African American circus workers had held James Sullivan and Irene Tusken at gunpoint, after which they were robbed and Irene raped. Six African American men were arrested on June 15 and held in the Duluth jail station on the corner of Second Avenue and Superior Street.

In their statements that the Duluth police made to the grand jury after the lynchings, none of these law enforcement officers could clearly identify who was involved. In Michael Fedo's book *The Lynchings in Duluth*, Sergeant Olson is portrayed as the most involved officer, doing the most and saying the most during the jail break-in; this is also the same police officer who joined the Duluth Ku Klux Klan after the lynchings. No attempt was made early on to disperse the gathering crowd. The mob forced its way into the jail and pulled all six men from their jail cells. Clayton, Jackson and McGhie were declared guilty and taken up one block to a light pole on the corner of First Street and Second Avenue East. The three men were beaten and then lynched—first McGhie, then Jackson and lastly Clayton.[27]

On June 16, at 7:30 a.m., the Minnesota National Guard arrived, secured Duluth and put under protection the remaining three African American prisoners. These men were finally moved from the downtown jail to the St. Louis County Jail. Judge William Cant convened a grand jury investigation on June 17, two days after the lynchings. Duluth investigators were bent on convicting the African American men still alive. Identifying the leaders and instigators of the massive lynch mob proved "difficult." Eight whites were tried. Four were acquitted, and one trial resulted in a hung jury. Three of the whites—Louis Dondino, Carl Hammerberg and Gilbert Stephenson—were

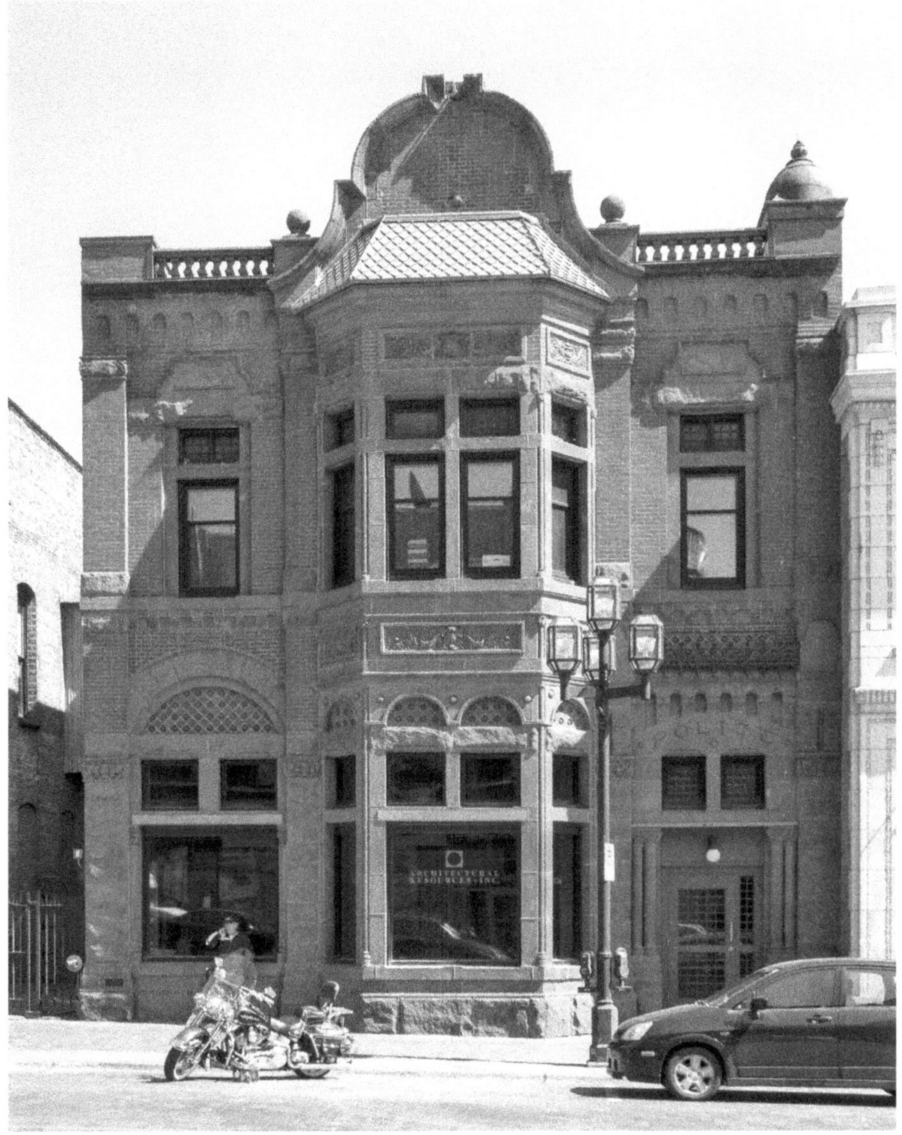

Duluth Jail, Duluth, Minnesota. *Courtesy of Kevin B. Hatle.*

convicted for rioting, each serving less than fifteen months in prison. No one was convicted of murder.[28]

Warren Read, author of *The Lyncher in Me*, is Louis Dondino's great-grandson. Louis Dondino was accused of inciting the deadly riot in Duluth that resulted in the lynchings. A prosecutor said later that without Dondino, there would have been no riot. He was charged with first-degree murder but convicted on a lesser charge, and he spent a year in Stillwater State Prison before moving to Washington State with his family, where Warren Read lives today. Warren said that he's always been reluctant to insinuate something like that—others may have been just as guilty that night. The chairman of the Clayton, Jackson, McGhie Memorial Committee, Catherine Ostos, who was one of the key members at the outset of establishing the Duluth memorial, told Warren Read that she felt that there were "big name" community members involved, people too important to be touched, and that Warren's great-grandfather was "just a guy from the West End" who was a convenient person to hold accountable.[29]

Of the twenty-eight written statements from police officers involved that night, twenty-seven were from World War I veterans—the jail that night was manned by men who had experience under pressure. Was there a "brothers in arms" issue that evening that led to the Duluth police officers not being able to identify men that evening? It must have been a real question of loyalty testifying against men with whom they had just recently been fighting in World War I. The *Duluth Rip-Saw* advocated a "thorough house-cleaning" and "elimination of every yellow member" of the police department who had failed to protect the African Americans from the mob. This was not done. Police officers who had been at the jail the night of the lynchings were still employed as police officers in 1925 and 1926, and some were now also members of the Ku Klux Klan.[30]

In Governor J.A. Burnquist's papers, there is a letter from a man named Anton Gronseth in Duluth, one of the owners of Gronseth & Olsen Grocers. Gronseth blames the lynchings on Townleyism. Mr. Gronseth's letter is dated June 19, 1920, four days after the lynching. He conveys in his letter that some in Duluth felt that the lynchings were due to the radical Nonpartisan League. About the lynchings, Gronseth noted, "This act in our City is a fair sample of what we can expect from Nonpartisan regime." The Nonpartisan League had nothing to do with the Duluth lynchings; blaming the league was just another way for the city to not take responsibility for what happened that night. Monroe N. Work, director of research at Tuskegee Normal and Industrial Institute, kept track of lynchings in the United States in a publication called the *Negro Year Book: An Annual Encyclopedia of the Negro.* It contains a chart called the "1920 Lynchings of Negros Distribution by States"; Minnesota is in the top five for lynching that year, yet the state had an African American population of less than 0.5 percent in 1920.

The first newspaper report of a Ku Klux Klan chapter in Duluth, Minnesota, is titled, "Ku Klux Klan in Duluth; Has 1,500 Members in City." The local Klan was "said to have been organized with a membership of 700 at the Owl's Hall on West Superior Street early last summer." On the 1925 and 1926 lists, close to 50 percent of the Duluth Ku Klux Klan members were World War I veterans; police officers are also on the Duluth Klan lists, as is Sergeant Olson, who was in charge of the men at the Duluth jail the night of the lynchings. The Duluth Ku Klux Klan held its meetings at the Owl's Fraternity Hall, less than a block and a half from the jail the young African American men were taken out of in June 1920.[31]

Walter White of the National Association for the Advancement of Colored People (NAACP) wrote a letter to Governor Burnquist after the Duluth lynchings on July 25, 1920, telling the governor how evidence secured since the Duluth lynchings had clearly established that the three who were lynched in Duluth were not guilty of criminal assault on the white girl involved. White asked Governor Burnquist to make a statement to the Associated Press for national release that the three young men who died in Duluth were not guilty. White pleaded with Burnquist, noting just how important such a statement to the nation would be, especially coming from Burnquist's office. Governor Burnquist proclaiming that a mistake had been made and that those three young men had been innocent would get wider publicity than such a statement coming from the NAACP. Governor Burnquist never made a local or national statement declaring that the young African American men lynched in Duluth were innocent.

John Quincy Adams was invited to St. Paul to revive a flagging African American newspaper called the *Western Appeal*, ultimately leading to his move to St. Paul. A *Western Appeal* office was opened in Minneapolis by Adams and his brother; at its peak, the Adams brothers' newspaper offices could be found in seven cities. Adams realized that Minnesota state laws established to protect African Americans were being subverted. The cost of bringing civil suits against discriminatory hotels, restaurants and real estate agents in St. Paul and Minneapolis was expensive for the average African American citizen. African Americans were "settling," living in segregated neighborhoods of their own in exchange for jobs, education and physical safety in Minnesota, versus living in the South. They knew that their business was not welcome in all parts of the Minneapolis and St. Paul area.[32]

Adams's newspaper, the *Appeal*, printed an editorial in 1922 about the poor relations between communities given the burning of a fiery cross on Bass Lake, which was seven miles northwest of the Twin Cities. Charles

Chapman, a local African American man, owned the property. More than one hundred Ku Klux Klan members, masked and robed, led a procession of five hundred people in a rally in a hollow close to Chapman's cabin. The same month of the editorial, J.Q. Adams was struck and killed by an automobile while attempting to board a streetcar at University and Fry Streets. Adams died the following day, and his funeral was attended by hundreds of people and out-of-town friends, according to the *Appeal*. The St. Paul newspaper gave coverage of Adams's editorial position in the community, declaring, "Adams was one of the recognized leaders of the colored people in St. Paul and was the first president of the Afro-American Newspaper Association."

Adams was hit by Otis Woodward, a "colored" driver, although he did not own the car. Reverend Joseph W. Harris, also "colored," owned it. A formal inquest was held after Adams's death on September 9, 1922, before a jury. Mr. Allen McGill, Ramsey County assistant attorney, appeared for the state. The cause of death was due to the injuries received in the accident. In the inquest made into Adams's death, there was another car involved (unidentified). According to all the people in the car that hit Adams, a speeding Ford forced Woodward to drive his car into Adams. Woodward did not testify during the inquest, stating that he wished not to testify. This other car's existence was ignored by Assistant Attorney McGill in the testimony. Was there really another car, or did Woodward intentionally hit Adams?[33]

Reverend J.W. Harris, the owner of the car that struck Adams, died in Ancker Hospital less than nine years after the death of John Quincy. Harris's death was due to numerous bullet wounds. He was shot by George Mundell, an African American man, in front of Mundell's home in St. Paul. Reverend Harris had come to the Mundell home with a gun. Words between the two men were exchanged. Mundell said that there had been an earlier phone call between the two men regarding a source of gossip said to have involved the reverend's character. The front yard of the Mundell home is incredibly small and less than fifteen feet from the sidewalk. The original house, built in 1907, still stands there today. The location where Adams's home once stood was only a few blocks from where the Mundell home currently stands.[34]

Adams's death was possibly seen by some in the community as intentional rather than accidental. Maybe not everyone in the African American community was happy with Adams becoming more "radical" in his viewpoints; perhaps some felt that change was needed, but why rock the boat and anger whites? John Quincy Adams no longer being on the scene in the 1920s, no longer being a voice for the African American community in Minneapolis and St. Paul areas, would possibly have been a relief for some.

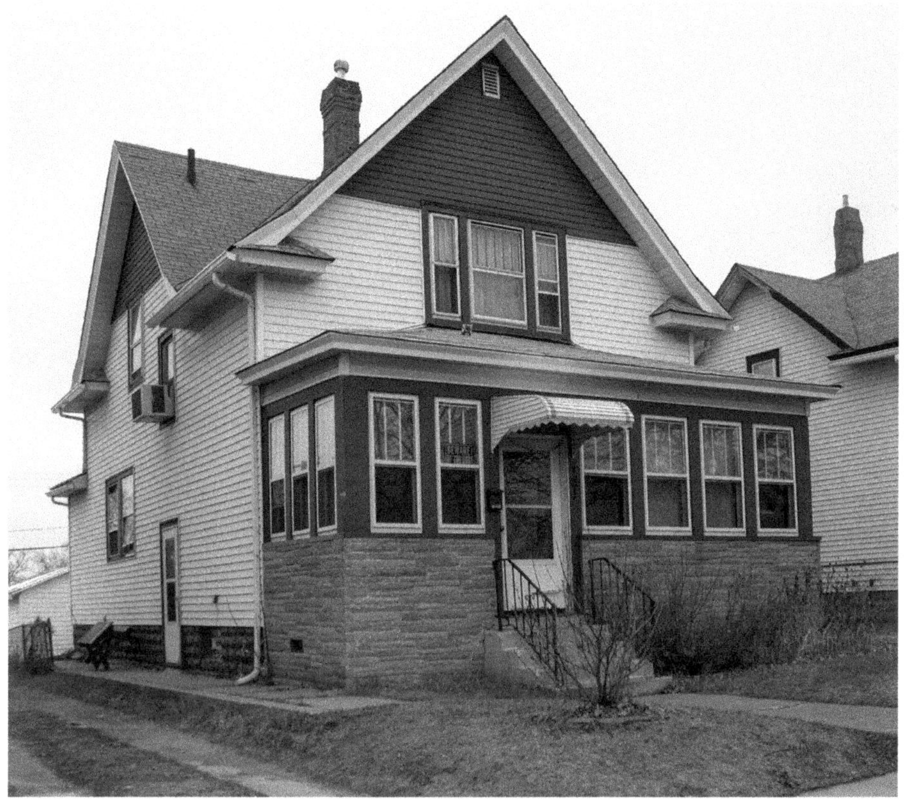

Home where Reverend Joseph Harris was shot, St. Paul, Minnesota. *Courtesy of Kevin B. Hatle.*

Mundell said that he did not write the letter or know what the contents of the letter were that had brought Reverend Harris to his home; he said that his wife had written it. Mundell's wife was a member of Reverend Harris's congregation; she had written the letter ten days before the shooting. J.E. Perry, the head of the company that published the *Twin City Herald*, an African American newspaper, would not give details of Mrs. Mullen's letter out to the St. Paul newspaper. George Mundell continued working for the U.S. Postal Service and died at the age of seventy, married to his wife.

Reverend Harris had started up a nonprofit corporation in 1926 called the Christian Center Inc., located at 603 West Central Avenue. Reverend Harris was in Minneapolis in 1922,[35] the year that his car struck and killed John Quincy Adams. Is it possible that Joseph Harris was the African American reverend in Arthur Jacobs's book that the Republican Party and Thomas Schall used to get the African American vote? In Jacobs's book, the reverend took bribes from the Minnesota Republican Party in exchange for black votes. The Christian Center, an impressive establishment built by Harris, was all financed by "small donations." The building was a gracious brick building with well-appointed interiors, its purpose "for Character-building Education among Negroes." Small donations would not have been sufficient to accomplish what Harris did, building such a large-scale complex in St. Paul.[36]

Bootlegging in Minnesota had sprung up in response to the Commission of Public Safety arbitrarily closing saloons in the state before prohibition became the law of the land. Waseca, a town six miles east of Otisco, had a problem with illegal stills—or, as the *Waseca Herald* described them, "keeping and maintaining nuisances"—which required constant legal supervision. An attempt was made to oust William C. Wobschall, an alderman of the first ward in Waseca, from his position due to raids on his residence for maintaining a "liquor nuisance." Wobschall stated publicly to the Waseca newspaper that he was "not in sympathy with the 18th amendment to the constitution of the United States." He vigorously defended himself at his ouster hearing, stating that he had not violated the city charter as it then stood and that he had done nothing wrong in his duties as an alderman. Wobshcall finished out his term as alderman but withdrew as a candidate for reelection as an alderman for the first ward.[37]

The *Waseca Herald* gave front-page coverage to the stills in Waseca County, noting, "The Moonshine game is hard to put down. It reminds one of the saying of the old Yankee regarding swatting the fly. When you kill one of the darn things, it seems a dozen come to his funeral." Due to the issue with illegal alcohol, this undoubtedly helped to bring in the Ku Klux Klan to Waseca County. First reports of the Ku Klux Klan being in Waseca occur on July 19, 1923, when Klan bills were scattered around town. A lecture by Dr. W.S. Harper was announced at Trowbridge Park. A resident on his way home from Albert Lea to Waseca was stopped in August 1923 by four robed Klan members on horseback as he drove by the cemetery south of Waseca. A Ku Klux Klan cross was set ablaze in September 1923 in Lew Sterling's pasture across from the Waseca fairgrounds.[38]

The congressional representative for Steele County, where Blooming Prairie is located, was Republican Allen Furlow (1925–29, World War I veteran). Letters written by Representative Furlow to constituents like S.E. McCarl of Winona, Minnesota, state how strongly Furlow was opposed to any modification of the Volstead Act: "Count on me to use all my influence to see that the law is enforced." Representative Furlow was adamant in

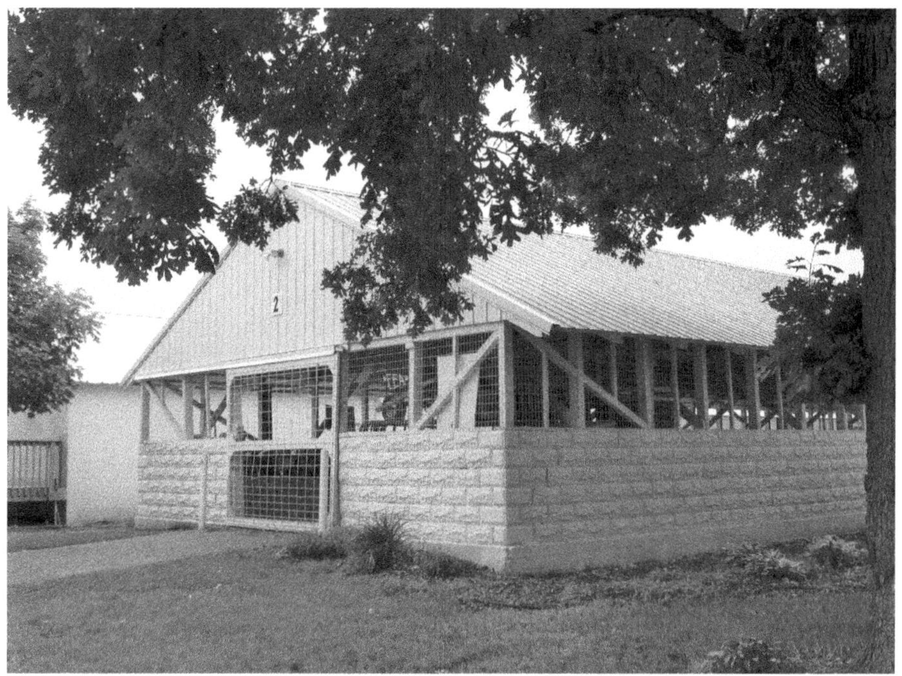

Waseca Fairgrounds. *Courtesy of Kevin B. Hatle.*

telling his constituents that he was strongly opposed to seeing the Volstead Act weakened. The superintendent of the Methodist Episcopal Sunday School of Winona also telegrammed Furlow noting how strongly he agreed with this viewpoint. "Urge strict enforcement," wrote C.A. Duncanson from Stewartville, Minnesota, to Furlow in 1926. "The world knows the liquor traffic was a curse to humanity and the better element of democracy had long and vigorously opposed it."[39]

As prohibition settled in, reports of the number of bootleggers killed by untrained enforcement agents looked good initially, but the body count disclosed that most victims were small-time neighborhood operators, and some were ordinary citizens killed just for having a bottle under their front seat. In Northfield, Minnesota, a twelve-year-old boy (Gilbert Fox) was shot to death by local law enforcement while he was riding in the back of his family's truck because the family ran a liquor roadblock. Governor Theodore Christianson received numerous letters from residents in the state reporting on their neighbors' illegal drinking habits. Mrs. Long reported to the governor that Adam Seha had liquor in his basement and that Charley Lamont, who lived a block south of the dance hall, had a ready supply in his home. The diligent Mrs. Long went on to report others in the areas that had liquor, as well as exactly where it could be located.[40]

Klansmen were staunch supporters of prohibition. Liquor raids by Klansmen, deputized or acting on their own, were logged in a majority of states. Gambling was also rife in speakeasies and roadhouses, evoking condemnation from the Klan. Premarital sex and excessive dating were also condemned, and simply skipping Sunday services might draw attention from the local Klan. Local law enforcement did not seem to be able to get a handle on the liquor situation in Goodhue County, and Goodhue resident T.W. Taylor asked for state help. Governor Christianson responded to Taylor that there was no state police to send to Goodhue. The occupations listed for the "good" people living in Goodhue County, according to Taylor in his letter to Governor Christianson, were the typical job occupations for middle-class 1920s Klan members. Goodhue County did have an identified Klan chapter, the Kenyon Klan chapter.[41]

Wright County residents wrote to Governor Christianson about a group of families located two and a half miles southwest of Annandale breaking the liquor laws. One of those families was William Ryan's family, who had been selling liquor for years. The residents were upset that William Ryan was warned before they raided his place, allowing William to hide any evidence of illegal activity. Bill Adams, who lived next to William Ryan, was an even more egregious offender of the prohibition laws and was not being stopped either, according to the outraged Wright County residents. Irma Long, president of the local temperance chapter in Elysian, Minnesota, wrote to the governor telling him how a group of women had been working for years to get their neighborhood cleaned up. If the governor would only send a prohibition agent there on a Friday night, he "would find plenty of evidence," she said.

A Ku Klux Klan sword was donated to the Minnesota Historical Society by Mrs. Ralph Plaisted from Buffalo, Minnesota, located in Wright County. Mrs. Plaisted was the wife of Ralph Plaisted, a polar pioneer who reached the North Pole by snowmobile on April 19, 1967. The KKK sword was found in the attic of the home of Mrs. Plaisted's in-laws. The Klan sword from Buffalo, Minnesota, is a second Klan officer's ceremonial sword. The front of the hilt has a mounted Klansman in high relief, and the reverse side has the letters "KKK." Such swords are a rarely encountered and were largely issued only when a Klansman had advanced to the second degree of the Klan. This particular sword signified that a Minnesota Klansman had achieved a high rank in the Ku Klux Klan.[42]

There is primary evidence noting how Archbishop Austin Dowling directed the fight against Catholic schools in the 1920s. Correspondence between Dowling and Father James Ryan shows how Dowling was on the front line, battling this divisive national issue that the Ku Klux Klan was using to stir up its followers. The *Masonic Observer* of September 18, 1920, reported of Archbishop Dowling's organization of the Catholic schools in Minnesota, "These schools are scattered all over the state and are attended by thousands of children who should be receiving the broad, American training of the Public Schools." The KKK expressed worries that Catholic schools were becoming too powerful. One goal of educational reformers during the 1920s, with Klan approval, was to create a federal Department of Education. The Ku Klux Klan's assertion that the Catholic Church represented a primary obstacle to the establishment of a Department of Education was essentially correct. There is correspondence between Ryan and Dowling suggesting just that.

The 1920s Ku Klux Klan identified Catholics as one of this country's most severe problems. At Klan rallies, "escaped nuns" and former priests would speak, outlining to their engaged audience tales of Protestant girls being turned into sexual slaves and nuns impregnated by priests. They were told that the pope in Rome was intent on taking over the United States. There is a Ku Klux Klan letter in which the KKK "complains" about Father Ryan's and Congressman Mullen's booklet on the danger of federalized education booklet. "Attached to this letter you will find a pamphlet called 'Private Schools are in Danger,' Mullen and Father Ryan discuss the question of federalizing education, the Oregon School Bill, and other items of interest to us."[43] Archbishop Dowling made a special point of having Ryan come work for him; Ryan was previously stationed in Indiana.

Dowling was also in contact with Catholics in the state of Alabama, telling them about the attacks that were taking place throughout the country on Catholic schools. J.K. Glennon thanked the bishop for sending him a circular letter on the Towner-Sterling Bill. The letter between the men read, "The forces behind this bill, I believe, are the same as those which passed the Oregon School law in November and if I am right in that supposition there is little reason for the friends of private parochial schools, to take comfort in the passage of the Sterling-Towner Bill." Mr. Glennon informed Dowling on January 30, 1923, that in the state of Alabama, Governor Kilby, elected on an anti-Catholic platform, as passed all the bills "[o]pposing our schools and orphan system." Mr. Glennon told Dowling that people with degrees from Loyola, Spring Hill and other Catholic institutions of higher learning—and

Catholic college graduates in particular—had to take teaching examinations from the board in Montgomery.[44]

In October 1923, the Scottish Rite Masons had their annual meeting of the Supreme Council in Washington. The whole day was spent devoted to education, and they voted money for "educational propaganda." The Masonic Service Association, which was also meeting there that month, decided that it was going to devote the whole year to propaganda in favor of the Towner-Sterling Bill and the public school. "I have some of the literature gotten out by the Scottish Rite People and it is dominantly anti-parochial school," Ryan wrote to Dowling. "Every indication points to the fact that American public opinion, particularly in the West and Middle West, is very rapidly going around to the Scottish Rite viewpoint. If they are permitted to go on unmolested in their propaganda for two or three years more, they will undoubtedly succeed in jockeying us out of position and attaining what they desire, a national sentiment in favor of the public school."[45]

A letter from the executive secretary of the National Education Association to Monsignor Joseph Smith in New York City was provided to Dowling by Ryan stating that if Catholic public school teachers would join the NEA, they could have guidance on their conduct, be represented at teachers' conventions and represent the rights of parochial schools. Catholic teachers may not have wanted to join the NEA because regardless of what was being presented to them (that it would be a good idea to join), they wouldn't be respected or treated fairly if they did join—this was possibly another method for Protestants to out Catholic teachers, removing them from teaching in the public school system. Father Ryan sent Dowling a newspaper article from the *Washington Post* about how non-Catholics were becoming more interested in religious education. Ryan stated, "I feel certain that they will make plans which will leave us out of consideration altogether and, by isolating us from the national current of education serve more and more to brand us with the stamp of un-Americanism."[46]

Ryan and Dowling gave a great deal of attention to a lawsuit involving the Hill Military Academy. In 1923, the Portland-based academy filed suit with the U.S. District Court against the State of Oregon to challenge legislation that would have outlawed private school education as a pupil's primary form of instruction. When the private school won the case, Governor Walter Pierce appealed the decision to the U.S. Supreme Court. The KKK called for uniform public schools that would foster patriotism and eliminate elitism. On June 1, 1925, the U.S. Supreme Court announced its unanimous decision in favor of the private schools. The Catholic Church helped pay the legal fees of P.J. Hanley, the lawyer representing Hill Military Academy. There is a copy of a letter from Hanley sent to the National Catholic Welfare Council noting, "I am taking the liberty of asking if you will kindly advise me the amount, if any, sent to you, and when we may expect to receive a draft to cover."[47] It would be interesting to know whether the Oregon Klan

National Catholic Welfare Council

ADMINISTRATIVE COMMITTEE
MOST REV. EDWARD J. HANNA, D. D., CHAIRMAN

REV. JOHN J. BURKE, C. S. P., GENERAL SECRETARY
REV. JAMES H. RYAN, PH.D. EXECUTIVE SECRETARY

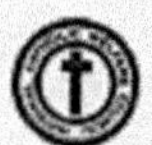

NATIONAL HEADQUARTERS
1312 MASSACHUSETTS AVE., N. W.
WASHINGTON, D. C.

November 11, 1922.

Most Reverend Austin Dowling, D. D.,
226 Summit Avenue,
Saint Paul, Minnesota.

Dear Archbishop:

I have not answered your letter sooner because it has been impossible for me, although I tried often, to get in touch with Dr. Pace. I have not yet been able to see him.

With reference to the meeting of the Department on the Monday that you will be here, we all feel here that such a meeting would be most desirable. I will, therefore, send out a letter Monday to all the members of the Department asking them to be here on that date. I will suggest the questions which you propose in your letter and, in addition to them, the problem of what the Department of Education is to do in the present emergency.

As for the other matter which you mentioned in your letter, I will write to you about it as soon as Dr. Pace and I have been able to go over the situation.

I am sending you enclosed a copy of a program for American Education Week which we will get out if you approve. It is simply a rewriting of the folder gotten out by the American Legion with the emphasis, however, placed on Catholic education. Two points worry us about this matter: First, some Catholics might take the point of view that this movement should be disregarded as its purposes are open to question. Dr. Pace, however, thinks, as well as Father Burke, that we should take part in this movement. On the other hand, do you think that the American Legion or the N. E. A. would be justified in saying that we are using American Education Week for propaganda and sectarian purposes? There is not much time left to make a decision in this matter. Whatever your decision is, would you be so kind as to wire it to me?

With best wishes to you and asking your blessing,

Yours very sincerely,

James H Ryan

Father Ryan's letter to Archbishop Austin Dowling. *Courtesy of St. Paul Diocese.*

knew that the Catholic Church was helping to pay the lawyer representing Hill Military Academy and if Archbishop Dowling in Minnesota was directly involved. Dowling succeeded in minimizing the damage from the KKK, steering Catholic schools and teachers who were Catholic through treacherous waters in the 1920s. A heart ailment gradually incapacitated Austin Dowling, and he died in 1930.

Another example of what schools had to deal with in Minnesota was a report submitted to the American Historical Association by Minnesota educators in December 1926. A.C. Krey was the chairman of this Minnesota committee, and his report recognized that people were concerned about religious issues. The report criticizes organizations not normally concerned with education, "some of them distinctly propagandist in their purposes have devoted increasing attention to social studies in schools."[48] One of those organizations interested in education where there had been no interest before was likely the American Legion. In 1922, Dowling had heard from Ryan, "It is simply a rewriting of the order gotten out by the American Legion with the emphasis, however, placed on Catholic education." There were two points that worried Father Ryan about the matter. One was that some Catholics might take the point of view that this movement should be disregarded as its purposes were open to question. But on the other hand, Father Ryan said that if the Catholics didn't work with the American Legion's demands, not doing so could be used against Catholic schools.[49]

Rochester publicly expressed anti-immigrant and anti-Catholic sentiments as early as the 1880s, and William Mayo, who came to Rochester in 1863, was a flashpoint for local criticism due to his pro-Catholic and pro-immigrant feelings. William Worrall Mayo's family background was English and Protestant. Being more open-minded and liberal may have been due to his being born near Manchester, England, which was fired with social and political unrest; in 1826, ninety thousand unemployed weavers and spinners smashed machines and burned factories there. Mayo's biographer, Helen Clapesattle, theorized that this early influence may have planted in Dr. William Mayo more of a social and political conscience, nurturing an inclination to champion the economic underdog, and set in him a growing conviction that government must be for all the people.[50]

Dr. Mayo's endorsement of evolution also shocked the citizens of Rochester, and John Edgar called him "an infidel and friend of demon rum," leading a successful campaign to defeat Mayo for reelection to the Rochester School Board in 1870. Dr. Mayo never belonged to any formal religion and was a registered Democrat in a Republican county. St. Mary's

Hospital was opened to serve all sick persons regardless of their color, sex, financial status or professed religion, but anti-Catholicism was an obstacle that Mayo and his sons (also doctors) had to overcome. Dr. Mayo tried to organize the staff at St. Mary's but was met with outright refusal by other medical professionals in Rochester. Ardent Protestants would not accept an institution that was managed by black-robed nuns and in which there was a chapel set aside for the exercises of popery, according to local newspapers.

Riverside Hospital, a new institution, opened for patients in November 1892. Rochester Protestants renewed their opposition to St. Mary's Hospital and pointed to rival Riverside as an institution that "Protestants and patriots could enter without doing outrage to their convictions by furthering an agency of the hated and alien Catholic Church." Once, when two important members of the Presbyterian community fell ill, they were taken to Riverside Hospital; however, they called on the Mayos to attend them. After deliberating, the Mayos refused to attend to patients or operate at Riverside Hospital. The Mayos' decision brought criticism from a segment of the Protestant community, with one enraged pastor calling the Mayos servants of the Catholics. The *Masonic Observer* reported its displeasure with the Mayos in May 1922, noting, "It is generally understood that the Mayos have made millions of dollars since they started as surgeons and first joined forces with St. Mary's." The article goes on to say that Rome is in the hospital business because the profits are huge there.[51]

CHAPTER 3

Fraternal Organizations and Protestant Churches

Fraternal organizations, churches and women's clubs were a staple of social life in the 1920s. It was not at all unusual having various memberships in fraternal organizations overlap. Klan Kleagles (recruiters) could and did use fraternal contacts to recruit new Klan members. In Duluth, the Klan chapter there used the Owl fraternity for its meeting place, and in Fairmont, the Klan chapter used the American Legion building. Imperial Wizard William Simmons was a member of fifteen fraternal organizations. Simmons had provided a club system with his new version of the Klan that people were familiar with, as well as a movement white Protestants could get behind and relate to. The new Klan modeled itself as a civic club for super-patriots. Minnesota Klan members likely saw belonging to the Klan as similar to belonging to a lodge on the same level as the Masons.

Women's clubs were also popular in the 1920s and were powerful political vehicles that women who belonged to the Ku Klux Klan had access to use. It was while speaking at one of these women's clubs that Stafford King got into trouble by admitting Republican responsibility when the Farmers' Credit Bureau, which was then under the Minnesota Republican Party's control, had done a bad administrative job. Alice Winter was the wife of Thomas Winter, the appointed superintendent of the safety commission's intelligence bureau. Alice was also half-sister to Charles W. Ames, a member of the Minnesota Commission of Public Safety, and her brother was committed to uproot all "pro-Germanism." Alice was also closely linked to the Minnesota Commission of Public Safety's power structure. In her book, *The Business of*

Being a Club Woman, "Americanization" was near and dear to her heart as an important goal in Minnesota.

The *Masonic Observer* was a national publication, with its headquarters in Minneapolis. In 1921, mentions of the Minnesota Ku Klux Klan begin to creep onto the newspaper's front pages. The *Masonic Observer* criticized other publications in the area for "exposing" the KKK. The newspaper went on to state that the Masons were also treated to this type of exposure and that "only those actually on the inside ever knew whether there was the slightest foundation for any of these 'exposures.'" It was pointed out that the Catholic Knights of Columbus have secret gathering and rituals, but the *Masonic Observer* did not report on their activities, so why report on Ku Klux Klan's activities?[52] Masons had survived condemning exposures like this, and only time would tell what the outcome would be for the Ku Klux Klan existing in Minnesota, according to the *Masonic Observer*'s editor.

The editor, H.E. Soule, went on in next month's edition, again stating that the *Masonic Observer* held no feelings against or for the Ku Klux Klan, but Soule also printed statistics concerning how the prison population in Minnesota for the previous three years was composed of 39 percent Catholics even though Catholics only composed 17 percent of Minnesota's population. The *Masonic Observer* pointed out again how exclusive memberships in fraternal orders did not make the Klan distinctive among American fraternities. You wouldn't find any Protestants in the Knights of Columbus, but no one complained about that, according to the editor.[53] After 1921, the *Masonic Observer* gave meeting times, places and dates for Klan activity throughout Minnesota. The newspaper reported how the KKK "has undoubtedly become a national factor, and will wield an influence in this country's affairs." Klan activities in other parts of the country were reported, including publishing written statements from Mason grand masters who support the Klan, like those in Texas. A Ku Klux Klan initiation, with all its details—including the exact oath used by Klan members—was given a detailed two-page coverage in the *Masonic Observer*.[54]

The Masonic Board of Relief of the City of Duluth Inc. had several Ku Klux Klan members on it, including Walter Gladson, second vice-president, and A.P. Cook, treasurer. Belonging to the Duluth Masonic Club were Elmer Johnson and Walter Gladson (both identified Klan members). The Old Settler's Association in Duluth, another type of fraternal organization, also had several KKK members as part of this fraternal organization, including W.S. McCormick (charter member), Joseph Becks, Joseph Berg, Henry Butler, Sydney Catherall and George Clark. The building where the Duluth Ku Klux Klan would meet was called the Owl's Hall, near where the Duluth lynchings occurred, and was affiliated with the Independent International Order of Owls, which was a Mason-related group. Only master Masons were eligible to join the Independent International Order of Owls.[55]

Records for the Moorhead Ku Klux Klan chapter were reported to have been found in Moorhead's old Masonic Temple before it was razed to make way for a parking lot in 1968.[56] Moorhead's police magistrate and its city attorney were both reported to have belonged to the KKK. At the Clay County Historical Society located in Moorhead, there is a photo of a Minnesota Klan organizer, a pilot named Mac McPhail. The *Hawley Clay County Herald* and, especially, the *Moorhead County Press* both reprinted Klan press releases and their advertisements without negative editorial comment on the Ku Klux Klan. Both newspapers' local correspondents made regular mention of Klan activities, and the *Moorhead County Press* ran a few (unsigned) letters written by Klan supporters.

An anti-evolution bill was introduced in Minnesota in 1927. This was a bill for an act to prohibit the teaching that mankind descended from a lower order of animals, as well as the adoption or use of textbooks that taught such in all the public schools, colleges and state teachers' colleges and at the University of Minnesota. The act was supported in whole or in part by the public education funds of the State of Minnesota, declared violations of this act to be misdemeanors and provided penalties for the violation of the provisions thereof.[57] Another bill, from Senator Edwin L. MacLean, a World War I veteran, was introduced in 1927 regarding the reading of or the use of the Bible in public schools or institutions in the state of Minnesota.[58]

Minnesota House representative Olaf H. Dahl's continued support of having evolution banned from schools may have personally aided his political career. "Mr. Dahl's industry was rewarded when the announcement of committee appointments was made. Mr. Dahl is vice-chairman of the important public highways committee." Did being a continuous supporter of the anti-evolution bill help Dahl become vice-chairman of the committee? Not everyone in Dahl's county was happy with his stance, though, as a newspaper noted: "We understand according to the publicity department of this movement, that the state wide campaign to purge school texts of pernicious evolutionary teaching started in Austin with the address of the gentleman from Kansas. Dr. W.B. Riley of Minneapolis has drafted his bill with the help of course of the man denounced so generally and impartially in Austin last week. The fundamentalists evidently have abandoned individualism in thinking and are going in for mass production. Believe and preach as we say or we'll sic the law on you."[59]

With the support of the Ku Klux Klan, the Tennessee legislature passed the Butler Act, which declared it unlawful "to teach any theory that denies the story of the Divine Creation of man as taught in the Bible." The 1925 trial of John Scopes in Dayton, Tennessee, was a legal battle over the Tennessee law that made it a crime to teach evolution in public schools. William Jennings Bryan and Clarence Darrow were the lawyers in the case. For Christian fundamentalists like Bryan, who believed literally in the Bible, the idea that human beings descended from primates contradicted the book of Genesis. The "monkey trial," which pitted Bryan against Darrow, an avowed atheist, foe of prohibition and defender of labor radicals, transformed Dayton into the news capital of America.

Minnesota was notably one of the few northern states to consistently have at its political forefront legislation that opposed the teaching of evolution. William Bell Riley was a prominent Minnesota minister and pastor of the First Baptist Church in Minneapolis; he was also known as the "architect of fundamentalism" and was Billy Graham's mentor. William Bell Riley was the founder of Northwestern College in 1902. He was the dominant person who led the fight against the teaching of evolution in Minnesota and was a key anti-evolution leader nationally. He stated that if liquor could be bottled up in legislative action, why not evolution? William Bell Riley was a close friend of William Jennings Bryan, and Riley helped pay Bryan's legal fees in the Scopes trial.

William Bell Riley published a sermon that he gave at the First Baptist Church in Minneapolis on August 2, 1925, commemorating the death of his great friend, William Jennings Bryan, who had died five days after the Scopes trial. In the sermon Riley delivered that day, he told his church audience that Bryan's best and last battle was the one against evolution. Bryan told Riley personally that the trial was no war of words but rather a "conflict between science on the one side and Scripture on the other." Riley also noted in his sermon how he was being attacked by a liberal magazine called the *Truth Seeker* on his Minnesota debate victories, pointing out how in his debates "[e] volution disposes of Christianity, not partially but absolutely!" Riley said that Bryan knew that evolution taught in schools meant the "final massacre of Christian faith."[60]

William Riley was to be the University of Minnesota's next challenge after World War I. Dr. Riley called the teaching of evolution at the University of Minnesota an example of trespassing against the word of God. Riley and the ministers of the Anti-Evolution League went after the University of Minnesota and used the Minnesota legislature as part of their plan to keep evolution from being taught on campus. Riley wanted to deliver an address at the university called "Should the Teaching of Evolution Be No Longer Tolerated in This State University?" Frederick J. Kelly, the dean of administration and assistant to the president, withdrew the invitation for Riley to speak. Riley felt that he had been turned away and "talked in anger of getting an injunction to bar from the university all textbooks teaching evolution."[61]

Riley brought a version of the Scopes trial to the state of Minnesota in a much bigger way than the Butler law in Tennessee had. Riley was trying to ban evolution not only in the public school system but also in all of Minnesota's colleges as well. Riley's speech was given to the joint session of the Minnesota State Senate and House on March 9, 1927. Riley asked if Minnesotans wanted the state teaching their children a philosophy of life and religion held "by only a despicably small section of its citizenship." And why should people in the state be asked to support these state schools in the form of taxation, Riley stated, "in support of such unscientific and non-effective philosophy of life and religion as is the atheistic doctrine of mere 'Humanism'"? Riley told the legislature that the state should not be able to claim their children from when they rise in the morning until the evening or to teach him doctrines that are not demonstrated by science and that directly oppose the Christian faith.[62]

Up to this point, University of Minnesota president Lotus Coffman had been diplomatic dealing with Riley, but now that the bill had reached the Minnesota legislature, Coffman felt having this bill pass would be a "police surveillance of the mind that would be imposed upon his teachers." One of Riley's strongest and fervent student opponents was Howard Haycraft, the student editor of the *Minnesota Daily*. Howard Haycraft was the son of the conservative judge Julius Haycraft from Fairmont, Minnesota. "There is a danger that the bill may go through," said Howard. "Riley's 'flying squadron' of evangelists has covered the state and members of the legislature from rural districts receive as many as 25 letters a day from their constituents asking that the bill be passed." After Riley's speech at the armory, there was a letter written from William B. Riley to Howard Haycraft. Among several things, Riley stated, "There were a score of them that thanked me personally; a number who told me that their shattered faith had been recovered to a large degree, and aside from a few atheistic Jews, my reception was more cordial than I had any right to expect."[63]

The joint hearing conducted by the Educational Committees of the Senate and House of Representatives of the State of Minnesota was held on

Wednesday, March 9, 1927. A brief on resolutions opposing the proposed bill to prohibit the teaching of evolution in tax-supported schools and colleges in Minnesota was also given at the time. The bill was defeated on political rather than theological grounds; Riley was unable to gain more than a fraction of the expected Lutheran support he had needed. In 1948, Riley asked Billy Graham to come speak at a fundamentalist conference sponsored by his Northwestern Schools in Minneapolis. Riley spoke to Graham privately afterward and told Graham that he believed he was "God's man to replace him as president of the Northwestern Schools." In February 1952, Graham resigned as president of Northwestern Schools. William Riley's son graduated from the University of Minnesota. Billy Graham later counseled Billy Sunday's grandson, Paul Haines, who later died suffering from alcoholism.

Arnold S. Rice wrote, "In all areas of the county the Klan attempted to ally itself with the Protestant churches." Of the thirty-nine national lecturers working for the Klan at one time, two-thirds were said to be Protestant ministers. Each Klan chapter had its own kludd (chaplain), and chapters worked closely with Protestant clergy—mainly the Methodist, Presbyterian, Baptists and other evangelical Christian churches. Chauncey Hobart, a Minnesota Methodist historian, reported that preachers in Minnesota "stamped and shouted and pounded the Bible, and were boisterous enough to break the pulpit down." A Methodist minister was very suited to identify with the type of people in rural settlements in Minnesota. Membership in the Methodist Church was offered only to those who gave lasting evidence of a change in their lifestyles, which mostly meant not drinking alcohol. If they departed from the Methodist way, they were nicknamed "backsliders," and they were denied the privileges of membership.

A *Mower County News* report, "Church Should Help Clean Out Slothful Police Officials, Prohibition Chief Tells Methodist Conference," noted that "if the enemies of prohibition have been taking comfort in the supposition that the Methodist church doesn't carry its war club and machine gun for liquor, an uncomfortable time is in store."[64] Temperance was a high priority with Methodists; old-time Methodists had seen "too much of the drink to have any patience with the habit." Methodist ministers placed more emphasis on political methods of attaining moral results, and the Methodist pre-prohibition policy of supporting only "dry" candidates continued with supporting verified "dry" politicians during prohibition. If a politician drank or supported drink, he was marked to be removed from office. There was a well-defined Methodist moral behavior to follow when it came to drinking, card playing, oath taking, dancing and theatergoing, as well as not attending church. The Ku Klux Klan loudly proclaimed its support of Methodist churches' social goals.

Methodist bishop T. Otto Nall wrote that after World War I, there was widespread enthusiasm for a white Protestant America, and there were Klaverns of the Ku Klux Klan in Minnesota. He also wrote how in Minnesota, "strangely enough," the popularity of the Klan was still strong after its relapse throughout most of the nation. Bishop Nall wrote of a state meeting of Minnesota Methodist ministers where instead of attending to Methodist Church annual business, the ministers from across the state marched in a Klan parade. A bugle had sounded, and Methodist delegates rushed to the church door to see Methodist conference members march by in a Ku Klux Klan parade. The conference that year was held in Winnebago, Minnesota.

On October 4, 1909, Methodist minister Ezra C. Clemans was appointed the superintendent of the Minnesota Anti-Saloon League, Duluth District. In his annual report, Clemans declared that the local Hinckley fire wasn't all bad since it had rid the area of all its saloons and stills.[65] Minnesota ministers had their speeches and sermons published in local newspapers, with Clemans getting a great deal of coverage. Ministers in Minnesota getting this type of front-page newspaper coverage declared themselves "100% Americans and anti-immigrant." Ezra Clemans, later of Owatonna and national chaplain of the American Legion, stated, "The American Flag stands for America. If those who come here want to speak another language than American, if they want to read other than American newspapers, they don't belong here. Go back to where you came from."

Ezra C. Clemans had a personal relationship with Stafford King, who sent Clemans a personal telegram on March 9, 1929, congratulating the reverend and his wife on their fiftieth anniversary: "I send that which is far more sweet, our love and friendship built over the past fifteen years."[66] Clemans was also a friend of Senator Thomas D. Schall. On May 28, 1924, "Padre" Clemans stated, "We don't want any but Americans in this country and we're going to put up the bars to stop the tremendous influx of foreigners while we take time to Americanize those who are here. The immigration bill was the wisest piece of legislation, next to the bonus bill, adopted by the present session of Congress." Clemans went on to say in that speech, "They say we are opposed to prohibition, but speaking for the bulk of the Legion, I will say that we are back of national prohibition until the last bootlegger is driven out."

Minnesota charities and churches were often the benefactors of Ku Klux Klan charity. Located at the Paynesville Historical Society are letters written by two individuals outlining a KKK group coming into a church in the Paynesville area to make a "donation." In April 27, 1990, Mrs. Emmett Hoeft wrote an account remembering her former Methodist church, which was having some remodeling done on its dome. The KKK apparently offered to give the church some money for the repair. She, along with friend Aileen Sanborn, were in their chairs one Sunday evening when a group of Klan members in their robes marched in and provided the donation. In many towns, there was little distinction between membership in the Klan and membership in a conservative Protestant church.

A Klan initiation ceremony was once held at the Moorhead National Guard Armory. Advertisements taken out by the Klan chapter in the area's newspapers referred to themselves as the "Klay Kounty Klan." In 1926, the Klay Kounty Klan had Congregationalist reverend J.N. Van Cleve of Northfield (Van Cleve is actually from Tapico, Minnesota, and was a minister there) hold a series of lectures near Barnesville, Sabin, in Moland Township and at least two other locations in the county. Mark Piehl is currently working on researching a set of diaries written by a Norwegian pioneer farmer, Levi Thortbedt, from northwest of Glyndon. There are several KKK references in the diaries, including a humorous one to a "mistake" that somebody made in inviting a leading Moorhead attorney to speak at the Klan gathering to "the Protestant people of the Buffalo River area." The attorney was Catholic and reportedly very anti-Klan. But after the meeting, Thortbedt was clearly relieved that the attorney did not mention his Catholic religion, writing, "He made a very nice speech."

Reverend J.N. Van Cleave spoke several times at Carleton College.[67] (First Convent is the church at which J.N. Van Cleave served. Today, the First Convent Church is the Evangelical Covenant Church, which currently operates Minnehaha Academy in Minneapolis, Minnesota.) Carleton College, established by the Congregational Church in Northfield, Minnesota, was known as "Karleton" College. A photo published in the school newspaper, *Algol*, depicted three hooded Klansmen, each with the letters "KKK" emblazoned on their chests, saluting a man in a corporal's uniform outside the Carleton chapel. Effigies of African Americans were often strung up during homecoming festivities, a tradition that continued at Carleton until the 1930s. The college also had the Carleton Cosmopolitan Club, an organization made up of Carleton's few international students. In an issue of the *Carletonian*, there is a photograph of the members of the club

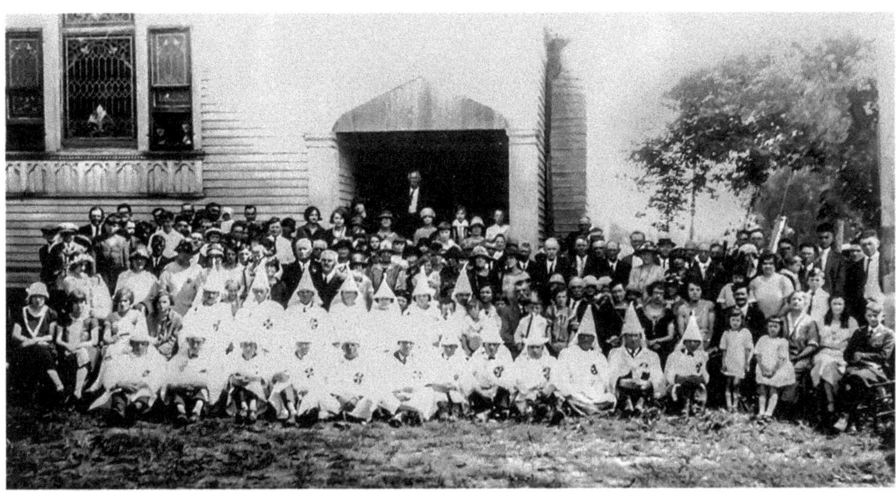

Claremont, Minnesota KKK chapter. *Courtesy of Ruth M. Murray.*

underneath a banner that reads "Karleton Kosmopolitan Klub." Howard Gilkinson, who appeared in the photo of the KKK robed students and had achieved the rank of corporal in World War I before coming to Carleton, had ties with the Carleton Klan.[68]

In the northwest part of Minnesota, there was Presbyterian involvement with the Ku Klux Klan. The *Moorhead County Press* reported on March 26, 1926, that the Ku Klux Klan was holding open revivals with Reverend John Sornberger, an evangelist from Duluth, lauding the Ku Klux Klan for its fearless stand on Protestant Christianity and law enforcement. Reverend Sornberger's funeral services were held on May 5, 1939, at the First Presbyterian Church. Sornberger was a resident of northern Minnesota for sixty years and was a Presbyterian missionary in rural areas for thirty-two years. A Presbyterian minister from Claremont, Minnesota, Reverend Walter Rothwell, wrote to the *Masonic Observer* defending the Ku Klux Klan, and front-page coverage was given to his impassioned letter supporting the Ku Klux Klan.[69]

Reverend Rothwell was a minister at the First Presbyterian Church in Claremont, Minnesota, from 1921 to 1925. Rodney Hatle has a friend who remembers his mother telling stories about cross burnings in Claremont, Minnesota, when she was young girl in the mid-1920s. The Claremont Klan chapter held outdoor movies at the band shell in Claremont in Memorial Park, and this is where they burned Klan crosses. Memorial Park is located one block off Main Street and a block and a half from

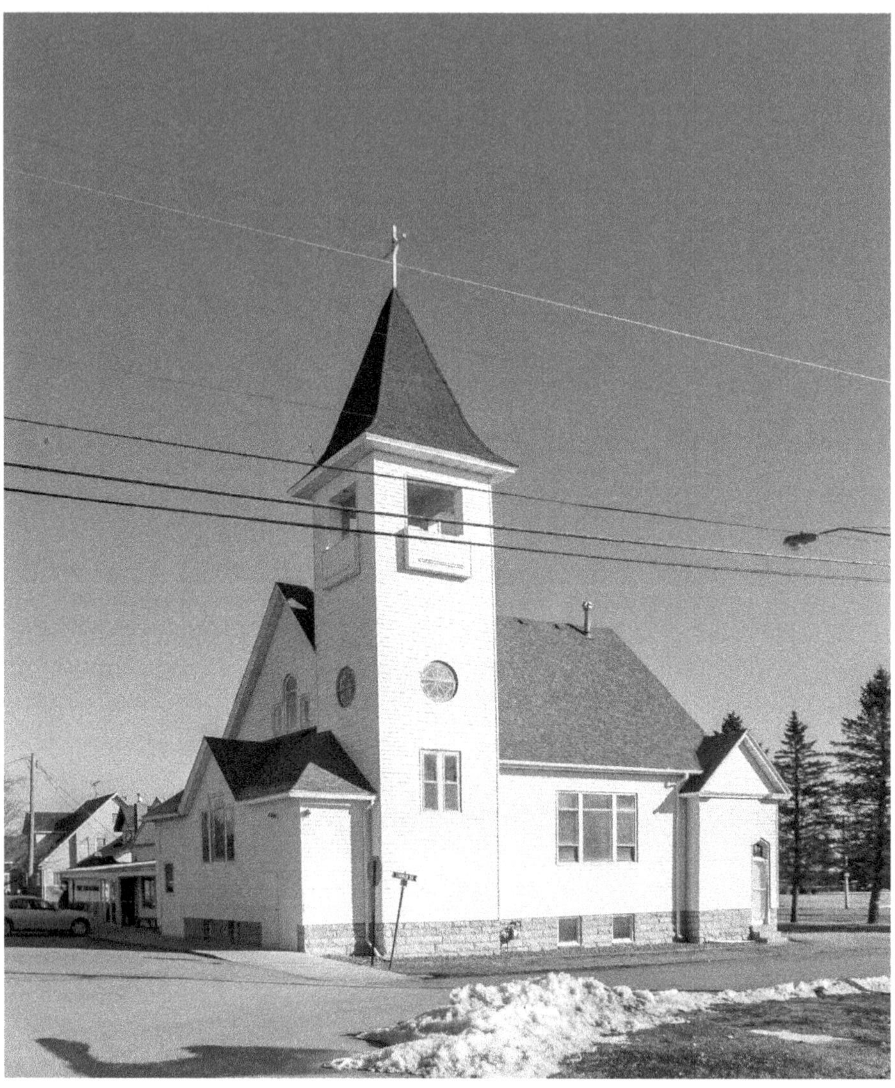

Claremont Presbyterian Church. *Courtesy of Kevin B. Hatle.*

Rothwell's Presbyterian church. Mary Edmond was a member of the Ku Klux Klan, and she is in the photograph of the Claremont Presbyterian Church; men and women belonging to the church posed in front of the church in Claremont in their Klan regalia. Mary Edmond's parents were both originally from Scotland, and she lived in both Steele and Dodge Counties during her lifetime. Her KKK regalia was found among her things after her death.

At a Moorhead Ku Klux Klan revival, a newspaper noted, "Rev. W.J. Hall of the Presbyterian Church will preach on Protestant Christianity and those who hear these ministers of the Gospel on Saturday night will have spent a very interesting as well as a profitable evening in the Klan Klavern." In Grand Forks, North Dakota, arguably the hotbed of Klan activity in the valley, the *Herald* bitterly opposed the Ku Klux Klan group and its leader, Presbyterian minister F. Halsey Ambrose. In April 1924, Klan-endorsed candidates won election to the city government and school boards and later took control of the city commission and police magistrate's office in Grand Forks. Dr. Edgar Allen Cowles was a Klan speaker in the Clay County area. His career as a doctor is listed on his death certificate, and he was also a dentist and farmer. Cowles's father was "native stock" from Connecticut, and Cowles left behind a wife thirty years his junior.

In 1925, newspaper editor Cecil Campbell of Ellendale outlined in great detail a local Klan wedding, "the first Klux Klan ceremonial wedding in the state." The Klan groom was James P. Hanson, and his bride was Miss Angeline Erickson; Mark Elliot, former pastor of the Church of Christ of Winona, performed the ceremony. A description of the Klan wedding held in Albert Lea, Minnesota, is quite detailed. This wedding did actually occur, and the couple's wedding certificate is recorded and listed at the Freeborn County Courthouse in Albert Lea, Minnesota. Toward the end of 1925, Campbell's Klan coverage began to drop off substantially. The Minneapolis Klan trial and Klan appeal in 1923 and 1925, along with his good friend Stafford King being outed as a Klan member in 1924, may have made Campbell tone down his newspaper rhetoric, but Klan activity in Ellendale did not abate.[70]

For the *Madelia Times Messenger* of March 26, 1926, a local woman wrote in telling how she was attending her church in a nearby community when the congregation was interrupted by a procession of white-robed people, "the so-called Klansmen and 100 per cent Americans." They marched up the aisle to the pulpit, pledged allegiance to the flag in the church, marched out and disrobed. She wanted to know what the point of that was and if it stopped the great drive that "Rome is making against the Protestants." The writer stated that bringing Klansmen into churches was unnecessary and questioned if there weren't any Mason or Odd Fellow lodges they could go to instead. In April 1, 1926, a nearly identical letter was reprinted in the *St. James Independent*. In this report, though, the name of the church is given. The Ku Klux Klan's effect was being felt in Minnesota churches. The pastor of the Evangelical St. John's Church at Fairmont was accused of being a member of the Invisible Empire of Klansmen. A woman at the church made the accusation, and the pastor resigned.

CHAPTER 4

Ku Klux Klan Sports, Parades, Fireworks and Family

In the 1920s, baseball was considered the most popular form of athletic competition in America and was one of the leading forms of entertainment and recreation. Baseball was seen by business owners as a constructive game that taught teamwork to employees (immigrant and non-immigrant alike) and encouraged them to start up baseball teams. At Minnesota Ku Klux Klan konklaves held at various locations throughout the state, baseball games were included as a part of Klan events. One identified KKK member and player in a Cannon Falls town team baseball league was James Fenton Mills, World War I veteran.[71] Some of those identified Minnesota baseball teams that played games at Minnesota Klan events included the Great Soo League Club, Albert Lea, Lone Rock, Rochester, Swea City and Fairmont. In 1923, ex–White Sox player Charles "Swede" Risberg played baseball at the Cannon Falls Klan chapter's event.

In September 1920, American learned that the 1919 World Series had been fixed. Chick Gandil and Risberg joined the Chicago White Sox together in 1917; they also conspired to fix the 1919 Series together. Eight players were indicted by a Chicago grand jury for intentionally losing to the Cincinnati Reds in the Series, three games to five. Risberg's standout career moments included punching out the likes of Ty Cobb after a game. The Swede was, as "Shoeless Joe" Jackson said, "a hard guy." After the scandal broke in late 1920, all of the White Sox players were banned from organized baseball, and Risberg came to Minnesota to play baseball. The Minnesota Ku Klux Klan would have been eager to employ the services of someone like Swede Risberg for their ballgames, as good baseball teams brought bigger

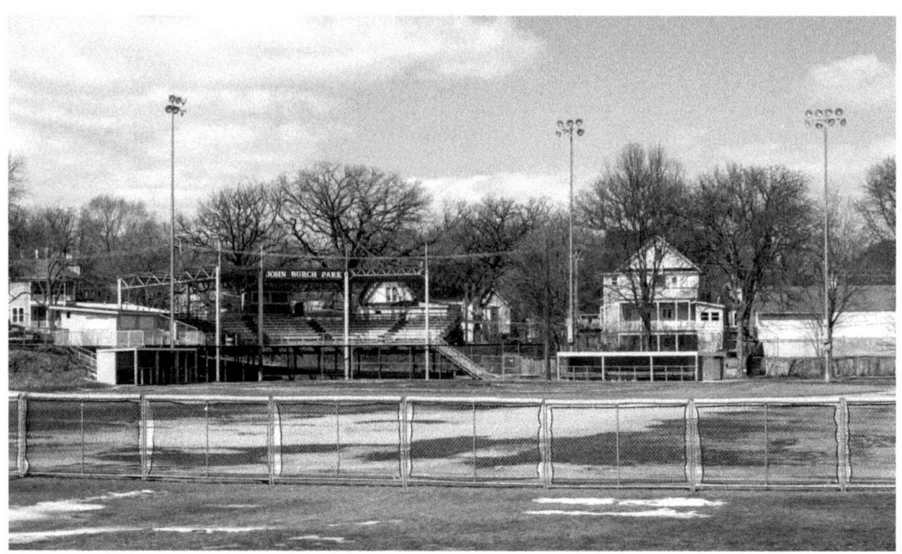

Burch Baseball Field, Cannon Falls, Minnesota. *Courtesy of Kevin B. Hatle.*

crowds to their events. In a newspaper article from Fairmont, it was reported that on Monday July 5, the Rochester baseball team played Lone Rock with Swede Risberg pitching that weekend during the Klan weekend celebration at Interlaken Park in Fairmont.

On September 28, 1923, Rochester awoke to find copies of the KKK's Minnesota publication *Call of the Wild* on the doorstep of every home and business in town. The publisher of the *Rochester Daily Bulletin* was also threatened by the Klan for publishing anti-Klan articles on September 29, 1923. The newspaper received threatening notes that were written on bedsheet-like material, and the publisher was told by the local Klan there that if he published anything further that was detrimental to the Klan, he would be asked to leave the city and that justice would be served on him by the Klan there. The *Rochester Daily Bulletin* did not run a follow-up article denouncing the actions of the local Klan.

In 1923, Rochester started its own independent baseball team, which Risberg joined that year. The Rochester newspaper gave extensive coverage to the games between Rochester and Gilkerson's Union Giants team. There must have been some trepidation, though, among African American players traveling through the state, as the Rochester newspaper also carried three articles that same summer about Ku Klux Klan cross burnings and initiation ceremonies around Mankato, Albert Lea and Austin.

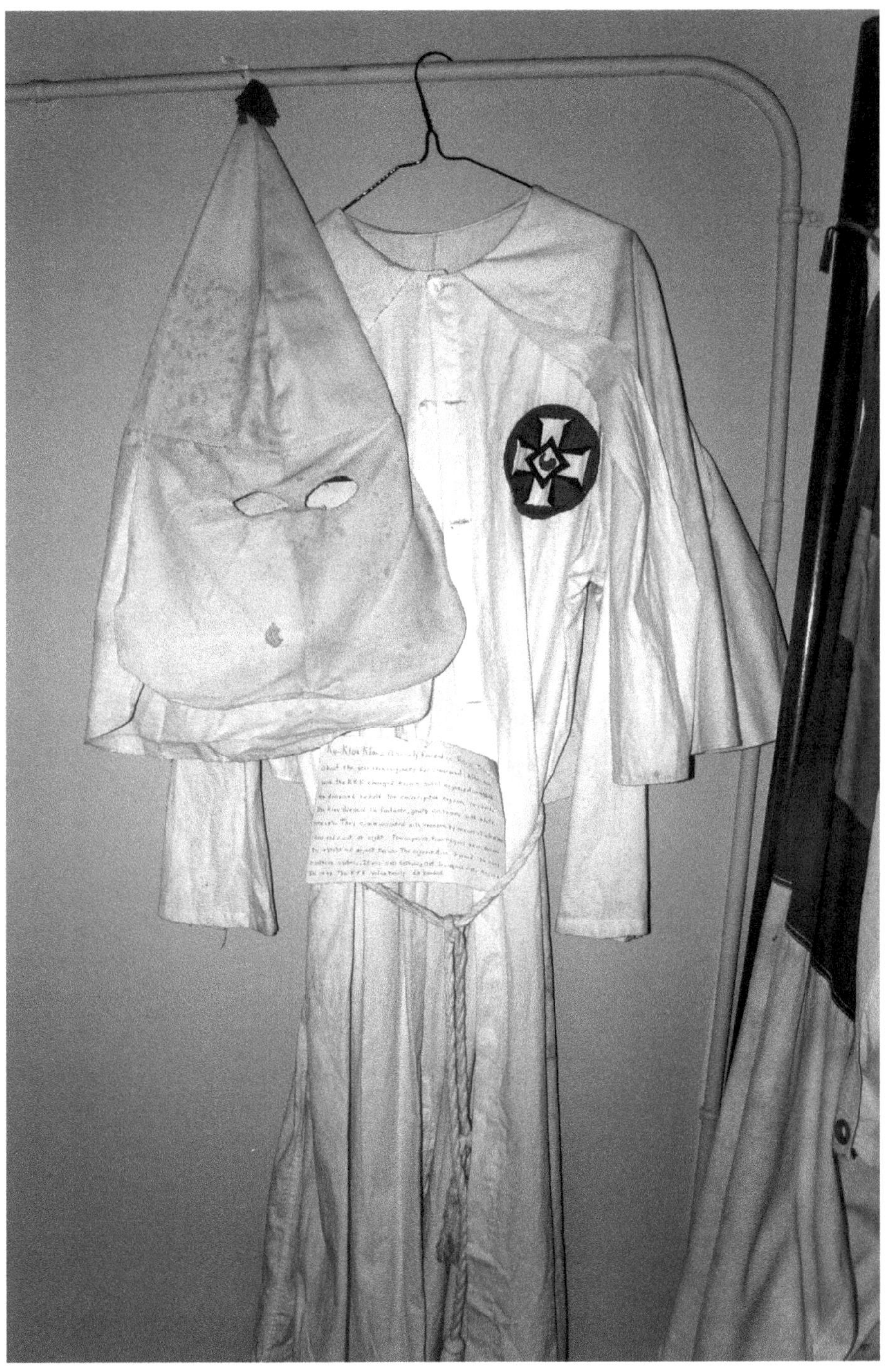

Askov, Minnesota Klan hood and robe. *Courtesy of Pine County Historical Society.*

On September 18, 1923, the Rochester newspaper reported that the Klan initiation ceremony in Austin drew Klansmen from Rochester and was attended by one thousand Klan members, along with two thousand spectators. In 1925, a Klan rally in Kasson attracted a crowd of five hundred, with the main speaker there having given an address the week before at Rochester's Flag Day celebration. In a photo of a Klan float from Rochester, Minnesota's Fourth of July 1926 parade, two men in Klan regalia are seen standing in front, while a third Klansman stands in back of the other two waving the American flag. Rochester had an active Klan chapter when Risberg lived and played baseball there. On March 3, 1924, a series of explosions sounded on a bluff to the north of Rochester, and people living nearby reported seeing a burning cross.

One southwestern Minnesota newspaper article makes mention of burning crosses, stating, "One burning cross represents 50 KKK members [who were now in the area]." In that particular article, three crosses were burned at the same time and in the same place; possibly meaning that there were 150 Ku Klux Klan members in the Heron Lake, Minnesota area. Heron Lake's population at the time was just 651 residents.[72] Minnesota newspapers seemed to make a particular point of covering the actual numbers of crosses that were burned at each location; was this to let the public know how many people the local Minnesota Klan chapters might have in an area? Other examples from the state also indicate how many crosses were burned in given areas: the *Minnesota Fiery Cross*, a Klan newspaper, reported on March 7, 1924, "Burn Fiery Cross at Virginia, Minnesota." "Some say that they have heard that the flaming cross appears wherever there is an increase of a hundred members." The reason behind using burning crosses was that they represented the Protestant churches standing for a living cross, while the Catholics supposedly worshiped a dead and meaningless cross.[73]

By the late summer of 1921, the Ku Klux Klan was flourishing across the country. There was a strong desire to get back to "normalcy," which included returning women to their "traditional" roles. In the 1920s, the divorce rate increased, and the use of the automobile was leading to greater mobility. Women who sought divorce, like in the case of Mrs. Radcliffe, a resident of Aitkin County, were fought in court by their husbands. Mr. Radcliffe claimed in court that his wife was insane and should be brought before the probate county for examination regarding her sanity. The husband also filed a petition in the probate court of Aitkin County alleging that his wife was incompetent to manage her affairs and "prayed" that he be appointed her guardian. In another divorce case (from December 17, 1927, at the State Hospital for the Insane in Rochester, Minnesota), Mrs. John Rosival wrote to Archbishop Dowling because her husband had managed to have her placed in a Minnesota asylum. The poor woman wrote to the bishop for help, begging him to get her out of there.

Minnesota newspapers in the 1920s are full of stories in which husbands aren't happy with their wives leaving them. In Worthington, Minnesota, in December 1923, a man angry with his wife for leaving him went to get her back. Instead, Henry Schumacher shot at his wife and then turned the gun on his son and eventually himself. Since their estrangement early in the summer of 1922, Mrs. Schumacher had been keeping house for Fred Wendt at Ellsworth. Schumacher shot at his wife, drew his gun on his son and tried to shoot the boy. The mother of the boy knocked the barrel of the weapon aside, and Schumacher ran to a barn, where he was later found to have shot himself. The vote had come for women, but there was also a desire on the part of women for more rights. Not everyone viewed women having a stronger voice in their own affairs as a positive step forward for the country.

As the Klan spread nationwide in 1920–21, thousands of women's auxiliary chapters sprang up, and Queens of the Golden Mask (another organization similar to the Women's Ku Klux Klan, or WKKK) was launched by David Stephenson. Imperial KKK headquarters founded the WKKK order of the Kamelia (a white rose symbol). Northfield, Fairmont and Owatonna had WKKK chapters. Klanswomen generally shared the concerns of their husbands, fathers and brothers in regard to fundamentalist morality, ultraconservative politics and racism. Klanswomen also proved to be a force in civic life in many towns, demanding strict enforcement of the vice laws and supporting charitable projects in the name of 100 percent Americanism.

Myrtle Cain was the first to make a public effort to outlaw Klan activities taking place in Minnesota; unfortunately, her papers at the Minnesota Historical Society were a disappointment. I spoke to Representative Phyllis Kahn to ask her why Cain's personal papers at the Minnesota Historical Society were so vague, as Myrtle was a good friend of Representative Kahn's. Cain's papers start in 1945, and there isn't any mention of the anti-masking bill at all. Phyllis spoke to Myrtle's brother on the phone soon after Myrtle's funeral in 1980 to make sure that he got her papers to MNHS. Since the brother was responsible for getting those papers to MNHS, this may be why they only start in 1945. Kahn said that Myrtle was very proud of her work on the anti-masking bill and in getting it passed. Myrtle was solely responsible for taking care and supporting her and her brother's mother.

Arvonne Fraser also confirmed this information about Myrtle's personal life. Myrtle's brother inherited her house due to Myrtle not having ever been married or having children. Both Kahn and Fraser think that the brother probably came into town after her death, took what he could and left again. Fraser also told me about Myrtle leading a strike of female telephone operators of the International Brotherhood of Electrical Workers. Socialist behavior like that would have been one more thing about Myrtle that would have put her on the Klan's radar.[74]

As noted in the *Voices of the Knights of the Ku Klux Klan*, "To make a long story short: Myrtle Cain is both a Roman Catholic and a member of the ladies' auxiliary of the Ancient Order of Hibernians." Myrtle had learned to not wear her Catholicism on her sleeve in Minnesota; Arvonne Fraser had not even known that she was Catholic. Cain had a Mass of Christian Burial in the Church of St. Anthony of Padua, and she was interred at St. Mary's Cemetery. The anti-masking law that Cain authored (Minnesota Statute 609.735, Chapter 160-H.F. No 138) was designed to keep Klansmen from hiding their faces in public. The Klan responded to the bill:

> *In view of the influence of the foreign pontiff to whose dictation she must yield obedience, if she is a loyal Roman Catholic it would be surprising if she had not done this. Although the Pope and all his satellites opposed equal suffrage to the limit, they are just smooth enough to realize that such a bill as the Cain Raisign bill would carry with it more of an appeal if introduced by a woman and the Papacy is ever ready to let a woman do its dirty work where there is work of that king that can be done for them more effectively by a woman than it can be done by a man.*[75]

G.F. Clarke, who said that he was active in putting over the campaign for the Oregon school bill, came to Minnesota to appear before the Minnesota legislature to fight Myrtle Cain's anti-masking bill. G.F. Clarke, also a Klan member, stated that the Cain bill was "a slap at the Ku Klux Klan." Clark went on to further state, "Now, that this king of thing has been started, we propose to give them what they want. We are going to put over the Oregon school bill in Minnesota." Frank Drill, a St. Paul attorney, said that he represented the Invisible Empire and wanted an amendment added to Cain's bill noting that that the bill shall be construed as prohibiting the wearing of masks in good faith for amusement or entertainment. Mr. Drill suggested further adding to this clause the words "or patriotic demonstrations, or for lodge purposes, or in the ceremonies of fraternal societies." This addendum was added to the bill.[76]

In 1921, Nellie Griswold Francis's successful lobbying efforts resulted in the passage of an anti-lynching law in Minnesota. Mrs. Francis, with the assistance of her husband, William T. Francis, formulated and wrote the bill and lobbied for its passage by the state legislature. It is likely due to the $7,500 fine it imposed on perpetrators and the dire consequences it promised law officers who permitted lynchings that effectively ended this type of atrocity in Minnesota. Mrs. Francis was from St. Paul, Minnesota, and was president of the Minnesota State Federation of Colored Women. When *The Birth of a Nation* came out, Nellie Francis's husband, an attorney, presented to the Minneapolis City Council a proposed ordinance to ban hate films. Mr. Francis was also a presidential elector of the St. Paul branch of the NAACP.[77]

When the anti-lynching bill in Minnesota was signed into law on April 18, 1921, it allowed for suspension of police officials who failed to protect prisoners from mobs. What Mrs. Francis had accomplished with her bill was proclaimed by NAACP activist James Loomis as "the most important piece of legislation affecting our race that has ever been passed in our state." The African American communities in Minnesota were aware that the Ku Klux Klan was now in Minnesota. The *Northwestern Bulletin*, a newspaper out of St. Paul, Minnesota, owned and run by African Americans, began newspaper coverage of KKK activity in Minnesota as early as 1921. On August 27, 1921, it reported, "KKK-1,000 Members Said to Be Active in Minnesota." On September 3, 1921, it reported, "Local African-American Lawyer Quizzes Jurors on KKK Membership." On April 21, 1923, it reported, "Mpls KKK Papers Subject of Grand Jury Investigation." And in June 1923, the *Northwestern Bulletin* began its coverage of the Minnesota Ku Klux Klan's actions in libeling Mayor George Leach of Minneapolis.[78]

Located in Minnesota governor Theodore Christianson's papers is a letter written to the governor from St. Paul by an African American named John. W. Willis, who signed his letter, "Respectfully, Your fellow-citizen." In the two-page letter, Mr. Willis points out to the governor what is happening to African Americans across the country. There is an eloquent paragraph noting why an organization like the NAACP is so needed:

> *Plans are laid for discrimination against the Negro and for his continued humiliation; and these plans are vigorously supported and furthered by an*

> *atrocious and beastly association, known as the Ku Klux Klan, founded in the Southern States, which has been extended into every State of the Union and not only proclaims loudly its diabolic purpose but also, hold secret conclaves in which measures are taken for their execution. Not only does it insult Christianity by burning the Cross—the emblem of salvation—but it also seeks to deprive multitudes of our fellow-citizens of their essential rights, to humiliate them in every way, and to force them into a state of civic ostracism which is akin to slavery.*[79]

William T. Francis was directly involved in the case of Max Mason, one of the young men who had been arrested but not lynched in Duluth. Francis raised funds for the impending trial through both Twin City branches of the NAACP. Francis wrote just a few days after the lynchings that neither James Sullivan nor Irene Tusken had told the truth about what happened that night. More than $150 was collected to defray ongoing investigative costs. Although no evidence was found connecting Mason to the crime, he was convicted of rape and received a sentence of seven to thirty years. Twenty-one-year-old Mason arrived at Minnesota State Prison in Stillwater in August 1921. He appealed his case to the Minnesota Supreme Court, but the guilty verdict was not overturned. In 1925, the Minnesota Parole Board finally discharged Mason from prison with the condition that he leave the state immediately.

Theodore Roosevelt had condemned the increasingly low birth rates of Americans, blaming them on selfishness. These deeply held convictions were translated into a national alarm about racial suicide and decline, giving credibility to eugenics-based and anti-immigrant prejudice. In the U.S. Census numbers for Minnesota, there was a dramatic birth rate difference between 1910 and 1930 between those of the native-born population and the foreign-born population. The Ku Klux Klan supported eugenics, which promoted 1920s Klan objectives of racial and immigrant stereotyping even further. After World War I, sterilization became a topic among Minnesota state officials and physicians. Dr. Charles Fremont Dight, president of the Minnesota Eugenics Society in Minneapolis, Minnesota, sought political and medical solutions to improve certain segments of the state's population.

Charles F. Dight took the position as resident physician at Shattuck School in Faribault, Minnesota, and later became professor of physiology at Hamline Medical School in St. Paul. Dight saw eugenic sterilization as a "modern" idea to give government control over sexual morals and reproduction, as well as a "social" movement to prevent the "degeneration of the race." From 1921 to

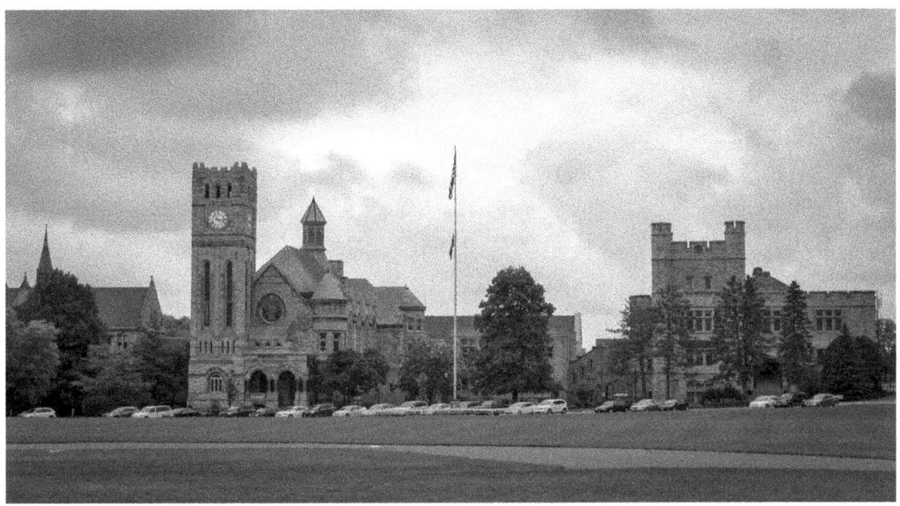

Shattuck Campus, Faribault, Minnesota. *Courtesy of Kevin B. Hatle.*

1935, Dr. Dight wrote some three hundred articles on heredity and eugenics that appeared in Minnesota newspapers. Dight also broadcast two series of radio talks on heredity and eugenics in Minnesota. The Minnesota Eugenics Society was organized in 1923, and in 1925, the Minnesota legislature voted on a bill for eugenics-based sterilization that passed both the House and Senate, with Governor Theodore Christianson promptly signing it. The first day the eugenic sterilization law in Minnesota was put into operation was January 8, 1926, on six adult "feeble-minded" females in the mental asylum in Faribault, Minnesota. On February 2, 1927, the Minnesota Eugenics Society held its first annual meeting as a corporation, with Dr. Dight elected as president and Sheriff Earle Brown as vice-president.[80]

Judge Searls had his oath administered to him by an identified Duluth Klan member, Arthur Davenport. Regarding these premature deaths in Minnesota, author Kathleen Blee referred me to a section in her book about the Athens, Georgia Klan chapter there taking matters into its own hands. Its Klan chapter had its law enforcement committee concoct a plan over one summer to bring to town a private detective. With the detective's help, Athens Klansmen collected evidence that resulted in a host of indictments, obtained illegally through deliberate entrapment of individuals and resulting in violent deaths for some men. Peter Sletterdahl (his Klan name "Twilight Orn") was from Minnesota. His book *The Nightshirt in Politics* made Sletterdahl one of the Ku Klux Klan's "enemies." Enemies of the KKK were those who tried to destroy the Klan movement. Enemies also included those who broke their allegiance to the Ku Klux Klan.[81]

Another ex-Klan member wrote that "frame-ups" and "poison squads" were common practices. "Frame-ups were the most numerous things. Usually a woman was used. At other times intoxicating liquor was secreted in a hotel room while the occupant was out or it was placed in his automobile while parked." Ex-Klan member Edgar Allen Booth wrote about the Ku Klux Klan that "[i]ts chief weapon, if not its only weapon, was the systematic spread of poisonous tales concerning men and women who would not do the bidding of the Imperial Kloncillium, and whom that body, or Dr. Evans, could not remove because of that person's large personal following in the Klan. This poison department maintained agents who went about the country losing tales of scandal against those who had fallen into the bad graces of the superbody of the Klan."[82]

Duluth judge Spencer Searls committed suicide in 1927, six months after he was sworn in as a judge, leaving behind a young wife and a six-year-old daughter. His judgeship was attached to the municipal division of the Duluth court system, but he had direct charge of the special conciliation court. Judge Searls was also permitted to practice law privately but not to appear in conciliation court—a perfect job for an up-and-coming judge with a young family. Spencer Searls had also been the Duluth American Legion commander and one of Stafford King's personal correspondents. Searls sent his own telegram to King upon King's father's death in 1922 and made an individual donation toward the purchase of Stafford King's new car. There is a very detailed letter in which King urges Searls to run for governor.[83] Searls was a rising star in the Minnesota Republican Party and seemed to be a man who had everything to live for with a brilliant future in front of him.

David's Sling magazine was the American Legion periodical published by the David Wisted Post No. 28 of Duluth from 1923 to 1925. In it are articles about Judge Searls from when he was a commander of the post—Searls is described as being actively engaged in post activities. He is also a featured speaker at the Duluth Legion post and spoke at other American Legion posts throughout Minnesota. What happened to Searls in 1927? The Duluth newspapers reported that war injuries resulted in Searls taking his own life, but why close to ten years after World War I and why at this point in his career? It looked as if Searls had everything to live for. Searls had told his wife the day of his death that he was going to St. Paul and had even packed a suitcase. He was found alone and dead in his Duluth office later that evening.

The *Winona Republican Herald* of April 23, 1926, reported, "Rev. Knute

B. Birkeland's, Former Minister and Financier of Mpls—Body Was Found in an Abandoned Apartment—Currently Investigating." Mrs. Hodges, who was accused of the murder, later brought three damage suits accusing two high Minnesota state officials, the Birkeland family and two members of the Hennepin County Sheriff's Office (Earle Brown's office) of libel, false arrest and malicious prosecution. Knute Birkeland's son, Harold Birkeland, wrote about his father's death in a pamphlet called *Floyd B. Olson in the First Kidnapping Murder*. Harold used the circumstances of his father's death to cause problems for Hennepin's county attorney Floyd Olson. Harold's pamphlet seemed less concerned about finding his father's killer and more concerned about Olson's job performance.

Mrs. Hodges's lawyer was William J. Quinn, who committed suicide in a downtown hotel room in St. Paul, Minnesota, on September 12, 1932, leaving behind a wife; his father, John Quinn; and three children. The *St. Paul Pioneer Press* headlines about Quinn noted that he had been prominent for many years in Democratic circles. Quinn reportedly opened the door and admitted a man into his hotel room before going into the bathroom and shooting himself. In 1926, the same year he represented Mrs. Hodges, Quinn was made chairman of the Democratic State Central Committee and later became a member of the national campaign advisory committee for presidential candidate Alfred E. Smith. The Ramsey County Bar Association in its memorial to Quinn stated that Quinn's personality was a pleasure and that "his quickness and speed of thought made him an exceptional trial lawyer and a feared adversary." Might there have been something in Quinn's personal life that the St. Paul Klan chapter used against this up-and-coming star in the Minnesota Democratic Party to cause him to take his life?[84]

Harold Birkeland put together another pamphlet called *To All Law-Respecting, Law-Abiding Citizens of Minnesota, Greetings.* Signatures of ministers inside were solicited by Birkeland for something else and then added to this pamphlet instead. Ray Chase, a political opponent of Olson's, had a copy of Birkeland's pamphlet in his personal papers. Essentially, this pamphlet is a blasting of Floyd Olson's record as county attorney, mentioning ballot tampering and election fraud. The ministers who signed a letter to Governor Christianson asking him to further investigate Reverend Birkeland's death, felt that they had been used by the son since he put their names into his pamphlet instead. The ministers publicly stated in June 1929, "We severely censure those persons who for political or ulterior motives are distributing pamphlets containing copies of this petition and containing other statements where were not in the original petition. We assure you that we have had no part in such printing and distribution and did not even contemplate it." The ministers did not know that in signing the letters to Governor Christianson, they would be used as a political ploy against Floyd Olson by Harold Birkeland.

Ray Chase also kept in his personal papers copies of radio speeches that Harold Birkeland made regarding Chase's father's death, as well as Chase's handwritten notes on the radio speeches that Harold Birkeland gave. One of Chase's suggestions is an attempt to link Olson with the Ku Klux Klan just because Olson's wife is Catholic—to a man like Olson, Chase remarked, that wouldn't have made any difference. Ray Chase's papers at the MNHS are described as such: "He collected a considerable body of correspondence, notes, and copies of official records, purporting to prove that Minnesota's Farmer Labor government was rife with graft, payroll padding, and other political irregularities, and that its leaders, particularly Floyd B. Olson and Elmer A. Benson, were of communistic leanings." Harold Birkeland worked for Thomas Schall as his chauffer and was murdered along with his wife in Mexico in 1972.[85]

Otto H. Diercks took his life on August 15, 1928, leaving behind a wife and four young sons. Diercks was superintendent of the Minnesota Timber Department from 1919 to a point several months before his death. His department was under the direct supervision of Republican Ray Chase. In the 1920s, the Minnesota Timber Department, at the state auditor's discretion, could sell state timber and swamplands without any direct accountability. The department came under scrutiny, with complaints coming from foresters Dr. Raphael Zon and Grover M. Conzet, who publicly criticized the timber diversion of the state auditor's office. Diercks was indignant and defended his division, declaring that not that much timber had been sold by his division and that if the foresters worked as hard as the men in Diercks's department did, the state's timber problems would be better understood.

Chase was not only Diercks's boss but also his personal friend, attending his marriage to his second wife in 1921. Chase stated to the press that he was shocked by Diercks's suicide, but in Chase's papers, there is a somewhat frantic correspondence that passed between Chase and several individuals about Diercks's suicide. Chase was being very obvious in pointing out how mentally ill Diercks was and how he was not surprised by the suicide. Diercks tendered his resignation to Chase several months before his suicide in Duluth and took a job with the Lehigh Briquetting Company in Fargo, North Dakota. Chase wrote to Diercks new employer, stating, "I wish to do everything possible to protect him in the tragedy which has occurred," asking for the name of Diercks's doctor to get a statement about Diercks's physical condition. Chase also released the information he got about Diercks to the press. A close friend of Diercks's, A.M. Welles, publisher of the *Worthington Globe*, wrote to Chase that Diercks had discussed with him the timber controversy, but news of his suicide came as a complete shock to Welles.

During the weeks before, during and after Diercks's suicide, Ray Chase wrote a series of articles in the *Anoka Herald* defending how he himself had handled state timber business. Absolutely no mention was made of Diercks's death in the paper (Chase's family newspaper, no less). Chase was vehement in his claim that "[t]here should not be any restriction as to the amount of timber to be sold." Diercks was not the person who made the decision about who received state lumber—that was Chase's decision. But why *was* so much timber sold, and to whom was it being sold or not sold? Chase stated that the controversies about the timber department were not "serious" issues, but they were serious enough to write four weeks of articles defending the department in his family's newspaper. Chase emerged unscathed from the controversy, but as for Diercks, who left his wife and four sons in his home state of Minnesota to work elsewhere, there were deadly and unfortunate consequences.[86]

CHAPTER 5

Persons of Interest "Brushing Shoulders" with the Klan

Charles Babcock made his home in Elk River and was the head of Minnesota Highway Department until 1933. Charles's brother started Babcock Hardware in 1916, when the Babcock family moved to Anoka, Ray Chase's hometown. Charles Babcock was appointed commissioner of highways by Governor J.A.A. Burnquist in April 1917. Senator Ole O. Sageng received a letter about Babcock in 1921 in which Thomas Cashman (from Steele County) wrote of his concern about Babcock's unlimited power. Cashman was absolutely opposed to the construction of Minnesota's highway system being placed solely under one's man's control. Cashman also talked about the possibility of abuse with contractors. Cashman could not understand "why conservative Legislators should leave so important a question and the expenditure of millions of money to the judgment of one man."[87]

In reelection information that Stafford King put out when running for state auditor, he noted, "As a member of the Highway Allotment Board, King has aided in the distribution of more than $20,000,000 to the Counties for good roads." King had regular correspondence with Charles Babcock, making job requests for county engineers whom King knew and wanted hired by the Minnesota Highway Department. One in particular, Paul Noyce Coates, was a good friend of King, who wrote that "arrangements had been made for me to speak at certain political gatherings which had been arranged for my friend, Paul Coates, who is a candidate for County Surveyor. I am Chairman of his committee and have promised him all the aid and assistance I can give him." Coates had a company that received quite a bit of work from the Minnesota Highway Department.[88]

The Ku Klux Klan was reported to have been involved in the Minnesota Highway Department. An interview was conducted by Roger Benson with Marlin Sigstad, a resident of Windom. Sigstad was a former Klansman and, when he was younger, a highway worker. He told Benson that in the western part of the state, highway jobs were "awarded" to certain people in the Minnesota Highway Department. Local Cottonwood county historian Lucille Nelson was told by Karl Mikkelson that when US 71 was being built near Delft, Minnesota, a motel-style building in the area was where out-of-town men who did highway work would stay. This is where the KKK crosses were burned, according to Marlin Sigstad's brother, Dale Sigstad. The organizer for the Ku Klux Klan—who came from Pipestone, according to Marlin—happened to be a close friend of one of the engineers working on Minnesota State Highway 62. There were four crews of young men from Windom employed by the state highway department at the time, and it was these men who were the first ones to join the KKK.[89] The *Cottonwood County Citizen* in September 1924 report C.L. Motl as being the district engineer for the Windom area.

In Thomas Schall's Senate reelection campaign against three-term governor Theodore Christianson, Schall traveled the state calling Christianson "Muskrat Ted" and linking him with the "fur farms fraud," resulting in Christianson's defeat in the primary. This scandal involved Charles W. Gillam, a grain dealer from Windom who was appointed state commissioner of securities by Christianson. Charles Gilliam's son, Stanley Gillam, a prominent Minneapolis attorney, said that Schall accusing Christianson and his father of this controversy over the fur farms was the determining factor in Schall defeating Christianson in the Republican primary. But was that necessarily the case?[90] In August 1924, Thomas Schall paid a visit to Windom in the company of Andrew Rahn.

Several weeks before Schall's visit, a cross was burned at a Klan meeting in Windom where a speaker made an address. Within ten days of meeting, another Klan event was held in Windom at the armory, with a large group in attendance. People who belonged to the Ku Klux Klan in Windom were encouraged to join by the local newspaper there, the *Citizen*. The Windom Ku Klux Klan chapter also publicly made a point of going after men who drank and were cruel to their wives. A Klan parade took place in Windom, with Klansmen marching down Third Avenue toward what is now the Travel Place. The Windom Ku Klux Klan chapter said that it was needed to help the sheriff keep order in town. Meetings of the Klan were held at the Windom armory, and members said that they only wore their hoods and robes when inside the building at meetings.[91]

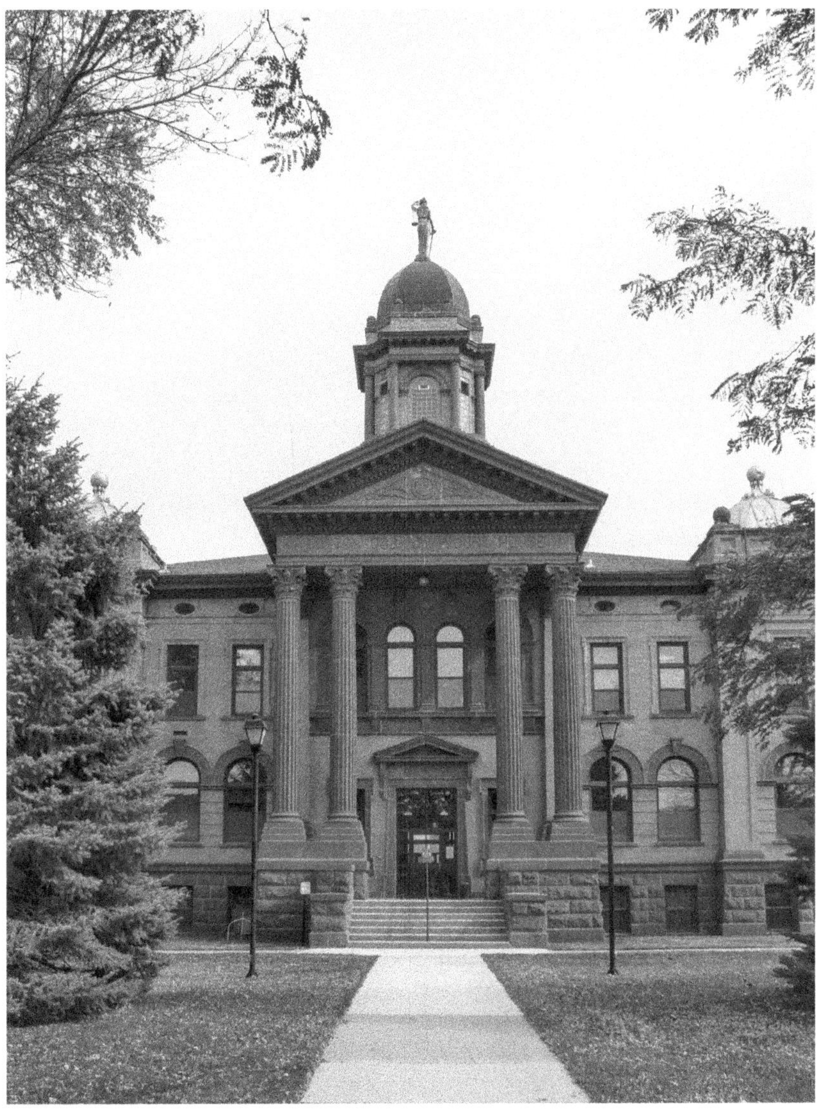

Windom Courthouse, Minnesota. *Courtesy of Kevin B. Hatle.*

Earle Brown was a Republican candidate for governor, the sheriff of Hennepin County and "Founder of the Highway Patrol." Brown was accused of and later admitted (to a Minneapolis grand jury in April 1923) to having joined the Minnesota Klan—membership no. 4. Sheriff Brown told the grand jurors that he joined the Klan because he realized it was becoming a powerful organization, and he wanted, as an officer of the law, to "be on the inside." Brown was solicited to join the Klan by a Mr. Henson of Omaha in the detective service of the Bell Telephone company in 1921. Brown was initiated in the Klan organizer's room in the Dyckman Hotel a few months before April 1923. The Dyckman Hotel was regularly reported on in the *Midway News* as being the meeting spot for Twin Cities Klan activities.[92]

As sheriff in the 1920s, Brown did nothing during his tenure to stop the Minneapolis Klan chapters from meeting or burning their crosses in Hennepin County. "Earle Brown candidate for Governor, Republican, is considered a Robbinsdale man, and keeps his fraternal and social relations here although he lives over the line in Brooklyn Center." The hill across from today's North Memorial Hospital's parking lot, in Robbinsdale, Minnesota, is where large and prominent Klan crosses were burned. Trudi Campbell, of Special Collections at the Minneapolis Central Library, remembered her mother telling her about seeing flaming crosses in Hennepin County. Her mother told her stories about vacationing in the Minnetonka area, and in the middle of the night, the Klan burned crosses in the middle of a group of cabins close to where Campbell's mother was staying. Lucille Beebe, a Robbinsdale resident, remembered a fiery cross being burned near Lowry Avenue and Highway 52 when she was growing up.

Andrew B. Robbins, passing though Robbinsdale in 1887, decided because of the area's proximity to Minneapolis and its natural beauty that the area

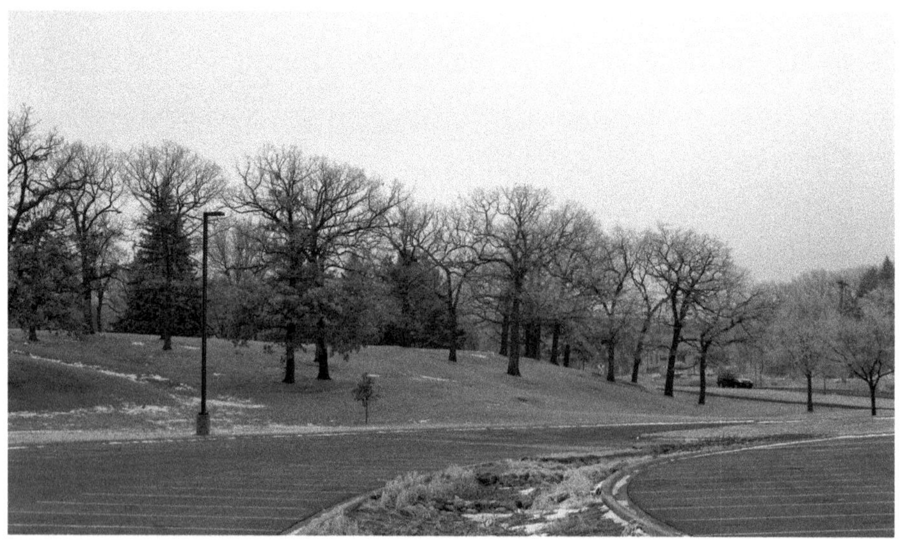

Minneapolis KKK meeting spot, Robbinsdale, Minnesota. *Courtesy of Kevin B. Hatle.*

could become an excellent suburb outside that city. The steep hill on Crystal Avenue (now West Broadway near Minneapolis) was a much-traveled road from Minneapolis to Robbinsdale. The hill where the Minneapolis Klansmen would meet to initiate new members and burn crosses overlooked Robbinsdale. Flaming crosses on top of this particular hill were reported by residents of Robbinsdale; Brown would have been aware of these activities. For two years in the early 1920s, the Ku Klux Klan of Minneapolis paraded in downtown Robbinsdale. The Klan would parade down Broadway from Forty-second Avenue to a gravel pit near the old traffic circle, and a former Robbinsdale mayor recalled that the line of marchers was four blocks long. In 1950, David Stephenson sought haven in Robbinsdale, which must have felt just like home to Indiana's former grand dragon.

Ray Chase worked for the Minnesota Commission of Public Safety and was also the Republican campaign manager for the Committee of One Hundred (Republicans). The *Anoka Herald* was accused in 1930 by the *McLeod County Republic* of having been favorable to the Minnesota Ku Klux Klan in the 1920s. German people were called "swine" in Chase's family newspaper, and Senator Shipstead of the Nonpartisan League ticket was called a "viper that crawls and besmirches the fair name of Minneapolis." The *Anoka Herald* defended the activities of the Ku Klux Klan in its editorial columns and criticized Hennepin's county attorney Floyd B. Olson for prosecuting officers of the Klan for circulating a paper called "Voice of the Knights of the Ku Klux Klan." Chase denied the charges, saying that he did not have any involvement personally with the *Anoka Herald*, although he was secretary-treasurer for the newspaper and one of its stockholders. The *McLeod County Republic* verified that Chase had intimate connections with the *Herald* up until 1928.[93]

Judge Spencer Searls—the young Duluth judge who committed suicide—was on Chase's Committee of One Hundred list. The *Anoka Herald* in April 1918 featured an editorial possibly noting the first clue that Klan organizers were in Minnesota already. It suggested that if Americans weren't 100 percent loyal, mob law should be an option in the state. The editorial further noted, "Ku-Klux-Klans and mob law are not indications of a healthy civilization, but they indicate that the United States will not submit to the rule of Bolshevics, Bentals and Townleys." Chase also was in close contact with Stafford King; in fact, the two men were on a first-name basis. King wrote to Chase telling him how appreciative he was having Chase (as state auditor) getting the board of review to reverse itself on three bonus board decisions, allowing the amount of their claims. Chase told King that this information was not for publicity purposes, but it was a sign of Chase's good faith toward King.[94]

Senator Ole O. Sageng, born in Norway, came to Dalton, Minnesota, located in Ottertail County, at the age of seventeen, graduating from Fergus Falls High School. Sageng and Judge Julius E. Haycraft put together a booklet "exposing" the Nonpartisan League with both men's "hearty endorsement." In Sageng and Haycraft's publication, there is also a copy of Joseph Gilbert's written endorsement of William D. Haywood; the same Joseph Gilbert tried in Minnesota in 1920 as an antiwar dissident. Another section in Sageng and Haycraft's publication features a poem: "If old Farmer John don't please us / His machine will visit Jesus." A typed note in the booklet on the bottom of the copy of the poem reads, "Some of the letters they introduced in the Chicago trial indicate pretty clearly what they meant when they suggest that: If old Farmer John don't please you, his machine will visit Jesus." Judge Haycraft was from Martin County, which contained a large and strong Klan presence.

During his lifetime, Judge Julius Haycraft spoke ardently for the temperance cause and made frequent patriotic speeches. Haycraft was the Martin County chairman of the American First organization during World War I. In 1915, Haycraft had a statewide reputation as a public speaker and a trial lawyer. He was appointed judge in 1925 and was reelected until his retirement in 1948 due to ill health. Haycraft refused to accept a pension that he had earned, saying that he would not become a burden on the taxpayers. Julius Haycraft's son, Howard, was the vehement adversary of Reverend William B. Riley, the man who wanted evolution outlawed in Minnesota schools and colleges. Howard did not move back to Fairmont after graduating from the University of Minnesota and is the only one of Julius Haycraft's children not buried with him in Fairmont; Howard lived and died in California after leaving Minnesota.

The Agricultural Credits Act of 1923 was passed in the Minnesota legislature, designed to support an avenue through which the farmer could obtain "intermediate credit." Loans from the rural credit bureau also provided for the purchase of farming equipment and live stock. Applicants were entitled to receive a loan under this act only if they could show to the satisfaction of the bureau that they were honorably discharged veterans of the war with Germany, that they were citizens of the state of Minnesota at the time of their enlistment and that they served on active duty as a part of the military or naval forces of the United States at some period between April 6, 1917, and November 11, 1918. Senator Ole O. Sageng was the president of the Minnesota

Department of Rural Credit (later determined to be corrupt) from 1925 to 1931. Chairman Sageng received a salary of $4,500 per year, with traveling and other expenses included.

In Minnesota, the rural credit bureau was accused of loaning money to big businessmen, who took that money from the government and stuffed it into their own pockets or loaned it to their friends, who never paid the money back. The secretary for the rural credit bureau was H.H. Flowers, from Cleveland, Minnesota. Flowers owned a large farm implement dealership. Sageng and his brother had been involved in an unsuccessful business venture in which they sold more than $200,000 worth of stock in a threshing machine company. The company went broke after only producing a few threshing machines. Also noted in the agricultural act is the order that the chairman and secretary should be of different political parties. Flowers and Sageng, however, were both Republican businessmen who sold farm machinery for a living, and they were in charge of the Minnesota Department of Rural Credit.

When he made an attempt for the governor's office in 1924, Sageng's main bases of political support were the issues of prohibition and women's suffrage. He said that any modification of the Eighteenth Amendment amounted to repeal. The Woman's Christian Temperance Union (WCTU) in Fergus Falls kept in regular contact with him—they did not want him to have 2 percent beer legalized and wanted to have pool halls closed on Sundays. Sageng wanted to be governor, but unfortunately for him, as his good friend Olai Lende, a lawyer and political sounding board for Sageng, pointed out, "I think it was Dr. Safford and Willie Norton who said that the Hennepin County machine would rather go down in defeat, defeated by a Nonpartisan at the election, than to surrender their machine to a Republican nominee not of their own choice." Sageng was instead put in charge of the rural credit bureau in exchange.

Governor Olson noted about the rural credit bureau, "The chief bank racketeer was a republican luminary in the state Senate, who happened to be president and majority stockholder of two banks. Through his influence this Republican politician succeeded in obtaining through his banks loans from the bureau aggregating between $500,000 and $600,000 refinancing frozen paper. Of these loans 51 percent already have been foreclosed, and on some of the loans not even an initial payment was made." H.H. Flowers (possibly the "luminary" aforementioned) also had troubles with financial irregularities that came to light in 1931. The alleged criminal amount involved was $47,000. Mr. Flowers owned a bank in Cleveland, Minnesota, a few miles from Elysian. Governor Floyd Olson charged that the Republican operation of the rural credit bureau during the 1920s was a "racket pure and simple."[95]

In 2008, Grace Rodgers, ninety-three at the time, gave an interview about her memories of the Pelican Rapids Ku Klux Klan chapter. "There had been a lecture at the Orpheum Theater about the Klan. A few days later, we heard of a rally up on the hill by Lakeview Cemetery. My fiancé and I went up for a look. Six or eight masked riders thundered up out of the darkness, cut some fancy horsemanship, set up a flaming, towering cross, then disappeared again into the night." Her memories are verified by *Daily Journal* coverage of this from June 6, 1924, reporting, "Klansmen…gathered on the hillside of a picnic ground about a mile from Pelican Rapids last night for one of their open air demonstrations. It is estimated that a crowd of 1,500 was represented and a class of 100 initiated." The *Daily Journal* reported on Thanksgiving night that a fiery cross was seen burning on the banks of the Mill Pond and that there were two hundred Klan members in the Pelican Rapids area.

Republican Roy Dunn was looked on as "Mr. Pelican Rapids" and served for more than forty years in the Minnesota legislature, entering the legislature in 1924 and stepping down in 1966. Dunn was a lifetime member of the Masonic Lodge in Pelican Rapids and belonged to the Congregational Church in town. The Dunn family owned a prosperous resort on Lake Lizzie, and for many years, nationally known figures and politicians spent vacations at Dunn's Lodge. When engines became available for boat launches at the resort, Dunn named one of the boats at the resort *Indiana* in honor of the hunting and fishing groups that had been coming to the resort from Indiana for years. To many people, Dunn was considered the one man who had done more than anyone in saving Minnesota from socialism. He stated, "Otter Tail always has been considered a rock-ribbed, conservative Republican county."

Roy Dunn did not like Arthur Jacobs, who had written a scathing book about the Minnesota Republican Party. In 1934, Jacobs, a former Republican, was strongly in the Farmer-Labor Party, and Dunn was "attempting to organize the Legislature and keep it from the control of Arthur Jacobs and the other Farmer-Laborites." Dunn had contact with Albert Pfaender from New Ulm and asked for his help stopping Jacobs from telling people in the state that Dunn was being financed in his legislative activities by the Northwest Banco group. Dunn condemned Jacobs for being part of the Olson machine and at the same time asked for Pfaender's help in controlling Jacobs. Dunn, in a letter to a different individual, referred to Pfaender's aspirations to governorship as being even worse than Olson's chances (possibly due to Pfaender's ethnic background and protest against World War I).[96]

In January 1922, Alderman Gottfried Lindsten reported to the Minneapolis City Council that some members of the Minneapolis police force were members of the Ku Klux Klan. A motion was introduced that read in part, "And whereas, it is a fact that the Ku Klux Klan wherever organized as a secret and extra-legal force has proved itself subversive to law and order." This resulted in Mayor George Leach forbidding Minneapolis police officers from Klan membership. The *Masonic Observer* wrote in April 1923 complaining how the "so-called reorganization of the Minneapolis Police force" under Mayor Leach is a disaster using one Mason's recent experience as an example. This Mason, a Minneapolis police officer, had been on the force for years, was widely known for his exceptional ability and was ranked a captain of detectives. He had recently been reduced in rank and was walking the streets as a patrolman; a Roman Catholic was placed in his job instead.

The Minneapolis City Council requested of the Minneapolis chief of police that he investigate the alleged activities of the Klan in the police department and report back at once to the mayor and city council. Alderman Chase suggested that the investigation should include all departments of the city.[97] This was done in March 1923, three months before the *Voices of the Knights of the Ku Klux Klan* was published with the affidavit from Gladys Kennedy (a prostitute, or "woman of the underworld" as the Klan called her) noting that Mayor Leach had visited her house and gone into rooms with women of her acquaintance. The declaration of the Minneapolis City Council and Mayor Leach that they were going to strip Minneapolis government jobs of Klansmen likely precipitated the Minneapolis Klan attacking Leach and Captain A.C. Jensen (also sometimes called Police Chief Jensen).

The *Masonic Observer* wanted Minneapolis cleaned up and reported that Mayor Leach had not done enough to get rid of its gambling, blind pigs, bootlegging and wide-open, questionable dance halls. "Ignorance of these conditions has repeatedly been claimed by both Mayor Leach and Chief of Police Jensen." A reference was also made to the 1923 Klan trial, saying that Leach and Jensen knew that these criminal activities existed and acknowledged this state of affairs in Minneapolis during their testimony. If it hadn't been for Sheriff Brown of Hennepin County providing deputies for the raids of these establishments, nothing would have been done at all in Minneapolis, according to the *Masonic Observer*.

The Citizens Alliance was established to maintain the open shop in Minneapolis. Rumor had it that Leach was for unions. The Citizens Alliance also relied on a group of "deputies" to police the city for those who weren't anti-union. Earle Brown also belonged to the Citizens Alliance. The Ku Klux Klan saw Minneapolis as a city in which it could get a political foothold, and it did. The Klan didn't like unions any more than Minneapolis business owners did. Another problem the KKK had in Minneapolis, it claimed, was that Catholics occupied more than 70 percent of the appointive and elective city positions even though the population in Minneapolis was over 90 percent Protestant. The first point was not actually the case.

William A. Campbell was the man who needed to replace Leach as Minneapolis mayor, according to the *Masonic Observer*. "William A. Campbell is a total abstainer from all alcohol and believes in promoting harmony by developing all racial types that comprise our citizenship into real Americans, solidly united for the best interest of America." Stafford King was asked if he was a Ku Klux Klan member by an American Legion member, and there is also a reference to Campbell in the letter:

> *You may think it insulting, unnecessary and presumptuous on our part to want a statement from you to the effect that you never joined, never were a member and never took the oath of the Ku Klux Klan, but the boys effect that you never joined, never were a member and never took the oath of the Ku Klux Klan, but the boys here in Hennepin remember the fact that Campbell, the Klan candidate for mayor, in answer to the charges that he was a Klansmen, denied that he was a member of the Klan or connected to them in any way.*

Colonel George A. Leach had personal correspondence with Stafford King in which Leach wrote that he was disappointed with the lack of support he received from the American Legion for his current run at being Minneapolis's mayor. In June 20, 1924, Leach wrote a personal letter to King, noting, "…to say nothing of the head of the Legion where I should have looked for my greatest strength." Mayor Leach sent King a copy of an anonymous letter sent to him from someone who signed himself "Service Man." The letter seems to imply that others with Klan connections, who have "better" American Legion ties, are more appropriate for mayor than Leach. Why did Leach send a copy of that particular letter to King? King assured Leach that the "Service Man" misinterpreted what King and some members of the American Legion were attempting to do. "Service Man" saw it exactly for what it was: "Klan-minded" American Legion members and American Legion members who directly belonged to the Klan did not want Leach as mayor due to the actions he took against the KKK in Minneapolis.

The *Daily News* of April 20, 1923, noted that "Mayor Leach this morning furnished the grand jury with a list of 200 alleged members of the Klan, which list included a half dozen city police detectives and one member of the Hennepin county district court grand jury, the body to which the list was submitted." An unidentified Klansman who was a witness at the 1923 trial revealed Klan political tactics, telling the grand jury that Klan members would support only one of their own, giving the Klan-chosen mayoral candidate their votes. In Mayor Leach's own words, "When I started to run for a second term the K.K.K. started after me in earnest, and on April 10, 1923, they circulated a paper in every doorstep in town with a slanderous statement from an under world character, Gladys Kennedy." Mayor Leach also stated that Grand Kleagle Hiram Evans came to town from Atlanta, Georgia, to help beat Leach for reelection. Leach added that he immediately went to County Attorney Olson and asked to have certain individuals indicted for criminal libel.

Minneapolis had at least ten Klan chapters. The location where the North Star Klan would burn crosses was on Liberty Drive, the old Jefferson Highway between Minneapolis and Robbinsdale. The *Masonic Observer* reprinted an image that a photographer from the *Minneapolis Journal* took of a nighttime Klan meeting there. The photo shows a large group of Minneapolis Klansmen standing around a very large cross. A group of new members was naturalized, with the Minnesota king kleagle presiding, assisted by his kleagles and field workers from all over the state during that particular gathering. The Minneapolis Klan accused officials of trying to keep Gladys Kennedy under wraps, even threatening her with sentencing to an asylum, thus leading to the need for them to talk to Kennedy in prison and have her affidavit composed there. In Kennedy's written affidavit, given to the Klan representative at her jail, her statement sounds as if Kennedy set Captain Jensen up, thus leading to his trial. Kennedy stated that Jensen asked her to come in and sign a statement regarding her affair with a police officer that resulted in an altercation with that officer's mistress. The agreement would mean that charges against the mistress would be dropped in exchange for the police not bothering Kennedy while she continued "operating her resort."

Gladys Kennedy's notarized statement against Mayor Leach appears in the *Voices of the Knights of the Ku Klux Klan*, published by the Minneapolis North Star Klan No. 2. It is notarized by Shurley Reichert, one of the defendants charged by Hennepin County. Above Kennedy's sworn statement, there is a note explaining why the Knights of the Klux Klan of Minneapolis were doing this. "Rum, Romanism and Rebellion" exemplified the state of affairs

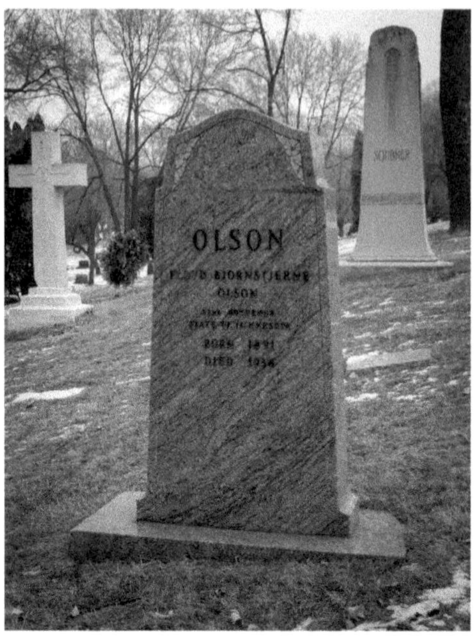

Floyd Olson grave site, Lakewood Cemetery.
Courtesy of Kevin B. Hatle.

when Lieutenant Governor Louis Collins went to defend Police Chief Jensen. Making sure that Jensen was vindicated would ensure the future safety of the present "Romanized Machine" dealing in state and city affairs, of which Collins and Leach were important factors, according to the *Masonic Observer*. Gladys Kennedy claimed that "George E. Leach, Mayor of Minneapolis, Minnesota, has upon three or four occasions visited my house and gone into private rooms with girls of my acquaintance and stayed in the room with them for several hours."

Olson had Gladys Kennedy examined by Dr. David E. Ellison. Olson asked Ellison during the 1923 trial, "From that examination did you arrive at any opinion or conclusion as an alienist as to her mental condition?" The doctor's testimony was blocked by attorney Donald Grant Hughes, which is understandable because the only thing the Ku Klux Klan defendants really had as evidence was her affidavit. If she had been portrayed as mentally unstable, that would have taken away the Klan defendants' strongest piece of evidence. Kennedy told the court that she was having an affair with a Minneapolis police detective, Ludwig Glarum. They began their relationship in 1922, and Detective Glarum's other mistress, Muriel Schwartz, found out about it. There was a vicious fight between the two women, thus leading to Captain Jensen's involvement with Kennedy.

Police Chief Jensen's trial took place in April 1923. The charge against him was that he had willfully neglected his duties. Jensen was seen as being responsible for the gambling and disorderly houses at the University of Minnesota. (Was this the hand of Shurley Reichert, the U of M student charged in the Klan trials?) Olson, the county attorney, told the media that he would only look at the legal points of the case and give close attention to the duties of the chief of police as stipulated by city ordinances. If Jensen had known of the existence of these gambling houses at the University of Minnesota, he might be proven to have been at fault. Within in a day of the end of Jensen's trial, he was found not guilty of neglecting his duties. Five minutes after the Jensen verdict was returned, Mayor Leach called Mrs. Jensen on the phone at the courthouse and told her that her husband was reinstated as chief of police.

At the 1923 trial, Olson stated about Kennedy, "These persons who circulated this canard spoke in that affidavit through the Kennedy woman and she I say is and was their mouthpiece, their oracle so to speak in this trial." Olson went on to say how the Klan was "as invisible in this lawsuit as is the principle of their organization." Olson continued, noting how Kennedy was used by the Klan. "Upon what meat is this Caesar fed? I say upon what meat is this Cyclops [Roy Miner] fed that he must come into a court of law and hide behind the skirts of a prostitute? She must take the cross-examination, she must take the fire, she must be the mouthpiece, and she must be the oracle." Olson asked why Kennedy had to be the target for the State of Minnesota—why not the Ku Klux Klan? "I say to you in conclusion that this action was better entitled the visible government of the people of the State of Minnesota against the invisible government of the Ku Klux Klan." This statement by Olson was used by the defense attorney, Hughes, to get the appeal trial in 1925.

The aforementioned Roy Miner had gone into the workhouse to visit Gladys Kennedy under an assumed name to receive this affidavit about the mayor's conduct and have it printed in the Klan newspaper. During the 1923 libel trial, Roy Miner received moral support at his courtroom table from the editor of the Klan paper the *Fiery Cross* and from H.E. Soule, editor of the *Masonic Observer.* Roy Miner was the exalted cyclops of North Star Klan No. 2 in Minneapolis. Miner was also the person in the Twin Cites area who sold paraphernalia and KKK regalia, regularly advertising his "Lodge Supplies" in the *Masonic Observer*.

Roy Miner's family settled in Mower County in 1863. He moved back to his hometown of Austin, Minnesota, after serving his sentence of ninety days when his appeal failed in 1925. According to his obituary, one of Roy's first jobs was that of messenger in the George A. Hormel & Company's office. At the time of his death, Miner was working at the Lincoln National Life Insurance Company in Austin as a district manager. There is no mention made in his obituary of his involvement with the Minnesota Ku Klux Klan or of his conviction.

William Campbell had received the second-most votes at a Klan gathering to be the candidate for mayor of Minneapolis. Miner could no longer make a run for mayor after his conviction. In the primary election held in the latter part of May 1923, there were eight candidates besides the incumbent, Mayor Leach. Campbell finished second to Leach, and his name went on the ballot opposing Leach in the general election held in November of that year. Campbell, though, finished far behind Leach, only able to carry the Lake Calhoun and Lake Harriet areas. Campbell never stated that he was a Klan member. Although convictions came out of the Minneapolis Klan trial, only light sentences were issued to the defendants. The trial also revealed the state's difficulties prosecuting law violations by the Minnesota Ku Klux Klan, especially in communities where the Klan had any semblance of strength.[98]

Defendants Miner, Sullivan and Reichert had been denied their separate motions for a new trial. Donald Grant Hughes was the attorney for the appellants. It was claimed by the *Minneapolis Journal* that three attorneys retained by the Ku Klux Klan came to Minneapolis to assist Hughes at the 1923 Klan trial. Hughes died in 1929, four years after the appeal. On his death certificate, it states that he was single and that the cause of his death was cirrhosis of the liver. An interesting fact about Donald Hughes is that on his death certificate, his birthplace is listed as Owatonna, Minnesota, a hotbed of Klan activity at the time. Another odd fact about Hughes was that Molly Regez, office specialist for the Hennepin County Medial Examiner's Office, could not find a file for Donald Hughes in its office, even though it had issued Hughes's death certificate.

Judge Royal Stone issued the opinion for the 1925 appeal trial. Stone stated that charges derogatory to the personal and official character of George E. Leach had occurred in the libel trial—this was in regards to the Klan's publication of *Voice of the Knights of the Ku Klux Klan* on April 10, 1923. The judge said that the evidence did sustain the guilty verdict and that the verdict from the 1923 trial would not be overturned. The attempt to involve Mayor Leach, who was busy in an election campaign, in the city's organized vice and alleged payment scheme by proprietors of public gambling houses for protection was libelous. Stone stated that the trial conduct of the county attorney, Olson, was subject to question, implying that Olson's anti-Klan stance during the trial was excessive. Judge Royal Stone, a Republican, was a friend to Stafford King. Stone seems more upset with Olson's conduct than that of the Klan attorney, Hughes.

In the files of Minnesota historical death certificate, there is a Shurley Reichert who died in Ramsey County at the age of eighty-five; his profession is listed as grain inspector. When first arrested in 1923 for the Leach libel trial, Shurley Reichert was a student at the University of Minnesota—an older student at twenty-seven, but this was not uncommon due to the effects of World War I. Shurley Reichert, a notary public, was fined fifty dollars with the option of thirty days in the workhouse. Reichert was a veteran, as was his older brother, Charles (whose death certificate notes, "World War I invalid"). Thomas E. Sullivan, the "truck driver" who picked up the newspapers from Silk and delivered them, had his profession listed in a Minneapolis 1924 telephone book as "investigator." That occupation is also listed on his death certificate, and he was employed by Walter Nelson, an attorney. Sullivan also had a World War I draft registration card.

The *Minneapolis Journal* wrote about a Ku Klux Klan initiation held in Austin, Minnesota, in September 1923. Clark F. Gross, a Klan organizer in Minnesota, stated that when the attacks on Mayor Leach were made and the five Minnesota Ku Klux Klan members were brought to trial, the Klan sent twenty-five of its best investigators into Minneapolis. According to Gross, the Klan spent $21,000 investigating the criminal conditions in Minneapolis. Mr. Gross, speaking personally to the editor of the *Masonic Observer*, assured the editor that the evidence the Klan investigators found in Minneapolis would be turned over to the proper authorities. The editor also said that the Klan should do a better job of protecting itself against these types of occurrences, which resulted in public trials like what had happened in Minneapolis.[99]

By 1925, the Klan defendants' attorney, Donald G. Hughes, knew the man who was actually involved with Gladys Kennedy: William G. Compton, Hennepin County's assistant district attorney. There are several affidavits from taxi drivers in the 1925 appeal trial who testified that it was Compton whom Kennedy was seeing. Debates the cab drivers had with Compton are clearly remembered; one cab driver revealed how Compton would be dropped off and then picked up half an hour later from Kennedy's residence. During the 1923 trial, William Compton testified that he did not know Gladys. Kennedy told her attorney about the taxi drivers and if they could be located, they could verify her information that she had slept with Compton. But those drivers weren't located in 1923, or their testimony was never sought. It was not until the 1925 appeal trial that the cab drivers verified Kennedy's claim. Kennedy had indeed been involved with a Hennepin County official, but it wasn't Mayor Leach. The Minnesota Klan had gone after the wrong man.

One glaring aspect of the 1923 trial was the fact that one of the jurors was a Ku Klux Klan member; two of the other jury members, Sarah Dunn and Hulda Hartman, testified to this being the case. Both ladies were also

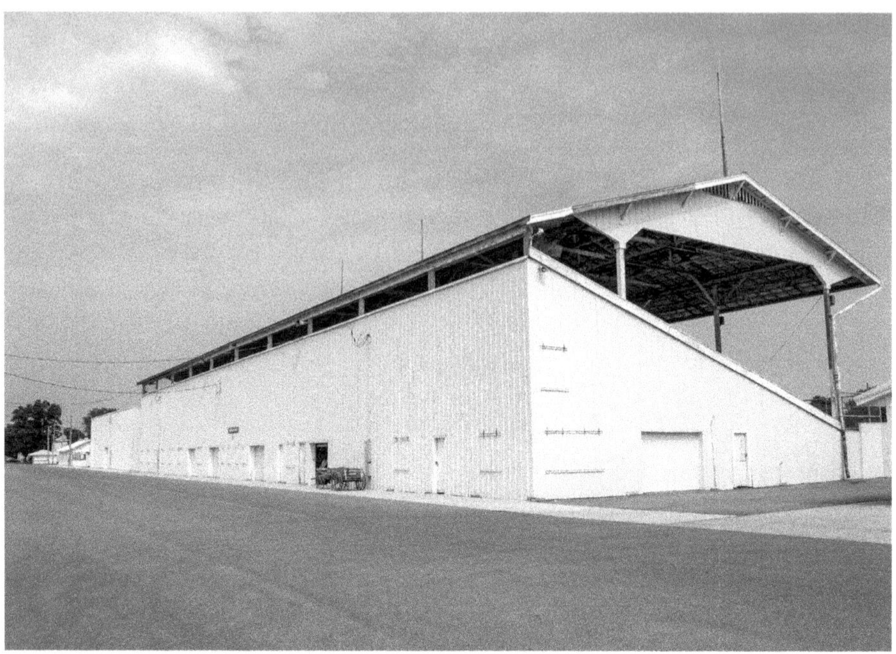

Austin, Minnesota fairgrounds grandstand. *Courtesy of Kevin B. Hatle.*

personally offended by the conduct of this juror, H.C. Payne, during the 1923 trial. Located in documents for the 1925 appeal is the card the juror had, and many recalled how Payne made a point of showing his fellow jurors this card. The title on the card read *Non Silba Sed Anthar*, which is the faulty Latin phrase, "Not for one's self, but for others." This phrase is also used on the back of Klan kreed medallions. Dunn, a native of Scotland, and Harman, a native of Germany (but then both naturalized American citizens), said that Mr. Payne gave quite a talk about joining the Klan to his fellow jurors.

From the 1923 trial, people came in to testify who looked to be Klansmen or "aspirants for that position," according to newspaper reports. Without the 1923 trial documents or transcript, it cannot be exactly determined who these other people were, but their testimonies seemed sympathetic to the Klan, or they were actual Klan members. Olson said that this trial was not about someone's character or what type of activities were taking place in the city. "Has there been one word uttered in this lawsuit about motive? Not a word. Not a bit of justification shown," Floyd Olson stated. There was something else going on here, and that was the Ku Klux Klan attempting to get a foothold in city politics.

Form P-217—100M—8-29-22

"NON SILBA SED ANTHAR"

Your friends state you are a "Native Born" American Citizen, having the best interest of your Community, City, State and Nation at heart, owing no allegiance to any foreign Government, political party, sect, creed or ruler, and engaged in a Legitimate occupation, and *believe in*:—viz.

The Tenets of the Christian Religion.
White Supremacy.
Protection of our pure womanhood.
Just Laws and Liberty.
Closer relationship of Pure Americanism.
The upholding of the Constitution of these United States.
The Sovereignty of our State Rights.
The Separation of Church and State.
Freedom of Speech and Press.

Closer relationship between Capital and American Labor.
Preventing the causes of mob violence and lynchings.
Preventing unwarranted strikes by foreign labor agitators.
Prevention of fires and destruction of property by lawless elements.
The limitation of foreign immigration.
The much needed local reforms.
Law and Order.

REAL MEN whose oaths are inviolate are needed.

Upon these beliefs and the recommendation of your friends you are given an opportunity to become a member of the most powerful secret, non-political organization in existence, one that has the "Most Sublime Lineage in History," one that was "Here Yesterday," "Here Today," "Here Forever."

Present this card at door for admittance, with your name, occupation and address.

Exhibit "A"

Name________

Occupation________

Address________

Discuss this with no one. If you wish to learn more, address Ti-Bo-Tim________

"DUTY WITHOUT FEAR AND WITHOUT REPROACH."

Minneapolis Klan trial juror's card. *Courtesy of Hennepin County Courthouse.*

The Minneapolis *Masonic Observer* was a strong supporter of Klan defendant George Silk. In April 16, 1921, the paper reported how "Brother George Silk, Worshipful Master of Albert Pike Lodge No. 237, Hopkins, Minn.," was wounded in a pistol battle in downtown Hopkins. Silk was a valued and prominent member of the Mason community in the Minneapolis area, according to the paper. Mayor Leach stated, "It gave me a hunch that the paper was delivered from Hopkins, where a man by the name of Silk, who was an officer of the Klan, published a paper." Leach's hunch most likely came from Silk running a newspaper in Hopkins called the *Hennepin County Enterprise.* Thirty days before the date of distribution of the Klan publication, Roy Miner approached Silk with Kennedy's affiant and asked if Silk could handle the printing. Silk had the type delivered to him, and he printed the newspaper. Silk said that he did not know Miner personally, according to his testimony.

Silk died in Two Harbors, Minnesota. A report of his death in the *Masonic Observer* was placed directly above a Ku Klux Klan meeting announcement for August 1924. "Brother George J. Silk of Hopkins Passes, editor and publisher of the *Hennepin County Enterprise* at Hopkins, Minnesota and former secretary of the Hennepin County Fair Association." Silk died of a heart attack while in camp at the headwaters of the Manitou River, near the Canadian border. "He was a fearless fighter for whatever he believed to be

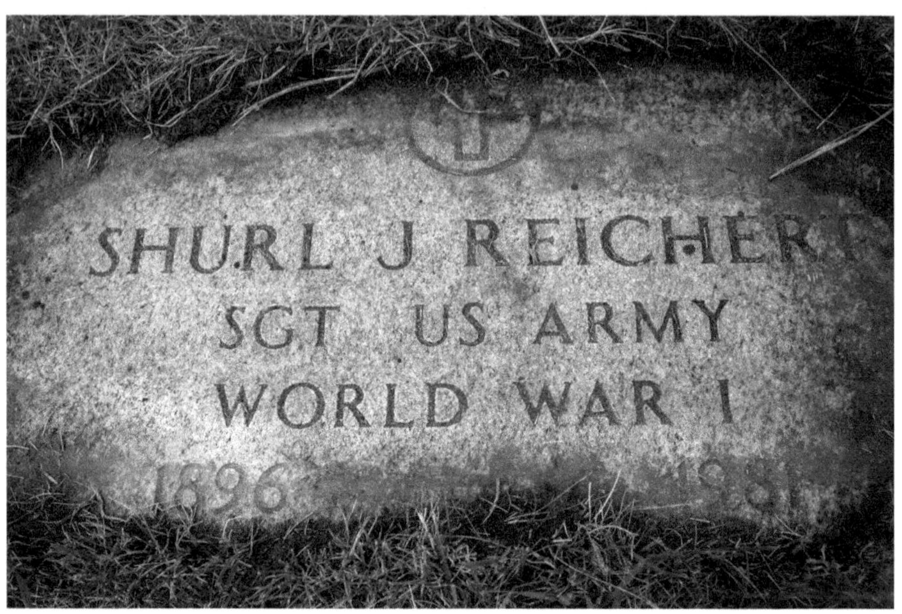

Shurley Reichert's grave site, Crystal Lake Cemetery. *Courtesy of Kevin B. Hatle.*

right; a good friend to those in whom he believed and square in his relations, even with those he opposed most actively and aggressively." No mention is made by the *Masonic Observer* of George Silk's conviction in the libel suit of Mayor Leach, but his death did get him out of ever having to serve any of the time to which he was sentenced for his conviction in that 1923 trial. Leach's belief about Silk's death was that Silk committed suicide to escape his sentence. Silk did die in 1924, before the 1925 appeal trial, but his death certificate does not list suicide as cause of death. It was unusual though. Silk's death occurred in an isolated, wooded area. It was difficult to reach to recover his body.[100]

CHAPTER 6

"100 Percent" Voters

The Klan was determined to put men who were "100 percent American in charge of the affairs of the nation," said C. Lewis Fowler (Tennessee grand dragon). Republican Minnesota senator Thomas Schall was accused by Arthur Jacobs of using Minnesota Ku Klux Klan chapters in rural areas to condemn the national Nonpartisan League. King has a copy of Schall's speech to the Senate in which Schall accused certain groups in Minnesota of attempting to destroy the Republican Party there. There is also an accusation in Schall's speech regarding the Hennepin Klan trial and how the county attorney (Olson) pursued this trial for his own personal political ambitions; it was suggested that there was no need to prosecute these Minnesota Klan members. Schall was on the House Committee of Rules during the 1921 Klan hearings. The official documents from the hearing list Schall's name on the front of the report as having been one of the representatives on that House committee. There is no condemnation of the Ku Klux Klan organization on the part of Schall during the hearing.

Thomas Schall's early life was one of poverty; his mother, unable to support him, allowed Schall to be adopted. In 1905, he married Margaret Huntley, who was from a wealthy family. In 1906, Schall was blinded by an electric cigar lighter, and because of his disability, he was limited in practicing law, and this resulted in him going heavily into debt. For Schall, there were other avenues open to him to gain money—namely politics.

Schall viewed his blindness as something that could be used to his advantage during a political campaign. There is hardly an instance in Schall's political career when Schall failed to bring special attention to his disability. Schall loudly claimed that his political opponents ran foul campaigns against him. In 1918, the Minnesota Republican Party asked Schall to run for Congress with their support. Schall's years in the House were uneventful, but his years in Congress led to his relationship with Andrew Rahn.

Andrew Rahn was a vice-president at the Shevlin-Carpenter-Clark Lumber Company and looked after company interests in the political sphere. There was an intense financial rivalry between two rival lumber interests, Shevlin-Carpenter-Clarke and the Backus-Brooks Lumber Company, for control of the Minnesota Republican Party. In 1923, Schall made his first attempt in a statewide election. Senator Knute Nelson had died, and Schall had little to lose by entering the Republican primary to replace Senator Nelson in the special election. There were nine Republican candidates, and Schall lost, with Governor Preus winning the primary. In the fall, Governor Preus lost against Magnus Johnson, who had won the Farmer-Labor primary. Minnesota now had two senators, Shipstead and Johnson, both from the Farmer-Labor Party, and neither of these Minnesota senators was very effective politically in Washington due to their third party status.

Magnus Johnson was elected halfway though Senator Knute Nelson's term due to Nelson's death. In 1924, there was to be another Senate election, and Schall ran again. The Minnesota Republican Party, though, was deeply divided between William F. Brooks and Fred H. Carpenter, from the two competing lumber interests, battling it out to take over the post of Republican national committeeman. Brooks won the post, but this was a serious defeat for the Carpenter forces because if the Republicans failed to defeat Johnson, they would lose their influence on federal patronage appointments in Minnesota. Andrew Rahn was playing both sides of the fence financially, supporting Judge Oscar Hallam, a traditional Republican, and at the same time providing aid to Schall. Schall found out that Rahn was also giving money to Hallam, and it resulted in a violent confrontation between Schall and Rahn, according to James Laughlin. This resulted in an intense hatred on Rahn's part for Arthur Jacobs, Schall's campaign manager, whom Rahn incorrectly held responsible for telling Schall that Rahn had been financially supporting Hallam.[101]

Andrew Rahn was also friends with Stafford King. Joseph Albert—a federal prohibition agent and World War I veteran—wrote to Stafford King asking for a promotion to group chief in St. Paul, with S.B. Qvale as his superior. Since Stafford King was a personal friend, Albert wanted him to be involved in recommending him for the position. Albert wrote to King that Rahn had a very good pull with Qvale. Within a day, King wrote a letter to Rahn, addressing him as "Andy" telling him that Albert was "a service man that is deserving and should be given reasonable preference." King also wrote that he would consider it a personal favor if Andy would intercede on behalf of Albert.[102]

Schall, Rahn, Arthur Jacobs and James Laughlin attended the national convention of the American Legion held in Minnesota in 1924. Schall received the legion's support and continued his attacks against Magnus Johnson, appealing to the religious and xenophobic inclinations of rural Minnesotans and telling them that Johnson was an internationalist. He stated in a speech in Winona that Magnus Johnson, by wanting a League of Nations, was "spoiling God's plan to have the United States lead the world onward." Schall asked to engage Magnus Johnson in a debate, but Johnson knew that against a skilled orator like Schall, he did not have much of a chance and refused. This is also the time when Arthur Jacobs printed in his newspaper how Magnus Johnson had been arrested for drunkenness. That newspaper report would later have Jacobs arrested for libel. Schall won the Senate election by the narrowest of margins.

Arthur Jacobs was brought to trial in April 1925, with the St. Paul and Minneapolis newspapers calling him Thomas Schall's campaign manager. Magnus Johnson stated, "While I was astounded that Mr. Jacobs should publish libel about me, now that the election is over I am not surprised at anything from that crowd. That is the way they licked me last fall." Johnson said that he had brought the lawsuit in the hopes of stopping campaign managers and candidates from carrying on campaigns the way his Republican opponent Schall had. Senator Schall disowned Jacobs, saying that he had never been his representative in any capacity of any kind. Jacobs admitted in court that one of his reasons for publishing the story about Johnson was the petition filed by Johnson in contesting the seating of Senator Schall.

The *Minneapolis Journal* reported on October 29, 1926, statements made by the ex-editor of the *Fiery Cross*, Milton Elrod of Indianapolis. Elrod told the newspaper that the imperial wizard had sent him to Minneapolis in 1924 to see whether Klan support was needed in the election contest between Johnson and Schall. Elrod reported that there was no need for the national Klan organization to get involved because the man the Minnesota Klan supported was as good as elected. Elrod was referring to Schall here, not Johnson. If the Klan was needed to provide additional help, it would be waiting in the wings for any assistance that it could give to Schall. Magnus Johnson said that Klan chapters in the state were working against him but may not have been also aware that the national Klan organization was willing to assist in his defeat.

In 1925, the *Park Rapids Enterprise* reported on Jacobs's new newspaper, the *Minnesota Republican*, stating, "This publication is evidently dedicated to Senator Schall, for his picture is large and his remarks plentiful." The Park Rapids newspaper went on to call Schall a hypocrite, telling state Republicans that if they had any kind of good judgment, they had better suppress this newspaper as quickly as possible. Jacobs was said to travel through the state, collecting money from postmasters for a political paper he was going to start. It was charged that Jacobs confined his activities mostly to places where federal patronage post office appointments were made on Schall's recommendations. In November 1925, Schall replied to a "shakedown charge" about his involvement in postal appointments. He said that he had turned this matter over to the federal post office department, and it had found nothing irregular, with the postmaster general telling Schall that they had nothing to investigate.

After serving his short prison term, Arthur Jacobs wrote a book called *The Tinhorn*, published in 1927. In the book, Jacobs exposed not only Senator Thomas Schall but also the Minnesota Republican Party. Arthur Jacobs made the accusation that radical elements within the Republican Party—Minnesota Ku Klux Klan chapters—were used to win the Senate race for Schall. The character in Jacobs's book representing him, Harry Porter, sees it as his job getting "Jim Hall" elected. A lobbyist named Andy Collier comes in and helps get Hall elected; he works for himself and the Minnesota Republican Party, according to Porter. Andy Collier, according to the St. Paul newspapers, is in reality Andrew Rahn. Collier (Rahn) wants Hall to run for the Republican nomination for senator and wants the Republicans to regain the Senate seat at any cost.

Characters in Jacobs's book are identified by St. Paul newspapers as Andrew Rahn, who was the secretary of the Hennepin County Republican Executive Committee of the City of Minneapolis; F.A. Carpenter; E.W. Backus, business owner of the Backus-Brooks Company and president of the N.W. National Bank; and William Frederick Brooks, treasurer of the Backus-Brooks Company. A "political cyclone" has hit the state, according to Porter (Jacobs), causing fear and concern in the Minnesota Republican Party. Jacobs wrote, "This new movement, known officially as the People's Party, because of the direct primary laws in the states in which there were operating, had gone and gained control of the party machinery." Here Jacobs is referring to the Nonpartisan League as the "People's Party." This new political party movement had to be stopped, according to Minnesota Republican leaders.

E.W. Backus, president of the N.W. National Bank and identified by the St. Paul newspapers as being "William C. Dempster" in Jacobs's book, called a meeting. Dempster (Backus) says at the meeting that there was a grave situation in Minnesota, and a particular movement has to be stopped before it engulfs all of the state. Dempster says, "What did the working man, the farmer, and the small business man know about running a country? We must crush them before they make any headway in our state." Edwards, another character, identified by Jacobs as one of Minnesota's keenest political brains, thinks that the banker has the wrong idea of how to handle the situation and states at the meeting that it is a time to move carefully. Collier (Rahn), also at the meeting, suggests that the way to stop this new movement from making any headway is to corrupt its leaders and disorganize its ranks. Jacobs states in the book that Magnus Johnson knew that the Ku Klux Klan was in the state and that it was being used against him during the Senate campaign.

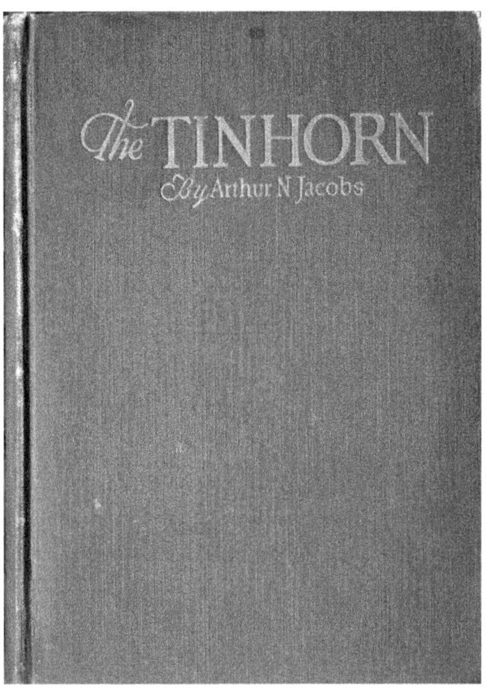

The Tinhorn, by Arthur Jacobs. *Author's collection.*

Edwards reminds Collier, Dempster, Carpenter and Brooks how the American Protective Association used religious prejudice to restrict Catholic immigration back in the 1890s. Edwards stated, "Politics is only secondary with a good church man. The Klan, to some extent, operates along the same lines as did the A.P.A." Edwards pointed out that, thus far, the future Minnesota Democrat Farmer-Labor Party hadn't drawn religious lines and that the IWW, labor unions, some Democrats and socialists had been working in unison. Edwards also pointed out that if the Republican Party could get the Klan's anti-Catholicism and anti-labor issues injected into the movement, "we can destroy it." Edwards related how the 1920s Ku Klux Klan in Minnesota was a party of passion, not politics; the Minnesota Republican Party, using the Minnesota Klan chapters that proclaim to be all-American and all-Protestant, could divide the Catholics and the Protestants in Minnesota.

According to Jacobs, the Minnesota Republican Party knew that "the Ku Klux Klan had an army of agents in the state soliciting membership to their organization. These agents could devote their efforts entirely within the ranks of the People's Party (the Farm-Labor Party) where they would find a fertile field for their work, which would prove to be very effective getting Schall elected." Jacobs claimed that agents from the Ku Klux Klan made a point of going into Protestant homes in Minnesota, and by insinuation and innuendo, they soon convinced some that the Farmer-Labor Party was not a political party at all but rather an adjunct of the Catholic Church. Jacobs also made the claim that Schall had secretly signed a membership card with the Ku Klux Klan. The Klan had proved to be a "most serviceable weapon in the hands of the enemies of the People's (Farmer-Labor) Party," according to Jacobs.

Politicians who kept mum on the Klan were politicians who received Klan political votes. The reason given by the Invisible Empire for entering into politics was a desire to "clean up" their county. Minnesota Klan member Peter Sletterdahl reported that copies of election reports were sent to the grand dragon of a realm (state) with information on all officials running for public office, if they were a Democrat or a Republican and whether they were a Protestant, Roman Catholic, Jew or Klansman. If the Ku Klux Klan wasn't into politics, why was this political information needed by Klan chapters? In a local political fight, the Ku Klux Klan would send speakers into the area, if deemed necessary, to distribute anonymous campaign literature where it would serve most effectively.

Located in the King files is a "Stafford King Testimonial," marked "personal." Included in the file is a letter responding to King's request for information about who made donations to the purchase of his car. A long list is sent to King revealing who gave what and how much, as well as which American Legion posts in Minnesota donated. A *Midway News* article headline on September 19, 1925, read, "Klansman King Gets Kar." The article told readers that in the display windows for the Golden Rule at Seventh and Roberts Street is a roaster automobile purchased as a testimonial gift to Stafford King, the American Legion adjutant. At the same time Stafford King received his new car, purchased with money collected throughout Minnesota, the *Fairmont Sentinel* reported that "that the King Kleagle was at one point provided a voluntary token of appreciation by the local membership due to what they considered his outstanding Americanism and leadership. This 'token of appreciation' happened to be a new automobile." Lenny Tvedten wrote that the king kleagle returned to Minneapolis in his

10

No. 1233 Name Stafford King (Surname) (Christian Name) Age

City St. Paul, Minn. Date Married Single

Res. 1076 Blair St. Res.

Add. Phones

Bus. Bus. Mi. 2533

Occupation With

Recommended By Don't call Car Pass

Frats

Remarks Old Card

KLANSMAN KING GETS KAR

On exhibition in the display windows of the Golden Rule, 7th and Robert streets, is a roadster automobile which Minnesota Legionnaires have purchased as a testimonial gift to Stafford King, department adjutant.

Subscriptions to the fund have come from every post in the state.

Every dollar contributed has been voluntarily offered.—St. Paul Daily News.

STAFFORD KING SIDESTEPS

Minnesota Adjutant of American Legion a Klansman

Denies Membership But Evades Demand for Court Action

Stafford King, Minnesota Adjutant of the American Legion, is a member of the Ku Klux Klan. His number in the St. Paul organization is 1233. His dues are paid up to date.

The above statement has been carried in the columns of The Midway News every week during the past four months. King has denied the charge before meetings of local posts of the American Legion, and at the recent convention of the Legion the same denial was registered.

Members of the American Legion in Minneapolis have offered to furnish King, at their own cost, with the legal services of attorneys in that city who are members of the Legion in any action he might choose to bring against the editor of The Midway News with a view of clearing himself of the charge that he is a Kluxer. Members of the Legion in St. Paul have repeatedly made the same offer to King, even going so far as to tender him with any amount of money necessary for the purpose, with the privilege of selecting legal representatives of his own choosing. King continues to sidestep. He knows he cannot verify a complaint, either civil or criminal, which contains a denial of the charge that he is a Ku Klux member without committing perjury. And the Midway News knows that neither King or any other member of the Klan will be permitted to start court action in St. Paul which would result in bringing prominent business men who are members of the Klan into court under subpoena. Daylight is the one thing

Stafford King's membership card. *Courtesy of Minnesota Historical Society.*

new automobile and was never heard from since. Fairmont citizens said that he got out "just in time."

In 1925, Stafford King began to feel the heat from the accusations and the newspaper coverage that he was a member of the Ku Klux Klan. Other American Legion members across the country also may have been feeling that same pressure to stand down from their American Legion positions due to suspected or actual involvement with the KKK. E.L. White wrote to King that he was stripped of his adjutant position at the American Legion department in New Haven, Connecticut. White's "acquaintances" in Indianapolis may have injured his reputation, resulting in the loss of his position, according to White. The *Midway News*' coverage of King continued and was relentless. King stayed with and visited Hanford MacNider during this time and was extremely grateful to MacNider for having him stay for what he called much-needed "vacation" time.[103]

The *Midway News* got ahold of a St. Paul Klan organizers' list and exposed a number of prominent citizens, including city and county employees, officials of the detective bureaus and staff members of the *St. Paul Daily News* who belonged to the Ku Klux Klan. Names, addresses, jobs and businesses of Klan members were published in the *Midway News* on the front page week after week. The editor explained that the Ku Klux Klan was out to control the schools and the employee departments of various firms and agencies. In June 1924, after the St. Paul Klan failed to bring a victory for Albert Wunderlich, a former commissioner of education and candidate for councilman, the *Midway News* began a campaign urging the citizens of St. Paul to remove any city or county employee owing allegiance to the invisible government of the KKK.

St. Paul had more public pressure on it than Minneapolis Klan chapters had given the *Midway News'* weekly publishing of St. Paul Ku Klux Klan members' names, occupations and addresses. The Klan chapter in St. Paul had some heavy hitters belonging to it, in particular detective Martin Ewald, assigned to the African American neighborhoods in St. Paul—the *Midway News* stated that this was absolutely disgraceful. Editor James H. Burns did a very brave thing, including challenging King publically. "Let's go to court and you can prove there you don't belong to the Ku Klux Klan." King never took Burns to court. In the 1930 U.S. Census, James Burns lists his father's birthplace as Ireland. Burns himself died in 1930 of stomach cancer at the age of sixty-eight.

In 1959, at the American Legion National Convention, an all-out fight took place to terminate the 40 & 8 organization, which did not allow nonwhite members. The 40 & 8 bylaws limited membership to white male members of the American Legion only. Stafford King separately kept track of the 40 & 8 membership numbers in the Minnesota American Legion, as there were two sets of membership books. The 40 & 8 knew from the start that the organization was not just about providing fun for American Legion posts but also that it was a separate organization within the American Legion that was restricted to white Protestants only, as exhibited by the letter King received from the organization from Grand Chef de Gare William D. Lyons. This letter informed King that all voyageurs (what members of the 40 & 8 called themselves) could not solicit others within their own American Legion posts for membership. Someone would be put in charge of doing that, finding the right people to be asked to join.[104]

King wrote a personal letter to a Mr. Parks from Texas, telling Parks that he cannot see him in person before a 40 & 8 convention in Texas. "In the meantime forgive me for my negligence in not answering your letter and for the feeble information which I can give to you. I do know that Texas has always been good to Minnesota, and I see no reason why we cannot cooperate." King wanted to run for American Legion national vice-commander. In the *Midweek News*, there are several mentions made of a visiting KKK chief of staff Parks, who left Minnesota after working for the Klan here. If this Parks is the same KKK chief of staff Parks, the two men being seen publicly together would not have helped King's future bid to become the American Legion national vice-commander.[105]

World War I had been over for nearly a year when delegates from across the United States came to Minneapolis in November 10–12, 1919, for the first official convention of the American Legion. By the time of the convention, there were 279 American Legion posts in Minnesota. Hanford MacNider from Mason City, Iowa, was at the Minneapolis convention and was defeated for the top spot of national commander that year. The prevailing mood at the convention was largely composed of reactions against illegal aliens, communists and others who threatened democracy. To increase "political awareness" of the American Legion, a form was devised and then used by the Minnesota members. The form was labeled, "Information is Desired Concerning Minnesota Legislators from your District" form. Minnesota American Legion members would fill out these forms with information about their local legislators. If you were a politician, having many of these forms filled out in a positive manner would have been a great help in getting the veteran vote, but it could easily mean the end of a political career if an American Legion post viewed you unfavorably.[106]

Jay Hormel of Austin, Minnesota, was a World War I veteran and not likely a member of the KKK; it's possible that he was not above using it for political purposes, though. Hormel was accused by Eric Sevareid and author William Millikan of being associated with the Silver Shirts. "In August of 1938, Pelley sent his top lieutenant, Roy Zachary, from North Carolina to Minneapolis with a list of Silver Shirt contacts and instructions to enlist 3,000 to 5,000 new members. Minneapolis, one of the most anti-Semitic cities in the country, provided an excellent environment for the spread of Pelley's doctrines. Among Zachary's Minnesota contacts was Jay C. Hormel, president of the Hormel Packing Company in Austin."[107] In the personal correspondence between Stafford King and Jay Hormel, on January 16, 1924, Hormel wrote, "If you will come down here, even other than a meeting day, it will be worth while because there are some things you can do and some things you ought to know about, but I am so tied up that I can't get chance to see you."[108]

Jay C. Hormel was the son of the founder of the Hormel Corporation, located in Austin, Minnesota, which had an active Klan chapter. It is difficult to believe Jay Hormel, being personal friends with Stafford King, did not know about the Minnesota Klan and which Minnesota Republicans belonged to it or worked with the Klan in the state. Roy Miner, Minnesota's exalted cyclops, worked at the Hormel plant at one time. James Hormel, Jay Hormel's son, stated that his mother had trouble fitting into the Austin community. His mother being Catholic, living in Austin may not have been easy. Jay Hormel's Presbyterian mother was from Blooming Prairie, Minnesota, and was not enthused about her only child's marriage; she had the couple sleep in separate bedrooms when Jay returned home with his French Catholic bride.

Like the Schall/Magnus Senate race, with accusations made of Klan involvement, there was a bitter Senate race going on in Iowa. When the tightly contested election between Smith Wildman Brookhart and Daniel Steck went to a Senate committee to resolve, Steck employed a noted attorney from the Ku Klux Klan, W.F. Zumbrunn. When Twilight Orn (aka Peter Sletterdahl, grand dragon of Minnesota and the Dakotas) resigned his position in 1926, he made public a letter he had received from Zumbrunn in which Zumbrunn threatened him to return sensitive Ku Klux Klan correspondence or else. In Hanford MacNider's papers at the Herbert Hoover Library, there is a letter to MacNider from W.T. Cozad in Shenandoah, Iowa: "That is the same way to stop Brookhart—I think it is the duty to carry this fight in the name of the Republican Service League right out in the open—Of course it is what we have been doing but not exactly out in the open." Also in the Hanford MacNider's papers is correspondence between Stafford King and Hanford MacNider. MacNider, the national chairman of the Republican Service League, was doing everything he could to elect a Democrat, Steck, as senator from Iowa.[109] The hometown of Hanford MacNider, Mason City, Iowa, had an active Ku Klux Klan chapter.

Writing to his son about Brookhart, after the vote, Hiram Johnson said that a "very remarkable combination" of "the Republican National Committee, the Democratic organization and the Ku Klux Klan" unseated Brookhart. MacNider used his American Legion contacts to get Steck elected, although the American Legion stated in its bylaws that it is "not a political organization." Brookhart took his close loss to Steck to the United

States Senate. It was a hair-thin victory for Steck, reliant on three counties. About 10 percent of the Iowa voters that gave Steck the win registered their political party as "the Brotherhood." National KKK lawyer W.F. Zumbrunn represented Daniel Steck at the Washington hearing on March 27, 1926, at the Committee on Privileges and Elections, which was authorized to investigate the unlawful practices in the election of a senator from Iowa.[110]

Luke Boyce was in contact with the American Legion National Americanism Commission, having correspondence with Frank C. Cross, its national director. Hanford MacNider, assistant secretary of war in 1925, was also in contact with these men. Boyce was head of the Northland Information Bureau, which was a detective agency operating from 1909 to 1933 in Minnesota. It specialized in spying on employees to see if unions were being organized at businesses. Boyce was hired by John McGee and Henry W. Libby of the Minnesota Commission of Public Safety; Boyce also did personal work for these two men. Cross wrote Boyce asking for information from him regarding what a communist home is like, giving particular attention to the treatment of the children in the home, and regarding typical conversions of some worker into the Communist faith for a series of American Legion magazine articles it would like to do on these topics.

In another letter between Boyce and Cross, the subject was evolution, described by Boyce as a "hot" topic since it "and the discussion and theory of evolution emanated entirely with the Soviet Government of Russia." Boyce told the American Legion that there was absolute proof and documentary evidence of this and that it was part of the policy of the Soviet government to destroy every ideal that Christian churches held. Boyce went on to tell Cross that the Soviet government sent a delegation into Africa composed of its most worthy medical men to study evolution and prove that evolution was a fact. Boyce also informed Cross that the Russians were planning to cross a human and an ape by impregnating a female ape with human sperm. Boyce wished that W.J. Bryan were still alive so he could give him a copy of his report on what the Communists were doing to prove evolution.[111]

John Bowe was from Canby, Minnesota, and was elected Minnesota's first vice-commander of the American Legion in 1920. In 1923, relations between Bowe and King broke down. There was an investigation of the trip that American Legion members took to Paris. King wrote to Bowe that he would tell him about it, but there was little to tell Bowe at this point, according to King. King made sure that a copy of his letter to Bowe was sent to Minnesota state commander Lindell. King was meticulous, making sure that others in the Minnesota American Legion knew that Bowe was asking him questions and writing to him frequently. In July 1925, the same year that Klan accusations were made against King, King decided to leave his position as American Legion state adjutant. There seems to have been a subtle implication from friends that it was the right thing for King to do.

King picked up his American Legion activities again within a few years. The acrimonious relationship between Bowe and King started again in letters between the two men in 1928. King's letter to Bowe begins with him accusing Bowe of spreading attacks on him throughout the state. King's friends urged him to reply to Bowe publicly, but instead King responded to Bowe with a letter. One of Bowe's accusations that King addresses in his letter is that King received pay from several different sources. Those sources are not named. King does not equivocally deny the claim that these sources exist or even attempt to explain where his money comes from. The letter goes on with King accusing Bowe of vilifying his character "by using my name in connection with the names of individuals and organizations with which I am in no way intimate."

This same Paris trip is again questioned in 1930 by L.L. Huntley from Grand Rapids, Minnesota. King wrote to Huntley telling him that he was informed while on a visit to his hometown of Deer River, that Huntley opposed his candidacy as state auditor. When Bowe questioned King about the Paris trip charges in 1923, King said that there were no reports yet on it. In his letter to Huntley, King denies having any connection whatsoever with the Paris Convention Committee. King asked Huntley to stop spreading "idle gossip." Huntley, a Democrat and commander of the McVeigh-Dunn American Legion post, replied back telling King that the Paris story had been in circulation for years. Huntley told King that if he found these charges to be groundless after checking into them, he would be only too glad to correct his statements, but "it also follows that in case I find them to be true, I would feel free to use them in opposing you."[112]

In a letter written to the *American Legion Weekly* on July 25, 1919, an African American World War I veteran felt that the jokes in the *American Legion Weekly* used insulting words that were not well received in his community. The veteran bravely wrote, "I am a member of the American Legion and have served the colors across the other side, and if the Legion stands for anything at all it should stand for different things than this. It is far from Americanism and tends to work a breach between the different integral parts of the nation." The newly formed American Legion considered forbidding African Americans from membership. In early 1919, the War Department reported that military tribunals had executed thirty-two soldiers during the war for charges ranging from murder to rape; twenty-eight of those executed were African Americans.[113]

There were only two American Legion posts for African American World War I veterans in Minnesota. The Leslie Lawrence Post in St. Paul, established in 1922, and the Johnnie Baker American Legion Post in Minneapolis, established in 1924. The commander of the Johnnie Baker American Legion post in 2012 was Evester Jenkins. Commander Jenkins said that he remembered hearing a story from an "old" guy that the Minnesota American Legion organization had the Johnnie Baker American Legion post charter members pick names out of a hat to name their post. White American Legion posts were carefully named after actual soldiers who were killed in action or died from war injuries from the areas where the posts were located. The only Johnnie Baker in the Minnesota historical death certificates files is a white Johnnie Baker from northern Minnesota who died of tuberculosis.

African American soldiers were held in such low regard by the American military that they were deemed only useful for labor. Two World War I veterans from Minnesota, Tela Burt and James Hodges, were members of the 809th Pioneer Infantry. The infantry was primarily composed of African American soldiers, with white officers. The men were used as a hard labor force, much as African American soldiers were treated in the Civil War. When African American soldiers arrived in France, the French military viewed this as a ridiculous waste of talent. Instead, they were trained as soldiers (with guns), fighting on the front lines and treated equally by the French soldiers. African American World War I veteran James Hughes wrote, "Well, I went shooting with a bunch of fellows today, 'Red,' Bob Harrison, Tela Burt (charter member of the Johnnie Baker American Legion post) Dave Malaricher, Lonnie and a little bunch of bullets. No one could shoot but myself."[114]

Minnesota judge Daniel Foley was instrumental in throwing out the Voitures/40 & 8 from the National American Legion, according to his son, Kevin Foley. Daniel Foley was the American Legion national commander in the 1960s and was from Wabasha, Minnesota. Al Zdon, communications director for the American Legion Minnesota Department in St. Paul, said, "Judge Dan Foley didn't have anything good to say about the 40/8, and he wasn't afraid to take them on, even though they included the who's who of the Legion in many cases. For years the Legion had nothing to do with the 40/8, even though the group was supposed to be kind of an honor society of the Legion. The 40/8 is still functioning, but it's withering away. There

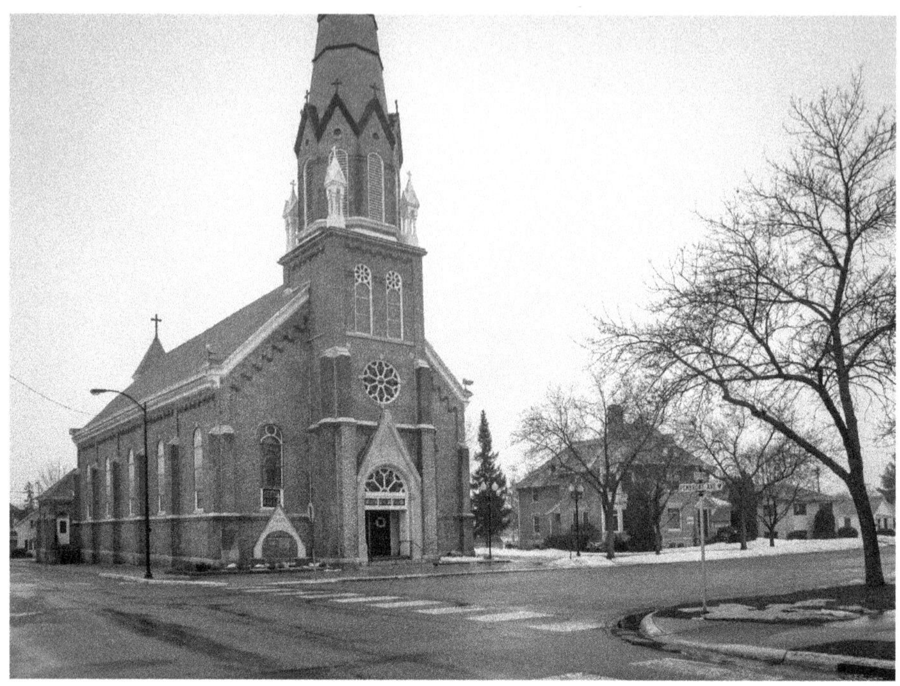

St. Felix Church, Wabasha, Minnesota. *Courtesy of Kevin B. Hatle.*

are still some fairly strong units in rural Minnesota."[115] Daniel Foley and his family were from Wabasha, and Kevin Foley remembered his father talking about Wabasha's Ku Klux Klan chapter.

Kevin's grandfather, John Foley, was appointed city attorney of Wabasha in May 1916 and also served two terms as district deputy. He was also great friends with Governor Floyd Olson, according to his grandson, Kevin. The Wabasha Catholic church is located three blocks off Wabasha's main street. St. Felix Catholic School was opened in Wabasha in 1915. Threats were made by the local Klan chapter to burn down the church next to the school in the early 1920s. John Foley arranged for a group of men with guns to be at the church to prevent that from happening. It is possible that the Mason building in downtown Wabasha is where the Wabasha Ku Klux Klan chapter would meet, just as the Clay County Klan chapter did in the downtown Mason building in Moorhead, Minnesota. The Wabasha Mason building is located on 200 West Main. "The building was altered in the 1920s when the second story windows were filled in." Klan crosses were burned at Coffee Mill hill, located directly across from Wabasha Highway 61, where the present-day Coffee Mill Golf course is today.

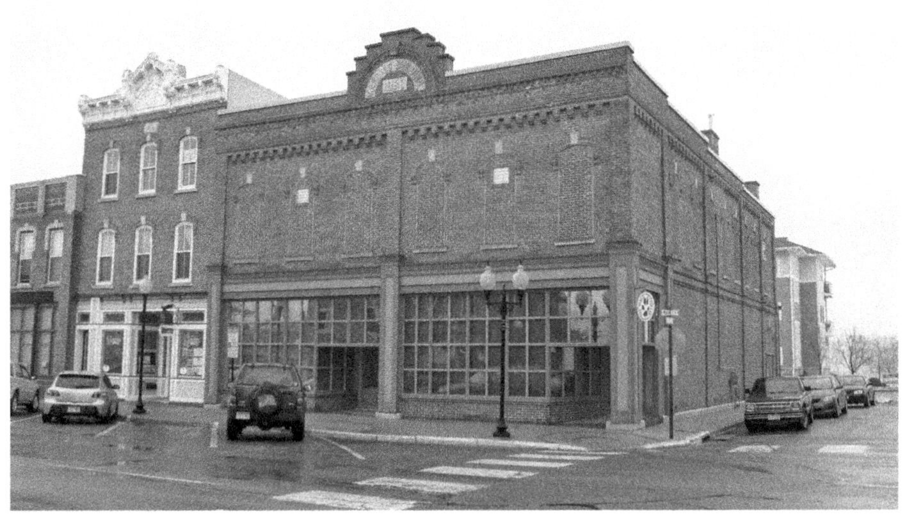

Wabasha ex-Mason building. *Courtesy of Kevin B. Hatle.*

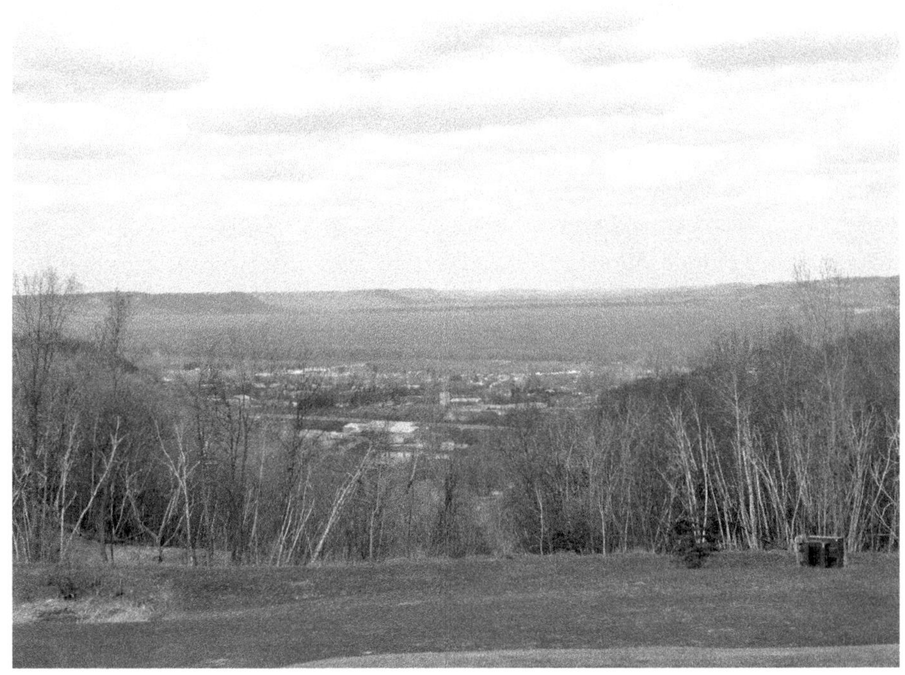

Coffee Mill Golf Course, Wabasha, Minnesota. *Courtesy of Kevin B. Hatle.*

Theodore Christianson was the editor and owner of the *Dawson Sentinel* and wrote fiery, anti-German, anti-Bolshevik editorials in his newspaper. Albert Pfaender from New Ulm was, in particular, a target of derision by Christianson, a future governor, who called Pfaender a Benedict Arnold, Kaiser Wilhelm and Judas Iscariot. Christianson stated, "The Bolshevik and their soul-relatives—the American I.W.W.—have no place in a sane world." In Fairfax, Minnesota, Christianson commented that on the school board there, "four [men] bear names that betray a Teutonic origin." The four had their houses painted yellow by citizens upset about the school board's opposition to the superintendent's reelection. The "red-blooded" school superintendent was doing nothing but attempting to teach "Americanism" to the students in Fairfax, Minnesota, according to Christenson, who wrote that America will get along just fine not having a new infusion of the Germans coming to Minnesota.

Letters from 1925 were written by Minnesota grand dragon H.E. Kettering to Governor Christianson. Kettering bemoaned the deplorable situation in Minnesota, with its difficulty enforcing the Eighteenth Amendment, and recommended L.G. Beach (*Midweek News* identified Beach as a Klan member) as acting divisional chief of the twelve prohibition divisions, with its headquarters in Minneapolis. In a letter on April 14, 1925, from the grand dragon to the governor, Kettering noted, "The first editorial is I believe a result of a bulletin I sent out immediately after seeing you last week."[116] The KKK Minnesota grand dragon wrote again to the governor noting that he was upset that when the Dakota County Knights of the Ku Klux Klan held their parade on August 22, 1925, the Hastings fire chief (M.L. Cline) put their burning cross out. Grand Dragon Kettering asked Governor Christenson whether the governor could let him know further information about that individual.

CHAPTER 7

North Minnesota Klan Activities

Glenn Donnay grew up in Paynesville, Minnesota, and his mother, Mabel Donnay, a schoolteacher, vividly remembered seeing Klansmen riding on horses in Paynesville as a child. She also recalled seeing the Klan crosses that were burned on the south side of Paynesville. Catholic farm families in the Paynesville area had robed Klansmen ride though their farmland at nights, intimidating their families. Finally, one night, two Catholic families trapped those Klan horsemen, pulled them off their horses and gave them a severe beating. When Glenn was eleven years old in 1959, he and his brother went out to an old barn, the Burr barn, and while playing around, they discovered a book buried in the wall of the farm's barn. Glenn took the book home to his mother. Inside the book were sheets of paper folded into it, and there was also a membership list.[117]

The book, likely a Kloran, was the handbook of the Ku Klux Klan. Glenn said that the family remembered reading about Klan ceremonies and procedures in it. Glenn's mother knew what it was right away and recognized Paynesville Ku Klux Klan members on the list. She showed the book to Jerry (Gerald) Burr, son of Frank Burr. Glenn related that his mother said that Jerry Burr's face was quite shocked seeing the book in Mabel's possession. The book was stolen from the Donnay house that following weekend. Frank, Elmer and Fred Burr, all brothers who registered for World War I, listed on their applications "native born," and their names were in the book that Glenn found. Both Glenn and Lawrence Donnay remembered very clearly seeing the Burr names on the membership list found in the book. At the

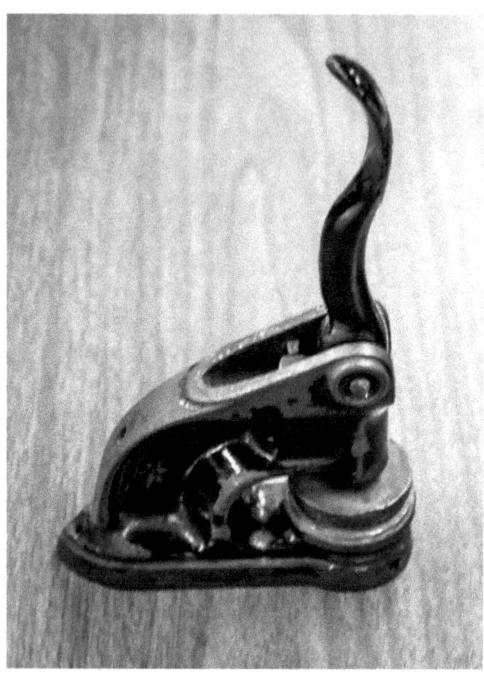

Paynesville, Minnesota KKK stamp. *Courtesy of Paynesville Historical Society.*

Paynesville County Historical Society, there is a metal seal with "No. #51 Paynesville Ku Klux Klan" inscribed on it.

Paynesville had a solid history of being anti-liquor. In 1870, Paynesville voted against a liquor license twenty-three votes to twelve, and by 1881, Paynesville had become the only town in Stearns County with no liquor licenses issued. A Klan cross was burned in Paynesville on July 10, 1924, and the *Belgrade Tribune* reported on July 18, 1924, that Klansmen burned another cross in Paynesville for the third time that season. The huge cross was fired on a hill south of the city, just outside the city limits. Klan crosses were also burned at the junction of Highway 55 and 124, south of Paynesville. The Paynesville baseball team's catcher was alleged to be an active leader in the Klan movement. A local priest liked Paynesville baseball and attended the games. At one game, someone suggested that the priest pitch, so he took off his robe and went to the mound. The baseball fans there at the game knew that the catcher was a Klan member and asked him how it felt to catch for a priest. The catcher said, "The Father put Holy Water on the ball and threw it; I put snooze on it and threw it back."[118]

Stearns County Historical Society has an oral history interview with Mrs. Mary (Harold) Bisenius from February 21, 1980, about the Ku Klux Klan in St. Cloud. Mary remembered seeing robed Ku Klux Klan in St. Cloud near a Catholic school burning a cross there. The *St. Cloud Journal-Press* reported on January 18, 1923, "Ku Klux Klan Now at St. Cloud," noting that the Klan in town had seventy-five members and an established headquarters in the city. A prominent St. Cloud professional man was approached by a representative of the Klan and was shown the membership application book, which contained the names of at least ten men prominent in the affairs of the city.[119] "Kluck, Kluck, Kluck" read the headline about a Klan

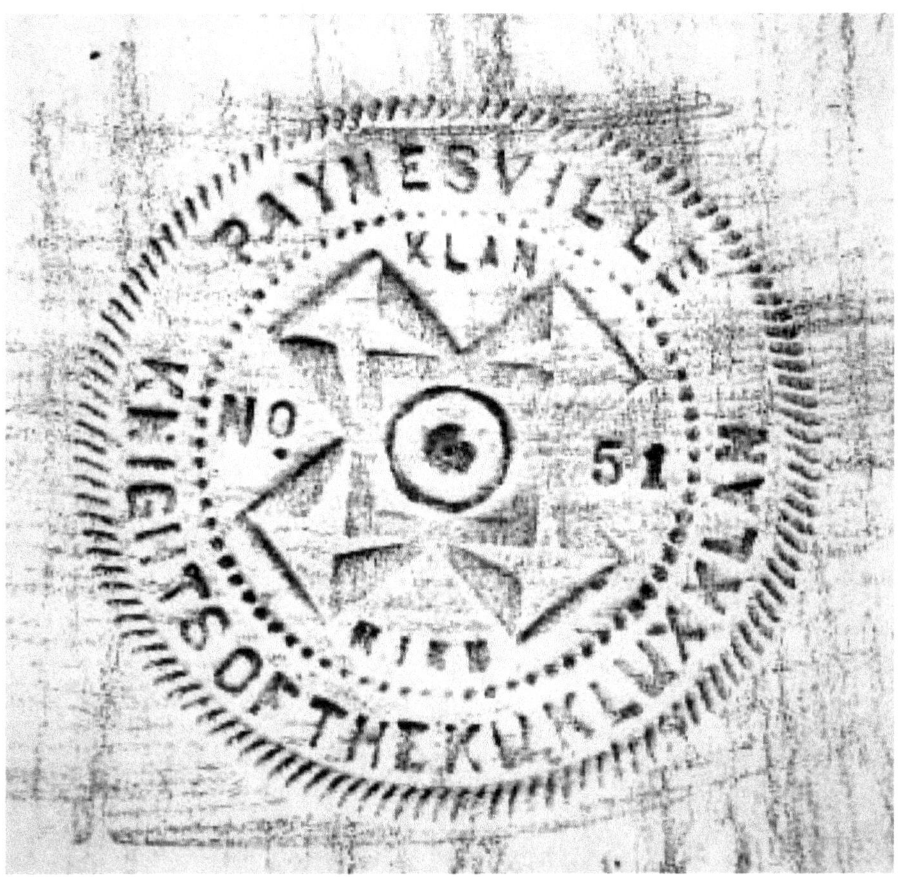

Paynesville KKK-stamped seal. *Courtesy of Paynesville Historical Society.*

chapter that was formed in Eden Valley. The *Eden Valley Journal* reported that the Klan chapter wasn't ashamed of its membership in the organization and even wanted to give a list of its members to the newspaper for publication.

Ku Klux Klan chapters also considered themselves law enforcement agencies in their communities, as in the Hoseas Mohlar case in St. Cloud. Mohlar, an aviator, was also president of the North Star Aircraft Corporation. He had a cross constructed of old automobile tire rubber burned in front of his apartment, and there was a note left in Mohlar's mailbox at his home advising him to leave the city and signed by the Minnesota Chapter No. 7, KKK.[120] Fred Eckhardt, from Boyd, Minnesota, west of St. Cloud, said that his father, Oscar Eckhardt, was a KKK member of the Boyd chapter KKK. "The *Boyd Bulletin* never made any mention of the Klan activities there at

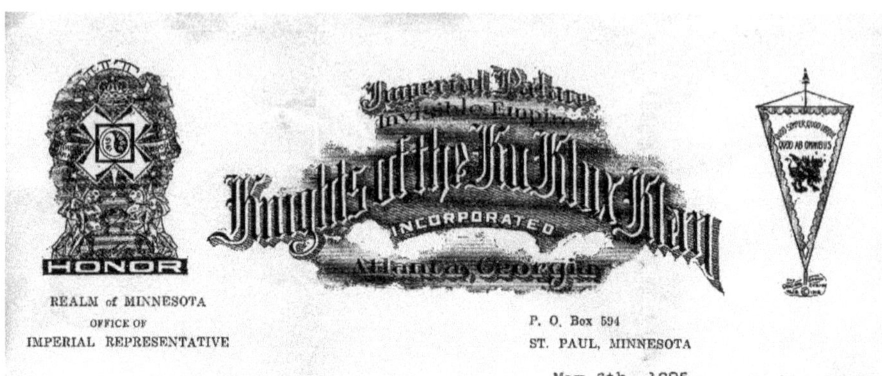

REALM of MINNESOTA
OFFICE OF
IMPERIAL REPRESENTATIVE

P. O. Box 594
ST. PAUL, MINNESOTA

May 6th, 1925.

Mr. A.R.Wohlstad,
Milaca,
Minn.

Dear Sir:

Some time ago you were extendéd the courtesy of being naturalized into our Order without first paying the required donation of $10. upon your promise to make payment within a few days.

We understand that you have attended several meetings but that you have not made good your promise to pay the required donation.

Unless your donation is mailed to this office immediately, it will have to be charged to our field representative, who we feel quite sure can ill afford to pay the donations of others, yet he is responsible for bringing you into the organization and unless you make prompt payment he shall be held accountable.

- May we, therefore, expect your remittance in the amount of $10. by return mail.

Very truly yours,

H E Kettering

IMPERIAL REPRESENTATIVE
REALM OF MINNESOTA

HEK:G

KKK dues letter from Minnesota grand dragon H.H. Kettering. *Courtesy of Jon Willard.*

all, including the two cross burnings," Eckhardt added. The editor of the *Boyd Bulletin* was Anthony Henry Nibbelink, a Methodist and ardent "dry."[121] A Minnesota KKK letter was sent to a Mille Lacs County Klan member, warning him to pay his Klan dues. The letter is dated May 6, 1925, and is from H.E. Kettering, representative for the KKK Realm of Minnesota; it was sent to Mr. A.B. Wohlstad of Milaca, Minnesota. "We understand you've attended several meetings but that you have not made good your promise to pay the required donation."[122]

In the possession of the Itasca County Historical Society, there is a handwritten note sent to James Connell, who was a Grand Rapids grocer. The Knights of Liberty sent the warning note to Mr. Connell saying the following: "Dear Sir, We have been informed that you are disobeying the law by selling groceries on Sunday which is a disloyal act and non-Americanism. If another such report is given your windows will get a coat of yellow paint of which you know the meaning. Hoping you will take heed, Knights of Liberty." The Knights of Liberty were but one manifestation of the anti-German hysteria that swept this country during World War I. Changing over to join a Klan chapter after the war would not have been difficult transition for members of the Knights of Liberty. Itasca was reported by the Minneapolis Klan newspaper *Call of the North* as having a Klan chapter as early as 1923; Klan crosses were burned there on October 5, 1923. There was also a cross burned at the top of Forsythe hill in Grand Rapids.

A fiery Klan cross in a Cohasset field signaled that there was a Ku Klux Klan chapter in the area. Cohasset is five miles west of Grand Rapids. A newspaper report about the cross in Cohasset goes on with the standard "instructions" on how a Klan cross is made "of heavy poles and lumber, firmly bound together with heavy wire." It was pretty commonplace to report not just that the Ku Klux Klan in the area was burning crosses but also detailed explanations on how to build your own Klan cross—what materials were needed to construct the cross, size and amount of fuel needed for it to blaze for several hours. If you could not be there in person to learn how to do this correctly, local newspapers provided detailed instructions how to effectively make Klan crosses. The *Herald-Review* of October 1925 reported a major gathering of the Ku Klux Klan taking place at the Itasca County fairgrounds. The fairgrounds were leased from the county commissioners by the local Klan chapter. It was quickly noted that on the day of the event, the thirteen-acre field would have trouble accommodating the large crowd. This Klan event did not have its parade downtown, instead holding it on the racetrack at the fairgrounds.

Crime in Moorhead made regular headlines in the newspapers there, and prostitution was also an issue in town. Changes in liquor laws due to a county option vote on May 16, 1915, saw the demise of Moorhead's great saloon district that summer. Stills popped up in the Moorhead area afterward, with regular raids conducted. Reports of local Klan activity began to surface in the Red River Valley in the fall of 1922. In February 1923, the Klan mailed out press releases to the local newspapers in the area. In October 1923, the *Moorhead Country Press* reported a lecture by Klan organizer Peter Sletterdahl (Twilight Orn) at Moorhead's Phoenix Lodge. Another Orn lecture, at Hawley's Garrick Theater, attracted "a large audience." Reverend G.F. Fink gave a Klan lecture in Barnesville in November 1923. The *Moorhead Daily News* and the *Moorhead Country Press* both reported that Police Chief Tim O'Leary tried to stop the meeting but had no grounds to do so, and Reverend Fink finished his speech. Reverend Fink had been the pastor of the Christian Church in Austin, Minnesota, until he resigned his position to serve the Klan as kleagle in Austin.

In December, the *Country Press*'s Hawley correspondent reported that another Klan organizer, Raymond Batty, had been "in Hawley during the past week lining up several new candidates for this order." The *County Press* also had in its news report notices that Pelican Rapids had gone solid in favor of the Klan and that numerous other villages in the territory were getting into line. On June 25, 1924, the Klan offered a presentation, "The Truth about the Klan," at the Moorhead Armory. Less than three months after that, a part-time policeman, Michael Hansmann, was shot and killed on September 17, 1924, as he arrived at the front door of his home in Moorhead. Hansmann's parents were both from Germany, and the murdered police officer was also Catholic. His murder is still unsolved today.

Seven months *before* the Duluth lynchings, a young woman named Edna Werner was murdered in East Grand Forks. Werner's murder was given intense news coverage in Duluth newspapers. It is possible that the mindset of Duluth's residents was that when the woman made her accusations against the young circus workers, these men in Duluth would not get off like the African American men in East Grand Forks. Did the Werner murder seven months earlier give Tusken, the "victim" in the Duluth lynchings, the idea to accuse the African American circus workers? The *Duluth News Tribune*'s steady reporting of the Werner murder was pretty sensationalized, with lurid front-page coverage. The Duluth newspapers described the murder as a "horrible affair." The two African American men who were accused in the Werner murder had something happen to them that saved their lives: law enforcement in that community took immediate action protecting the prisoners.

The most important legal agency to respond to real or imagined African American criminality is the police department. Its officers' actions or inaction set the stage for how an African American person suspected of committing a crime against a white person will be treated. Placing African Americans accused of crimes in a local jail is an inflammatory action and liable to set off lynchings in such communities. Moving an African American prisoner out of the jail in the area where the crime is committed to another jail can save a prisoner's life. Police officers often determine whether an African American man will face a trial or a lynch mob. Accounts of lynchings reveal that mob action was averted only when local law enforcement removed a potential victim from the jurisdiction or conveyed clearly to the members of the lynch mob that they will be shot if they proceed with the lynching.

Edna Werner's death certificate notes the cause of death on October 7, 1919, as, "Violence—by being shot in head. Was murdered, assaulted and shot by Negro." At the postmortem examination of the body, Coroner Nelson of Polk County stated in his report that Werner had been shot twice and that she was thrown from the bridge down to the riverbank; it appeared that she had been sexually assaulted after succumbing to her wounds and also that she had fought her assailant with all her strength, according to local newspaper reports. Before anyone was even tried for a crime, Miss Werner's death certificate stated that she was murdered by a "Negro." Edna Werner died on October 7, and on October 8, her autopsy was completed.

James Smith apparently confessed to the murder but attempted to place most of the blame on Tom Thomas, another African American man. On December 30, 1919, a newspaper article confirmed rumors of an attempt to lynch Smith the night after the murder. James Smith pleaded guilty on January 17, 1920, and received a life sentence in Stillwater prison. Smith changed his confession after being jailed, and this exonerated Thomas, who was released from prison. Jim Smith was a porter at the local barbershop at East Grand Forks, Minnesota, and had begun working at the shop in July 1919. The bullet lodged in Miss Werner's neck was fired by a .38-caliber Iver Johnson gun. A .38-caliber revolver was found in Jim Smith's room, and an examination showed that two shells had been emptied recently out of the weapon. Sheriff O.K. Bolstad of Polk County felt that the prisoners' physical safety was threatened and removed the two suspects from East Grand Forks, first to Crookston and then into the care of Ramsey County officials.

Oscar K. Bolstad became the sheriff of Polk County at the age of forty. What law enforcement did not do in Duluth, Minnesota, Sheriff Bolstad did in East Grand Forks. He got his African American prisoners out of town to keep them physically safe. When Sheriff Bolstad was called at the Polk County capitol building to see if he had arrived in Crookston safely with the prisoners, Bolstad answered that the prisoners were elsewhere to prevent a lynching in Crookston. Bolstad then immediately removed the prisoners from Crookston that night, sending them down to the Ramsey County Jail. Sheriff Bolstad did everything he could, constantly moving his prisoners and making sure that the two men were tried in a court of law.

The Klan burned crosses fifty feet high in Fergus Falls on May 31, 1924, according to the *Fergus Falls Daily Journal*. The newspaper reported that seventy-five men were initiated at the fairgrounds and that a national spokesman for the Klan spoke at the gathering, telling the crowd there that the Ku Klux Klan was not interested in politics while at the same time denouncing Mayor Leach of Minneapolis, saying that Leach had been elected largely by the underworld of Minneapolis. In 1926, Hans Ronnevik, a Norwegian immigrant farmer in the Fergus Falls area, wrote a novel called *100 Percent*. Hans and his wife, Lillie, were well-educated, Lutheran and open-minded citizens. Lillie would nurse and help deliver babies for their non-English-speaking German neighbors.

Ronnevik's novel is set against the background of a Minnesota town (Fergus Falls) during World War I. The main characters in his book wonder if the prominent townsmen were truly the "super patriots" they claimed to be or if being "100 Percent" actually meant some people getting what they wanted at the expense of others less fortunate. At the end of the novel, the main character's hometown is completely destroyed by a tornado. In 1919, Minnesota's second-deadliest tornado killed fifty-seven people in Fergus Falls. The town did not allow a liquor store to open there until 1959, and at the time of Fergus Falls' 100th anniversary, it contained only one Catholic church. The first African American families came to Fergus Falls in 1897 from Kentucky; none of the descendants of the original African American families who settled in Otter Tail County still live there today.[123]

Fred L. Gifford was a Minnesota native and Mason, born in North Branch, Minnesota, where he lived until he was ten years old before moving to Oregon with his mother. Fred Gifford's father was Benjamin L. Gifford, from Maine. Fred Gifford used his Portland, Oregon base to recruit Klansmen from across the state and was the grand dragon for the Oregon Ku Klux Klan between 1921 and 1924. The Oregon chapter focused on the perceived growing threat of Catholicism. Fred L. Gifford was a member of the Episcopal Church, a member of the Portland Fire Department and, at the time of his death, was a bailiff in the court of circuit judge W.L. Tooze. For a number of years, Gifford was associated with the Portland office of the International Detective Agency.

North Branch, Minnesota, is located in Chisago County and the Chisago County Historical Society helped me find Fred L. Gifford's family. The Ku Klux Klan dragon's two oldest brothers by his father's first marriage were half white and half Indian. Fred Gifford most likely didn't make mention of his half-brothers living back in Minnesota at Klan meetings in Oregon. The St. Croix River marks the eastern boundary of Chisago County and was very convenient to the logging industry's needs. Benjamin L. Gifford came to Chisago County from Maine to log. As Benjamin aged, logging being a very physical job, and he soon became a North Branch saloonkeeper. It wasn't likely that Grand Dragon Fred Gifford brought that fact up at Klan meetings either.

Gifford's brothers were likely to have been Ojibwas because that tribal group was most prominent in Chisago County, living nearest to where the logging camps were at the time. Fred's father was twenty-eight years older than Fred's white mother, his second wife. The census lists the two older brothers, George and Edward, as "H.B." (half-breed) for race. By the time the family left for Oregon, Benjamin Gifford had passed away in Minnesota. Did the family leave for Oregon because the wife had relatives there? Or did Fred Gifford's mother get them out of Minnesota and away from her husband's half-Indian sons? Benjamin Gifford is buried at Oak Knoll Cemetery in North Branch, Minnesota. Benjamin's wife left with the younger children for Oregon in 1889. George and Eddie Gifford are listed as having been in Minnesota in 1890, as they stayed there. So almost everyone was in Oregon, except for the two "H.B." brothers. Their names, George and Eddie Gifford, are not mentioned in Fred Gifford's obituary.

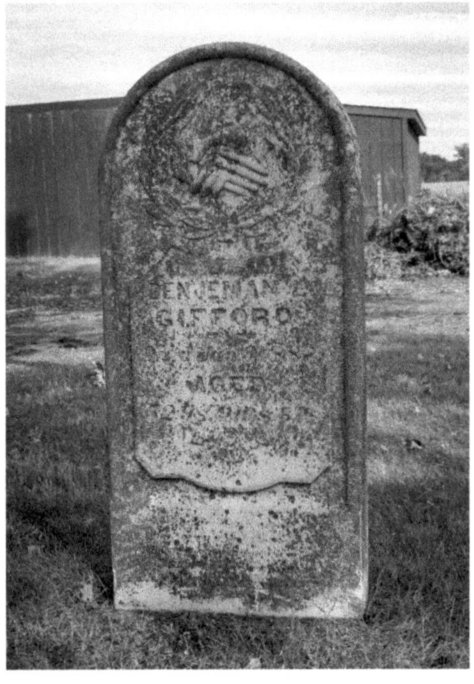

Oregon grand dragon Fred Gifford's father's grave site, North Branch, Minnesota. *Courtesy of Kevin B. Hatle.*

William Carver, the sheriff of Martin County during the 1920s, was outed by the St. Paul *Midway News* as being a Klansman. The *Midway News* reported on November 6, 1926, "In Martin County, this state, former Lieutenant Governor Frank A. Day defeated his Ku Klux opponent for the Senate, while William S. Carver, present sheriff of that county and a Klan leader, was defeated by Gus Jorgensen, anti-Klan. The Klan candidates for county treasurer and court commissioner were both defeated. Martin County has been a Klan hotbed for the past four years." William S. Carver moved from the Fairmont area to the state of Oregon, where his wife, Mary, was from. He died there in 1940. Oregon was a Klan state, with every county having a Klan chapter and Oregon's Ku Klux Klan grand dragon having been born and raised in Minnesota.[124]

In Virginia, Minnesota, which had its own Ku Klux Klan chapter, a battle took place regarding the Bible in the public school system. School boards were a popular Ku Klux Klan political niche. In Duluth, there were two KKK members listed as being on Duluth's school board: Henry Kern, board member and secretary who signed off for each meeting, and Daniel Williams. Virginia's school board most likely had Klan members on it as well. Max Kaplan, a Jewish kosher butcher living in Virginia, challenged the practice of Bible verse reading in the Virginia's public schools. Some in Virginia felt that exclusion of the Bible would cause morals to decline and crime to increase. Virginia, Minnesota, had a small Jewish population living there at the time, and the community organized the B'nai B'rith chapter to lodge a protest against the city plan on the basis that the school board's action "was contrary to the spirit of the doctrine of the constitution."

A delegation from the Jewish community, led by John Mesberg, appeared before the Virginia School Board to ask that the resolution to have the Bible read by teachers in the school be rescinded. The school board declined, and the practice of Bible reading was instituted by the school superintendent, Mr. Duffield, who selected the Bible readings that teachers were to read their students in their classes. Max Kaplan, who brought the case against the Virginia School Board, operated a meat market in Virginia and lived with his family above his shop, buying a home in Virginia in 1920.

There is extensive newspaper coverage of the battle to read the Bible in Virginia's public schools. Included in that coverage is what Bible readings the schools were using and what days they used particular Bible readings. The constitutionality of reading the Bible in the public schools of Virginia was upheld in a decision by Judge Edward Freeman. Judge Herbert A. Dancer of Duluth was the attorney representing the Virginia School Board. Judge Freeman's court said that the Jews maintained a separate school in

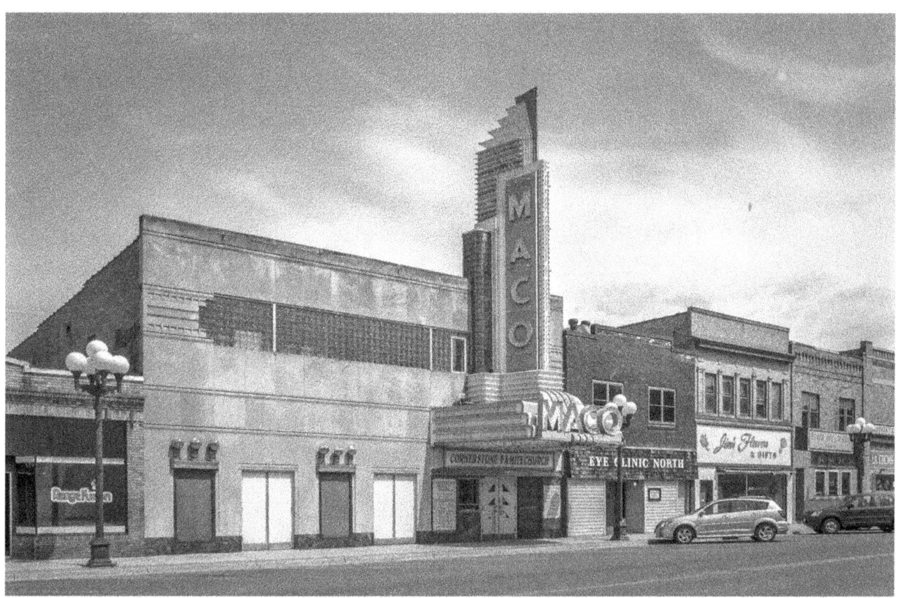

Virginia, Minnesota movie theater. *Courtesy of Kevin B. Hatle.*

Virginia where boys are taught the Jewish belief and given Jewish religious instruction. Attend those schools if reading the Bible in the public schools was offensive to the Jewish population, Judge Freeman stated.

Virginia had a special visitor one year: the Ku Klux Klan's national leader, Imperial Wizard Hiram Evans, from Atlanta, Georgia. The *Queen City Sun* on July 29, 1927, noted, "Klan Leader Attacks Smith." Imperial Wizard Evans held a public meeting at the ballpark on Saturday as part of the Klan's nationwide campaign against a candidacy of Governor Al Smith for the Democratic nomination for president. Evans said that the Klan would have no quarrel with the Catholic Church if it would recognize the sovereignty of this nation's laws as other religious denominations in this country are required to do. The newspaper estimated that there were about ten thousand to twenty thousand people who came to see the Klan parade of delegates from Klan units from all across Minnesota that day in Virginia. Fireworks for Evans's visit were provided by Northwestern Fireworks, Duluth. "The police department reports no cases on the blotter and not even a bent fender on Saturday night." The Ku Klux Klan still had an active presence in the north part of Minnesota as late as 1927, well after the rest of the country had rapidly lost its enthusiasm for the Klan.

Peter John Sletterdahl's son, Winston (still alive as of 2012), was born on May 7, 1922, in Chisago, Minnesota. Sletterdahl (aka Twilight Orn) listed his occupation on Winston's birth certificate as "salesman." His home address in the 1920s was 23 Ninth Avenue South, Hopkins, Minnesota, and his occupation was listed in the telephone book as "public speaker." His wife's name was Winifred Allen, and her hometown was Canby, Minnesota. Canby, Dawson and Boyd, Minnesota, are all within twenty miles of one another; future Minnesota governor Theodore Christianson resided in Dawson.

Peter Sletterdahl, before joining the Ku Klux Klan, once taught in the Hutchinson, Minnesota public school system and was an assistant superintendent for the district. What is not listed in the Minneapolis telephone book is that Sletterdahl was also the editor of the Ku Klux Klan Minnesota newspaper *Call of the North*. Sletterdahl wrote in his book *Nightshirt in Politics*, "A Klansman became a candidate for mayor in a Minnesota City. The Klansman didn't know exactly what course to follow in his campaign. He went to the state head of the Klan for advice. 'Since there are only a few Klansmen in your city, make a plea for toleration and denounce the Invisible Empire,' advised the Kockroach." The Klan-backed mayoral candidate referred to was Minneapolis candidate William Campbell; his run for mayor was unsuccessful.

Matthias Koll, a prominent Catholic businessman from Cass Lake, had threats made against him by the local Klan. Koll wrote to the St. Louis County sheriff in Duluth for help with the KKK threats. In Koll's personal papers, there is a letter to Owen Morical, then sheriff of Walker. Sheriff Morical evidently had hired a deputy who was a Klan member, and Koll attempted to have the deputy removed from Morical's office. On April 4, 1923, Koll wrote to Duluth's sheriff outlining in great detail what was occurring in his community. With his letter to the sheriff, Koll included three notices of Klan intention to blow up three different individuals in the Cass Lake area, including Koll himself. All the notices to the three men were signed with the letters "KKK." Koll wanted the sheriff in Duluth to have the notices tested for thumbprints or fingerprints. Another letter was written to Owen Morical on April 7, 1923, again asking that a particular deputy be ordered to resign because Koll had been told that this deputy was a Klansman.

Mr. Koll was pretty frightened by the KKK's written threats and hired a private investigator named Edward B. Armstrong to investigate the notices at a personal cost to him of $200. After visiting the area and speaking to several people, the detective told Koll that the notices were written by girls "as a joke" and that no fingerprints could be found on the work because, as the investigator put it, "there were no fingerprints made, which indicates that the persons who did the work are well posted on such work." So, if the threats were the result of teenage girls, were the girls criminals in training, enough to know not to leave fingerprints? Koll did not see these threats as any kind of "joke" and was not pleased with the investigator's report on the situation.

Koll told Sheriff Morical, "I am out to fight with every means at my command the gang that is trying to put a reign of terror into this town. I do this because I have been threatened with death. I have a right to fight. If you are with the side of law and order I am sure you will recognize my right to work to undo the work they are threatening to do." Koll did not have any type of response from state officials on the concerns he had, and nothing was done about discharging the Klan deputy, nor was any law enforcement investigation made regarding the threatening notes. Because Catholics lived in Cass Lake or due to other reasons, it was not just the Klan chapter in the Cass Lake area that was being ignored by law enforcement, but it was also the physical state of the town itself. Little aid was coming into Cass Lake to improve its road or infrastructure.

There was correspondence sent to Charles Babcock from Matthias Koll, with Koll asking some hard questions why the Minnesota Highway Department was not doing work regarding the roads in the Cass Lake area. Charles Babcock's letter back to Koll is abrupt and condescending in tone. Stafford King has in his papers a letter to someone he knew from where he grew up, telling that particular person exactly what they would need to do to get good roads where their farms were located. King knew what had to be done and outlined it in this letter to his "friend," telling him what he had to do to get the Minnesota Highway Department in his area to do what he wanted. Deer River, King's hometown, is less than ten miles from Cass Lake. Koll's letter from C.M. Babcock, dated September 11, 1929, related to Koll that the Department of Highways "did not have in mind" extending road treatments in the Cass Lake area.[125]

The second movement of the Ku Klux Klan in the 1920s was up and possibly in operation in Minnesota before 1920. Whether there were Klan recruiters in Duluth in 1919 cannot be firmly determined. There was a climate in Duluth, though, that was very receptive to Klan recruiters immediately after Clayton, Jackson and McGhie were lynched in June 1920. There may not have been Klan involvement directly with the lynchings, but it is possible that after the lynchings, Klan connections may have helped in the cover-up of whoever played a role in the lynchings. Many of the "right" people in Duluth joined the Ku Klux Klan less than a year after the lynchings—people who could have made sure that no one was further punished or charged with murder and that the lynchings would be forgotten as quickly as possible. There were some powerful Duluth citizens who belonged to the Duluth Klan chapter.

Being elected a county commissioner was a prime political spot to have; county commissioners had control over the county purse strings and could hire and control the road overseers, as well as road gangs, county clerks, law enforcement positions and other employees numbering in the hundreds in some counties. Not only was one Duluth county commissioner a Klan member (Thomas H. Little, Second District), the St. Louis County auditor and county commissioner of the Fifth District, Walter H. Borgen, was also a Duluth Klan member and the president of the Minnesota Association of County Auditors. K. Stanley Duff (also a Duluth Klan member) was the director of the Duluth Safety Council. Luther B. Arnold, land commissioner for the Duluth and Iron Range and Chicago, Rock Island and Pacific Railroads, as well as president of the St. Louis Country Club for two years, was a Klan member.[126]

On September 13, 1924, a national lecturer of the Klan, C.S. Cammer, told an audience of several hundred in Duluth that the Klan was not anti-Catholic, anti-Negro or anti-Jew, but rather was for true Americanism. St. Louis County seems to have had a preference for Klan-favored political candidates. The *Midway News* reported on November 13, 1926, "Miss Kaercher was cut in other localities where the Klan has shown strength." (Her opponent was George Higgins from St. James, and both were Republicans. Higgins, a friend of King's, may have gotten the votes in the Minnesota Klan localities.) Another possible reason for Duluthians to have found Klan candidates attractive was what was occurring to their churches in Duluth. In 1916, the three top Protestant church groups by numbers in Duluth, Minnesota, were the following: seventeen Lutheran churches, eleven Methodist churches and ten Baptist churches versus the thirteen Catholic churches, one of which was a Polish Catholic church. By 1926, "panic" must have set in with the Catholic church numbers going up to twenty-three, close to doubling in less than ten years. The 1925 and 1926 Duluth telephone books, which list all the Duluth churches and the ministers of those churches at that time, had at least one confirmed Klan minister: Reverend Harry W. Siefert.

There is correspondence between Stafford King and KKK Duluth members. Of particular note is a letter between Dutch Jerominus (Duluth Ku Klux Klan member and initial organizer of the 40 & 8 in Duluth). King thanked Jerominus for getting the "old club" out to vote for him for his first term as Minnesota state auditor. Another Duluth Klan member, "Rus" Mather, enthusiastically told Stafford King, "I'm with you 100%." In the papers of John Regan, there is a man named Siefert (only the last name is given) whom John Regan mentioned as offering him a bribe, accompanied by a threatening letter to Regan to lay off the highway department. This man was from Duluth, Minnesota, according to Regan. There is an Arthur Siefert, who worked for U.S. Steel, listed in the Duluth telephone books. I could not prove positively that Reverend Harry W. Siefert, Duluth Klan member, was related to Arthur Siefert, but both men lived in Duluth at the same time, disappearing from the Duluth telephone book at the same time in 1930.[127]

CHAPTER 8

South Minnesota Klan Activities

Harold Wade was the son of wealthy Fairmont business owner Frank Wade. Harold returned home from World War I to work in the bank where his father was president, later becoming head of Fairmont's largest industry, the Fairmont Railway Motors Inc. Harold Wade was also a Stafford King correspondent and an American Legion commander in Fairmont, Minnesota. Harold's father founded the Fairmont Boat Company several years before he began to build Interlaken Park; the Fairmont newspaper reported that this is where the Martin Ku Klux Klan chapter held its "events." The Wade family members were Christian Scientists. Christian Scientists were typically "drys."

The *Fairmont Sentinel* reported on August 17, 1923, "Mysterious Gathering at Legion Hall Said to Be Konference of Kluckers." The Fairmont American Legion eventually kicked the Klan meetings out of the legion building, but that's where the Fairmont Klan did meet for one year. The Fairmont Klan chapter then went to Interlaken Park to assemble until it bought its own klavern building, but it wasn't kicked out of the legion until Harold Wade was no longer post commander. The *Windom Reporter* of August 20, 1926, reported on a Ku Klux Klan Konklave and Harvest Festival held in Fairmont where Judge Wheeling (Wayne Ellsworth Wheeling) of Duluth delivered a speech. At this particular Klan event, there was an announcement of the presentation of the Martin Klan charter, a "mighty impressive ceremony worth going miles to see."

Judge Wheeling (or sometimes "Wheeler") was said "to be one of the leading Klansmen in Minnesota." Born in 1888 and an attorney from

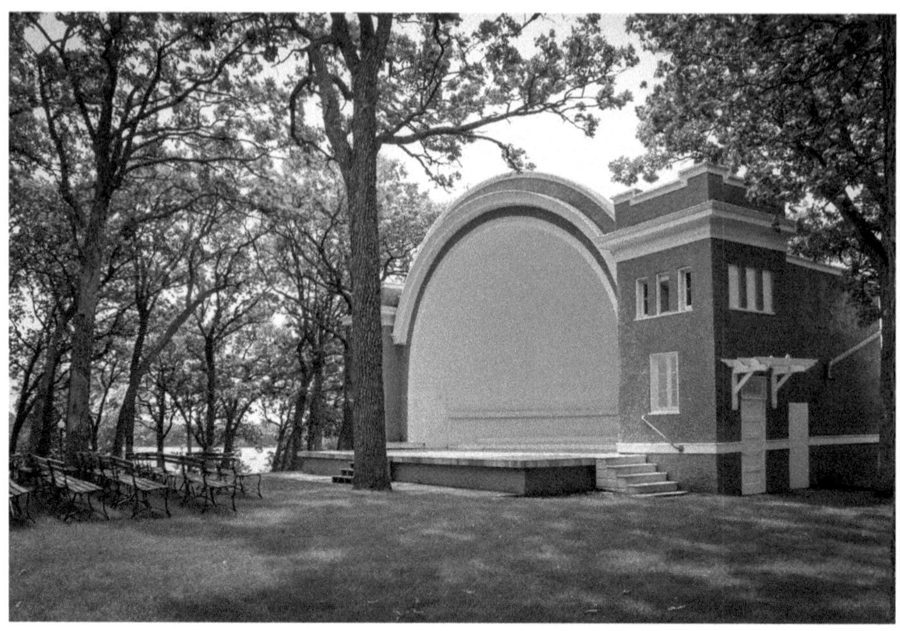

Interlaken Park band shelter, Fairmont, Minnesota. *Courtesy of Kevin B. Hatle.*

Duluth, Minnesota, Wheeling was a member of the Duluth Klan chapter. Wheeling made quite a few trips throughout Minnesota, speaking at Klan events. On Wheeling's World War I draft registration card, he printed in capitalized letters, "NATIVE BORN."

In his speech, Wheeling declared, "The little sparrows are saying that the Knights of the Ku Klux Klan of Martin County are figuring on erecting a hall or temple in Fairmont. The sparrows further depose and declare that one of Fairmont's wealthiest captains of industry [Harold Wade?] will donate the ground, provided the Kluxers build something that will make a flash in the skies like the Wrigley chewing gum building in Chicago." The Martin County Klan did not build a new building, but maybe that's where the $3,500 came from to buy the building—"one of Fairmont's wealthiest captains of industry." The Martin Ku Klux Klan's klavern still exists in Fairmont today, although now it is a Mexican grocery store. The property, at 105 Fourth Street Northeast, was bought by G. Fred Anderson in 1926, the Martin County Ku Klux Klan representative. Anderson sold the property on March 6, 1930, for $5,000. A.D. Johanson and Harold Axford also have their names listed as sellers in the transaction.[128]

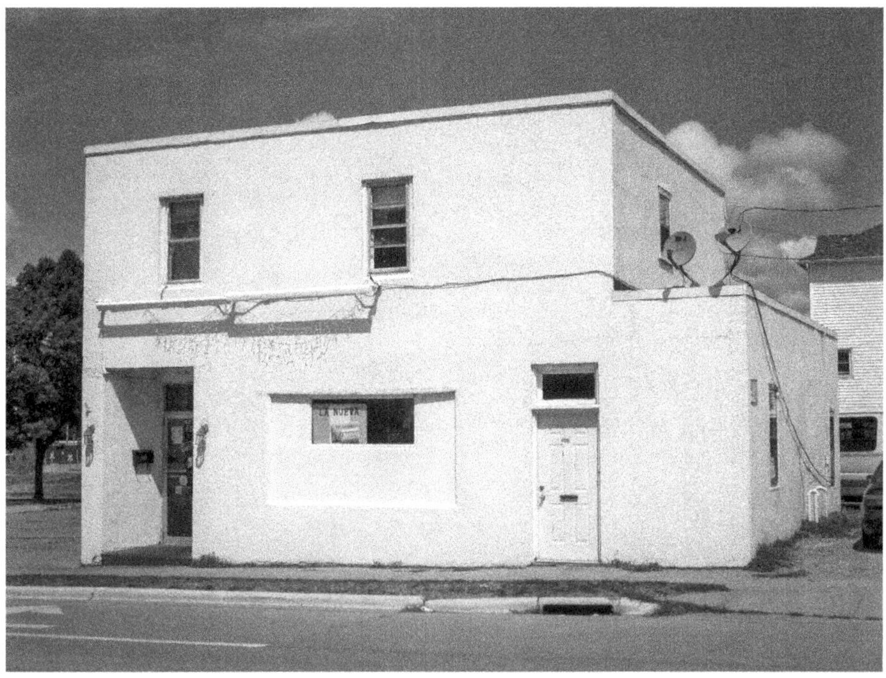

KKK-owned building, Fairmont. *Courtesy of Kevin B. Hatle.*

The Fairmont Ku Klux Klan klavern is located one-third of a mile from Interlaken Park (now called Sylvester Park). The original band shell from the 1920s still exists today; the hill park was a perfect spot for the Martin County Ku Klux Klan chapter to burn crosses during Klan events. Burning crosses would have been easily seen from town, across the lake and within open view of the Martin County Courthouse. G. Fred Anderson did not make his personal residence at the klavern, although there are living quarters located above the building. Martin County Historical Society telephone books from 1924–30 show G. Fred Anderson living at 236 South Elm in 1923–24, and then he lived at 209 East Webster. An occupation for Anderson is listed for one year, 1926, when he had a second phone number under his home phone, at the abstractor's office.

An article in the *Fairmont Daily Sentinel* on May 28, 1926, was headlined, "Seek to Rent Fairgrounds for Gathering—Board Ask $500, KKK's Offer Percentage of Gate Receipts to Society, Double Event if the Legion Celebrates." The matter had been under discussion between the Martin County Fair Board and Klan officials for several weeks. The board was standing out for a flat rental fee of $500, whereas the Klan wanted to put

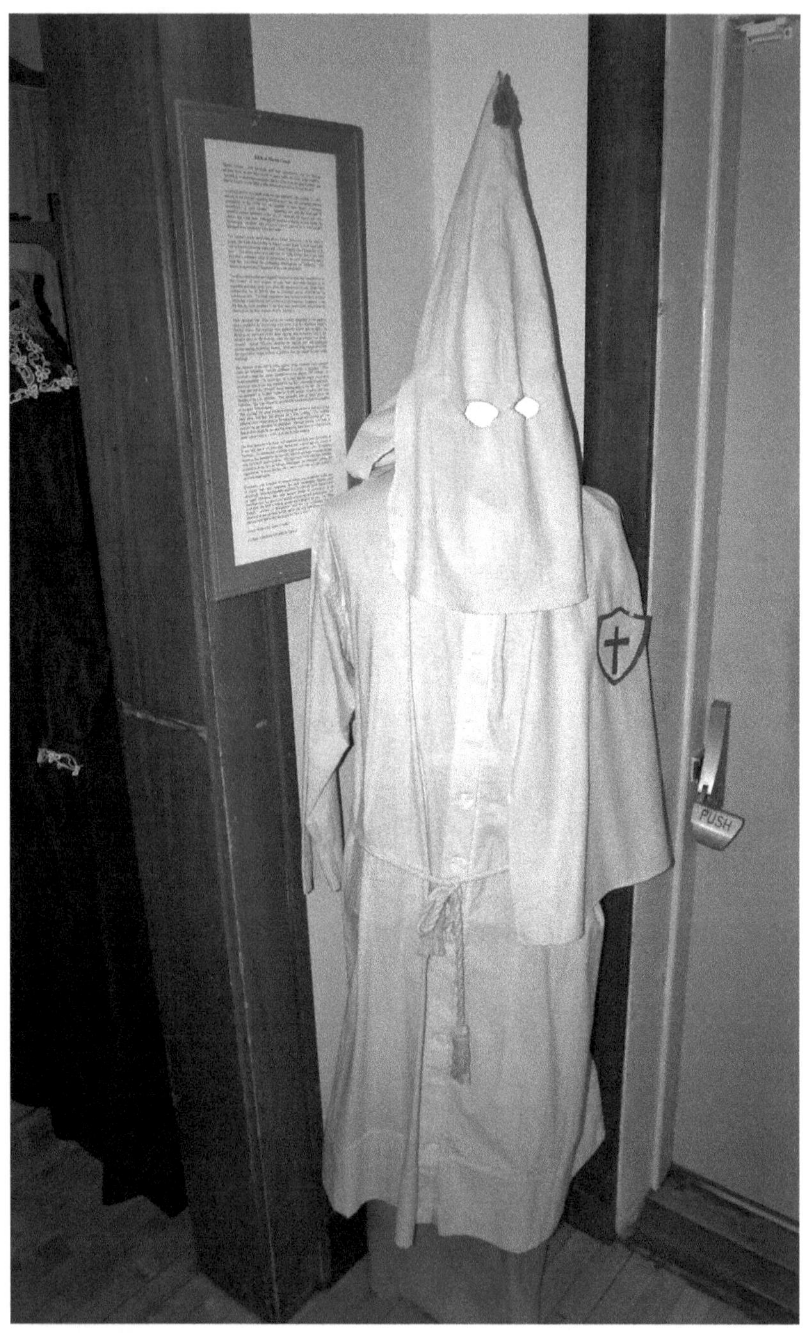

Fairmont, Minnesota Klan hood and robe. *Courtesy of Martin County Historical Society.*

up 10 percent of the gate receipts. If the Klan and the legion joined their celebration, it would have ensured one of the largest crowds ever for a Fourth of July celebration in Fairmont, according to G. Fred Anderson. On June 2, 1926, the *Fairmont Daily Sentinel* reported that the Martin County Fair Board had not yet made a decision on letting the Klan use the Martin County fairgrounds. It's wasn't that the fair board couldn't have used the money, they explained, but that they could not afford anything that would make trouble for the community. G. Fred Anderson wrote an article explaining how he, the Klan representative, told the fair board that a huge parade in the city had been further added to the Klan event; according to Anderson, this was a very important Klan date to celebrate because it was the 150th anniversary of the signing of the Constitution.

The fair board expressed concerns about how using the fairgrounds on July 4 would affect the upcoming fall county fair. Klan representative Anderson reassured them that the Klan would come in to help and even offered to put on a Klan day at the county fair that fall. Anderson wrote, "The Klan believes in equal rights and that is all it asks and as an organization will not order a boycott of the county fair on account of this refusal." On June 4, 1926, it was announced that the Ku Klux Klan would be celebrating in Fairmont on July 5, 1926. This publicized information was given by Claude Small, Easley Smith, Reverend William Bader, G.I. Thieman and Anderson (listed in the 1924 Minnesota Republican directory as a secretary for the Second Congressional District).[129] The *Fairmont Sentinel* on June 9, 1926, reported that the Klan's request to use the fairgrounds was turned down. F.J. Driscoll told a *Fairmont Sentinel* reporter that he plans to stay open both July 4 and the fifth and put up a sign in his window that reads, "Klansmen Welcome."

The *Fairmont Sentinel* of July 6, 1926, reported that twenty-one thousand showed up for the Klan celebration at Interlaken Park. Just thirteen thousand paid admissions and passed though the gate. There was not a single case of disorderly conduct, and not a trace of liquor was observed at the event, according to the newspaper. The Fairmont Klan chapter made an offer to pay ten dollars for information leading to the arrest of any bootleggers who may have attended the event. Also that July weekend, there was a "living cross" at the event composed of 250 robed Klansmen, each holding a red torch. The voices of several hundred Klanswomen, set aside from the crowd a quarter of a mile away, could be heard singing to the crowd in perfect pitch and harmony to their large audience. The Martin County Klan chapter did not get to use the county fairgrounds but had a highly successful event at Interlaken regardless.

Chris Milow's great-grandfather, Leo A. Milow, was a Martin County Board commissioner for thirty-six years. Leo's parents were from Germany, and Leo was the first in his family to have been born in the United States. Leo was known as a fighter, and in his thirty-six years on the board, he often had the last word. Leo was on the board that did not allow the Fairmont Ku Klux Klan to have use of the Martin County fairgrounds. Chris said that Floyd B. Olson visited the family farm to speak to his grandfather. Floyd Olson was the type of man who personally reached out to those who helped him politically in the rural areas of Minnesota. In the case of the death of Gerhard Hatle (a county secretary for the Farmer-Labor association), Olson sent a personal telegram of condolence to Hatle's widow and their ten living children, the youngest under the age of five, upon learning of his death.[130] Olson undoubtedly knew about the Martin County Klan chapter through Leo Milow. Leo said that he had never been bought off. "They tried—just once—that's all," Leo noted.

The Martin County Ku Klux Klan sent hate mail to the Milow farm. Chris found a postcard when the family farm was sold. The postcard was sent to Leo Milow in September 1923 in response to what he had said to the

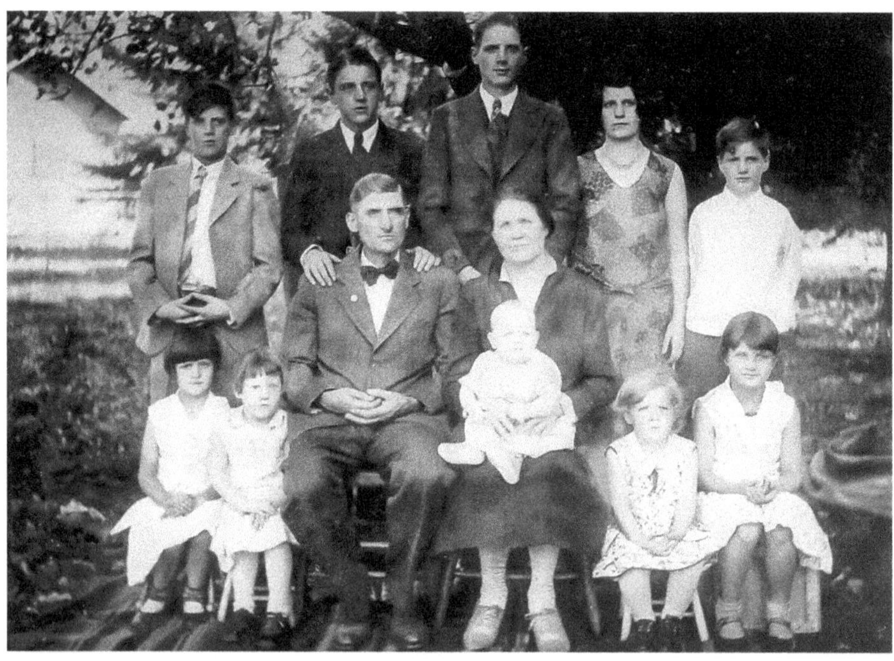

The Gerhard Hatle family. *Courtesy of Rodney Hatle.*

local newspaper. Leo, speaking of the Ku Klux Klan, said, "It looks to me like a political move and believe me it won't get very far in Martin County where citizens stand for law enforcement in the open by the regular officers of the law." That section of the newspaper was taped to the threatening postcard sent to the Milow farm. Below the newspaper section was typed, "You shoot off, half cocked, as usual, like all the rest of the GERMAN tribe. You will know more if you but keep your mouth shut and eyes and ears open."[131]

Editor C.R. Campbell made the Minnesota Ku Klux Klan regular front-page news in his newspaper, the *Ellendale Eagle*. In July 1924, Campbell wrote about a large crowd gathering in downtown Ellendale to hear "an ordinary chap" speak on the steps of the Ellendale State Bank. During his speech to the crowd, the Klan speaker informed the crowd that he was a Methodist preacher from somewhere in the state of Minnesota. The speech the man delivered "could be heartily endorsed by every American," Campbell remarked. There was a rush afterward to get the Klan literature, according to Campbell. The following week, Campbell reported on the front page about a Ku Klux Klan parade held in Hartland, noting that "at least there were no qualms of fear or dread among Hartland people over the first appearance here of the much talked of Klan."

Labor leader A.C. Townley visited Ellendale in August 1923. Did Townley's visit spur an interest in Klan membership in the area? In September 1923, there was a detailed account on Ellendale's front-page news of the Klan gathering held at Albert Lea's fairgrounds. Campbell described every aspect of the meeting as "one of the most spectacular scenes ever witnessed in this part of the state." An October 28, 1925 *Ellendale Eagle* headline noted that a "Ku Klux Klan Meeting Was to Be Held at the School House in Dist. 34 Monday Evening." The *Ellendale Eagle* reported on November 4, 1925, that "the Klan meeting at the Ellendale School a week ago last Monday was well attended in spite of the bad weather. Two ministers were the speakers." Cecil Campbell moderated school board meetings and would have been part of the decision-making process allowing the local Ku Klux Klan in Ellendale to use the school for its meeting. The *Ellendale Eagle* of January 8, 1926, reported that the "Klan Holds Meeting Here": "Members of the Ku Klux Klan of the Ellendale vicinity held a meeting Monday evening in the old Baptist church building, which they recently rented."

Cecil Campbell was also the American Legion Post No. 296 commander in Ellendale and a member of the American First Committee for that area. Campbell was the postmaster of the Ellendale Post Office in 1926 and again from 1954 to 1955. His wife, Ruth A. Campbell, whom he married in 1940, took over the position of postmaster for the next several decades. Postmasters were appointed by the postmaster general, usually on the advice of the local congressman. The local congressman at the time who likely backed Campbell's postmaster appointment was Allen J. Furlow. Born in Rochester, Furlow served as congressman in that area from 1925 to 1929. Furlow, a Republican, was an unsuccessful candidate for renomination as a congressman.

In Governor Theodore Christianson's papers, there is a letter from W.A. Kanorr regarding the post office and the Ku Klux Klan. Mr. Kanorr outlined the disgrace of the Ku Klux Klan taking over postmaster positions across the country. "Do the people of the U.S. want other departments of the federal government to become like there is evidence the Post Office Department has become under present Postmaster General [the same Postmaster General who cleared Schall of any postal misuse], a bureau of information an aid of Ku Klux Klan Konspirators?" The Ku Klux Klan wanted its people in post office positions, handling their neighbors' mail and keeping track of their activities. In Morristown, Minnesota, the local Ku Klux Klan chapter there attempted to take over the post office.[132]

The grandfather of Mr. Don Gorrie, the former Ramsey County medical examiner, was threatened by the Ku Klux Klan. Peter Walker Gorrie was postmaster in the 1920s for Morristown. Don remembered his father telling him stories of how the KKK threatened his father with the loss of his postmaster job. Don was also told that his grandmother was a friend of a woman whose husband was a local Klan member and that this Klan member's wife helped to get the Klan to leave Peter Gorrie alone. Don's father married a Catholic, rather a bold thing to do back then, according to Don, but that's the kind of family the Gorries were. That type of open-mindedness is probably what bought Peter Gorrie to the Klan's attention, and not being able to control the mail in Morristown was also an irritant for the local Klan.[133]

In Otisco, Minnesota, Janet Bauman Roeglin related how a Ku Klux Klan cross was burned at her great-uncle's hotel in Otisco during the 1920s. Janet noted how her family had gone to the hotel for a Sunday breakfast of pancakes. The family saw the remnants of the burned Klan cross in front of the hotel from the night before. Otto Bauman was German, and the family felt that this was the reason. The Ku Klux Klan had a meeting at the Otisco Town Hall in October 1926. Bauman was arrested by Sheriff Wadd after a complaint was sworn out in 1928 by Sigurd Niberg, who was said to have been a member of the Klan. Otisco

Klan members wanted Bauman's place shut down because it was thought that Bauman was selling liquor out of his hotel.

Rose Underwood Trom, from Blooming Prairie, also related how the local Ku Klux Klan chapter visited their home. Rose's father remembered his father telling him how the Klan came to their farm wearing robes and hoods and carrying guns. Rose's father said that his grandfather, with his five grown sons, came out on the porch with their rifles and said, "Go ahead and start shooting, but we will get some of you first." Rose's father said that he believes this happened in 1920 or 1921.[134]

A kleagle was a Ku Klux Klan recruiter and often adjusted his recruiting approach based on the area's ethnic composition and level of religious strife. Combining voting records with census information, adding the census religious body information, which told what churches were in a community and what kind of churches, would have allowed a kleagle to go into any community and know exactly what buttons to push to recruit members. Klan organizers would stir up sentiment in communities, playing on people's fears to get newspaper coverage and boost membership numbers. The KKK called doing this "kluxing." In Ellendale, Minnesota, a "figure" was hung on an Ellendale telephone pole on September 30, 1925, as noted in the *Ellendale Eagle* ("Thought It Was a Lynching Bee"). Edgar Allen Booth wrote that doing things like this was an excellent example of "kluxing, because any kind of newspaper coverage was good coverage for the KKK."

Within a year of the Duluth lynchings in 1920, there was a trial of an African American male charged for the murder of a white man named Curtis D. Joslin. The death actually occurred in Redwood County, but the murder trial was held in Redwood Falls, which is located in Renville County, next to Redwood County. Hall Green, a twenty-six-year-old African American and a Paxton township farmhand, was given a life sentence for the shotgun slaying of Joslin that occurred on April 7, 1921, beside a road two miles east of Redwood Falls. Joslin was shot once in the shoulder and once in the head. Green was tried on April 28 and 29, 1921. Hall Green's father was John Green, who was living in Le Sueur. Hall Green's mother was white.

The prosecutor in the case was Albert Enerson. The defense lawyers for Hall Green were A.C. Dolliff and A.R.A. Lauden, appointed by the court to be Green's lawyers. The prosecution brought twenty-eight witnesses; Hall Green's defense called only six witnesses. The trial took only two days, and the case went to the all-white jury on April 29 by 8:50 p.m. The jury returned a verdict of guilty. Hall Green did not speak for himself, nor did he testify at his own trial. There was time after the murder to file a motion for continuance before the Green trial, which wasn't done. There was no request for a change of venue by Green's white defense lawyers. Hall Green was a World War I veteran who had completed one year of military service in France during World War I. Green was sentenced to life imprisonment. He was granted an unconditional release on May 16, 1960, by Governor Orville Freeman and is buried at Fort Snelling Cemetery.

A Redwood Falls man by the name of Hugo Fesenmaier was the driver for the prosecuting attorney, Albert Enerson, and Fesenmaier made the claim that the Hall Green trial was unfair because of what Enerson had mentioned to Fesenmaier about the trial. Fesenmaier said that there was a "conspiracy" between the judge and the lawyers not to give Hall Green a fair trial.[135] The identification of Hall Green as being the murderer was unclear; the witness was not certain whether it was Hall or his brother, Henry, who purchased the shells that resulted in the shotgun death of Joslin. The trial judge, the county attorney and the lawyers for the defense knew that the eyewitness testimony was shaky, but they conspired to keep that detail secret from the jury. One of the witnesses who testified against Hall Green at the trial later committed suicide. Albert Enerson became country attorney and then later a judge.

Julius A. Schmahl, a Republican, became a partner in the *Redwood Gazette* newspaper in 1892. Few newspaper editors wielded the influence that Schmahl had with Minnesota Republicans. The 1920 U.S. Census shows Renville County as having one African American living in the county, while Redwood County had eleven African Americans listed living there. The African American population in Redwood County dropped to zero after the Green trial. Another fear in Renville County was the Nonpartisan League. Coverage of A.C. Townley was constant in the *Redwood Gazette*, and the newspaper patted Minnesota on the back for not making the grievous mistake that others had by putting Townley on trial and throwing him in jail. There was relentless and negative coverage of Townley by the *Redwood Gazette*.

Mrs. Arvonne Fraser (née Skelton), senior fellow emerita at the Humphrey School of Public Affairs, University of Minnesota, and wife of former Minneapolis mayor Donald Fraser, was born in Redwood County. She told me that her father had said that her grandfather, Percy Skelton, belonged to the Ku Klux Klan. Percy Skelton was a farmer and a Republican, dying at the age of sixty-eight in an automobile accident. The *Redwood Gazette* announced on September 27, 1922, that the "Enforcement League Is Organized." A meeting was held at the Presbyterian church in Redwood Falls that resulted in the organization of a Law Enforcement League, with cooperation with local and county officers as its purpose. Not exactly a "Klan" notice, but this new

Redwood Falls organization shared a lot of the same goals of the 1920s Ku Klux Klan. The membership was reported to have been large, including many of the prominent men in the county. "Bootleggers and unsupervised dances will come under the immediate attention of the League."

Danube, Minnesota, was perceived by the Renville County Republican chairman, Otto J. Zorn, as being too strong for Farm-Labor in 1926. According to Zorn, Danube was "the hot-bed of the Farm-Labor movement in Renville Co." Zorn did not approve of a German Emil Voelz of Danube being appointed as chairman for the Near East Relief Fund (a Christian charitable organization). Zorn pointed out to Governor Christianson that Danube was filled with strong supporters of Minneapolis mayor Leach. Mr. Zorn was not happy with how his town's business was being conducted and also spoke of being a candidate for postmaster of the village of Danube. He was upset at not receiving the postmaster appointment in Danube. "Something" had to be done about the town of Danube, according to Zorn.[136]

Dr. W.S. Harper, co-editor with Twilight Orn of the Klan's *Fiery Cross* newspaper, was reported addressing a crowd regarding the Ku Klux Klan in the Red Wing, Minnesota area. The Klan in Red Wing and Goodhue County kicked off its 1924 demonstration season in White Rock, where Dr. W.S. Harper addressed a crowd of five hundred on July 21. The following evening, two thousand gathered at Cannon Falls, with another meeting set for Kenyon. The *Daily Eagle* identified Harper as a local doctor in the Red Wing area. Harper's announced topic was "Putting the Bible Back in Schools." At the July 23 Klan gathering, a large Red Wing audience attended an 8:30 p.m. Central Park lecture by Harper, who was dressed in full Klan regalia for the occasion.

N.P. Olson was born in Sweden in 1855 and came to Red Wing in 1909. His wife, Fredrika, was born in Minnesota of German immigrant parents. When N.P. Olson's newspaper started in Red Wing, the news of a new daily making another attempt in Red Wing was just, according to the *Republican Eagle*, "talk emanated from people who had a grudge against the *Republican* for standing by its guns and advocating what it knew to be for the best interests of the community morally, financially and politically." The *Republican Eagle* reported that Nelson's *Daily Eagle* would "fight prohibition and county option." Before Olson came to Red Wing, he ran the *Minnesota Democrat* in Minneapolis. For the next several decades, the two Red Wing dailies attacked each other in print and competed vigorously for readers and advertisers.

When World War I broke out, the *Daily Eagle* supported the U.S. war effort but questioned the necessity of war and deplored that diplomacy had not been used enough to prevent boys from being killed on the battlefield. With Olson's wife being of German descent, this must have been a difficult road for N.P. Olson to negotiate as an editor, dealing with anti-German sentiment in Minnesota at the time. The *Republican Eagle* was a strong supporter of the Republican Party, so Olson's *Daily Eagle* found its friends and readers among the labor and liberal elements in Red Wing. This may explain why the *Daily Eagle* extensively covered Klan activities. It wasn't that the Olson family supported the Klan; instead, it seems that they were exposing the Klan every opportunity they could get.

In early July 1923, circulars were placed around Red Wing announcing that a lecture "on the history, aims and principles of the Ku Klux Klan" would be held at the public square (Central Park). A sixteen- by twenty-foot burning cross was placed at the highest point on Barn Bluff overlooking downtown Red Wing, Minnesota. The *Daily Eagle* claimed that sixty-seven Ku Klux Klan members erected the cross that night. The paper, in its follow-up story on the burning cross, noted that thirty-two candidates for membership were initiated that night. On September 21, 1923, Klan members from the Twin Cities, Albert Lea, Mankato, Austin and other locales gathered on Trenton Island across the Mississippi River, where they prepared for their demonstration. The *Daily Republican* reported "solid walls of humanity," including Klan members and the curious crowding the streets and expectantly awaiting the 8:30 p.m. KKK parade.

The *Northfield News* in July 1924 reported that a Klan lecturer attracted thousands, who crowded City Park to hear the speech. The Klansman said that he was a minister of the gospel and lived in Minneapolis. Before the Klan speaker came to Northfield to speak, *Northfield News* reported on May 30, 1924, that a fireworks demonstration, which included the burning of a large cross on the island in the Cannon River south of the Fifth Street Bridge, was staged in Northfield. "Not being equipped with submarines or aircraft the fire fighters were unable to negotiate the open span of water separating the island from the city."

That same night, a Klan cross burning occurred in Faribault. Local resident Maggie Lee remembered a Klan parade from her childhood in downtown Northfield; her father belonged to the Northfield Klan chapter. This major Klan event that Maggie remembered was front-page news in Northfield in July 1925. A pasture had also been rented on Jefferson Highway on the north side of Northfield where secret ceremonies were to be held during the day before the Klan lecture that was to be given on Bridge Square at 7:30 p.m.; afterward, in downtown Northfield, the largest Klan parade in Minnesota would be staged.[137]

On that last Saturday of July 1925, several hundred white-robed Knights of the Klux Klan arrived in Northfield, Minnesota; 150 men were said to have been added to the organization that weekend, according to the *Northfield News*. Two national lecturers from Georgia were there, a Klan wedding is reported to have taken place, there was a wrestling match and a game between Owatonna and St. Paul kittenball teams (girls' softball teams) also occurred that day. The Klan parade that night not only included several hundred Klanswomen and Klansmen in full uniform but also numerous floats. A Northfield resident of note living in Northfield when the Northfield Klan was active was O.E. Rolvaag, author of *Giants in the Earth*, a classic book about the difficulties immigrants had in their American communities. Rolvaag conveyed in his book how an immigrant arriving in American could hold on to his cultural heritage and still remain loyal to his or her adopted country. Rolvaag was a professor of Norwegian language and literature at St. Olaf College in Northfield from 1906 to 1931.

Mrs. Persons was the president of the WCTU and was the one who started the move to have all saloons in Northfield be removed. Seventy-three Northfield women belonged to the WCTU in 1923; it is quite possible that these same women also belonged to Northfield's WKKK chapter that Maggie Lee said existed and that her mother was asked to join. The *Carletonian*, Carleton College's school paper, reported on April 19, 1924, that the Knights of the Ku Klux Klan conducted a conference, inviting Carleton college students. A number of Carleton men who were interested in the Klan attended the meeting, according to the school newspaper. A visiting Ku Klux Klan officer from one of the Twin City chapters spoke at this gathering. A cross was burned at this meeting, and plans were formulated for associated memberships for students to be part of the Klan at a reduced fee. Maggie Lee's father was a KKK member and employee of Carleton College.

A national Ku Klux Klan speaker came to Worthington in July 1924 to address more than two thousand listeners in Chautauqua Park. The park is located on Lake Okabena, close to the business district, and faces downtown Worthington. The speaker opened his lecture noting that Protestants had just as much right to have their own organization as "the Catholic, the Negro and the Jew." The speaker said that the white race had to remain supreme. The unnamed speaker also spoke about how the Bible was needed back in the public school system. It was pointed out to the Worthington crowd that the door must be closed to immigrants from Russia and how northern European immigrants could more easily assimilate. The Klan speaker declared that the

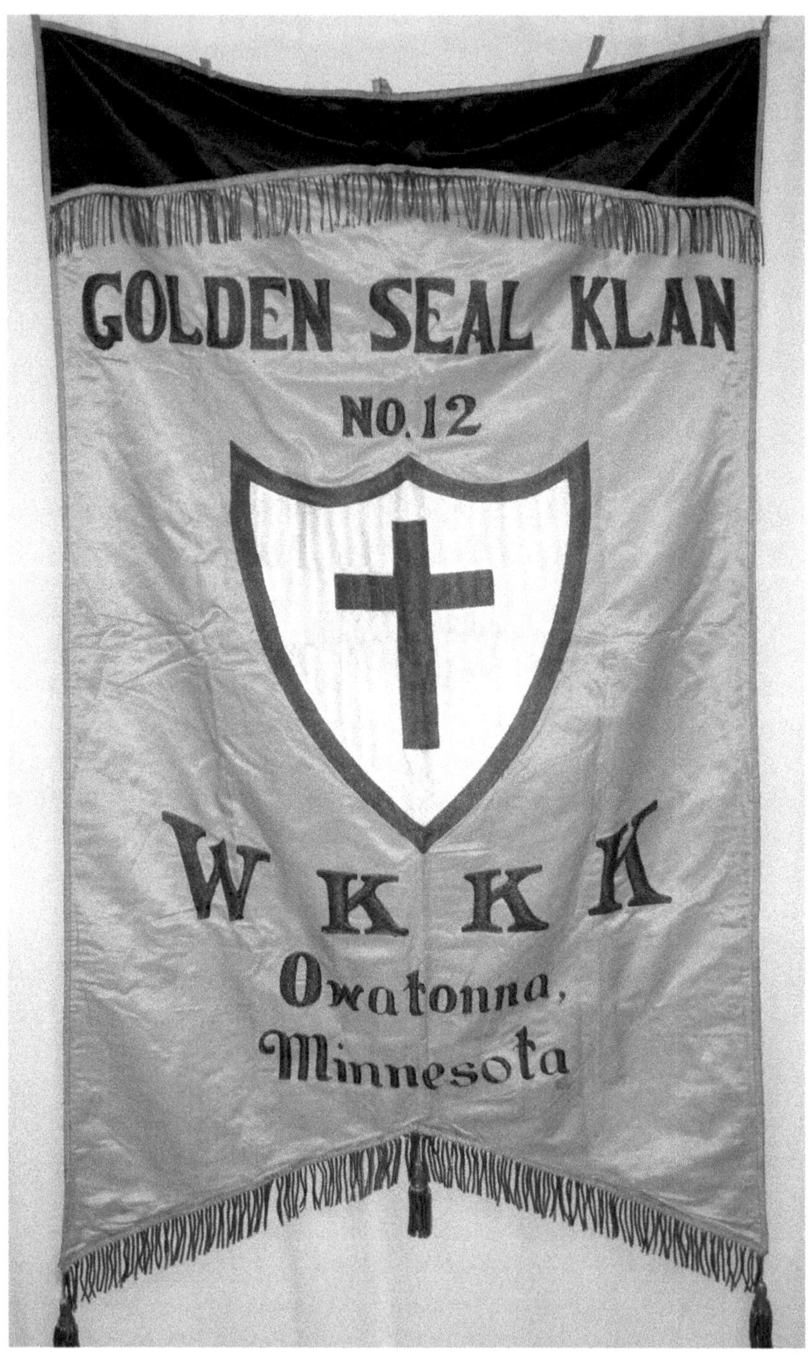

Owatonna WKKK banner, Steele County Historical Society. *Courtesy of Kevin B. Hatle.*

KKK's fiery cross, one of which was burned before the meeting that night, was the standard of the ideals that he had outlined in his speech.

The *Nobles County Times* of August 21, 1924, reported, "Klansmen in Protest at Lakeside Pavilion." The Lakeside pavilion dancers performed at the resort area, which is twelve miles southeast of Worthington. During one particular dance, visiting Klansmen from the Nobles County organization, white robed and unmasked, surrounded the dance floor with folded arms. When asked why the Worthington Klansmen had come to the dance, they merely stated that it was a silent protest against the conditions said to exist at the resort. The leader of the Klan was seen in conversation with the Jackson County deputy in charge of the dance, and "good will appeared to exist between them."

The *Jackson Republic* of August 6, 1926, announced a "Klan Konklave at Fox Lake Park." On August 29, a Ku Klux Klan Konklave was scheduled for Fox Lake Park with the typical Klan features: barbecue, a concert, a ballgame and fireworks. It was reported on August 30, 1923, by the *Lakefield Standard* that a fiery Klan cross was lit on a Monday night on Lover's Knoll, a high spot across the river north of Jackson. Again, a description of the cross and what it was made of were provided. "It is alleged the fiery symbol has thrown a good scare into moonshiners in that locality." Pastor P.A. Millard, from the Worthington Congregational Church, opened this Klan meeting with a prayer. The minister's speech addressed why the Ku Klux Klan denies admission to the organization to certain classes of American citizens and the desire to keep the white race white.

The July 3, 1924 article of the *Lakefield Standard*, headlined, "Klansmen to Hold State Konklave at Spirit Lake," reported that a group of "well behaved, native born American citizens" were planning a large July 4 celebration at Spirit Lake. The local Klan there was to have a sixty-five-Klan-band from Sheldon, Iowa, to head the list of entertainment that day. The local Klan also had some famous Klan speakers coming that day, and the list includes J.A. Brown of the Imperial Palace Flying Squadron, Dr. W.A. Smith and Reverend A.C. Such. Again, there was typical Klan fare: a parade at 8:00 p.m. through the business district and ceremonies at the fairgrounds, "at which time all eligible candidates will be initiated into the mysteries of the order and will be witnessed only by the men and women members of the organization." The *Noble County Times* of August 28, 1924, noted that a "Klan Speaker Talks to Large Crowd." Four thousand people were reported to have attended the speech given at the local fairground. The lecture took two hours, and the "crowd remained in good humor and perfect order."

A flaming cross of Ku Klux Klan was burned at Luverne on August 29, 1923, and later that same night, a second cross was found burning. Several copies of the Ku Klux Klan newspaper, published in St. Paul, were found near the first cross. The *Luverne Herald* found it strange that no one saw or heard anything while these crosses were set up. Klan organizers visited Luverne to speak at the park, but as far as the local newspaper was concerned, none of it was to be taken seriously. The *Rock County Herald* scorned any Klan crosses burned there. In the *Herald*, there was regular front-page coverage of a Catholic church's activities (which was not typically the case in other Minnesota newspapers), and there was even a front-page article about a favorite priest, Father Mangan, on November 13, 1925, moving to Mankato and how greatly he would be missed by Luverne's St. Catherine's Catholic Church and the citizens of Luverne.

The *Pipestone County Star* of September 11, 1923, noted that "a large audience assembled at the Gem Theatre Saturday evening to hear a lecture on the purposes and activities for the Ku Klux Klan by Dr. W.S. Harper, one of the national speakers of that organization." The *County Star* was owned by the Hart family and was viewed as the Republican paper. On August 27, 1924, a Klan cross was burned in Murray County, next to Cottonwood County, which was considered moonshine and bootlegging county by the KKK. Lake Wilson voters resisted attempts on the part of the Methodist Men's Club to rid the village of its saloon. A Klan chapter was active in the area, according to the *Lake Wilson Pilot*, and the Klan chapter's primary targets in the area were bootleggers. Klan crosses were burned in the area, and the local Klan chapter seated several hundred at a Klan event in the Lake Wilson area on a Saturday, watching movies in the open air and lighting up a cross during the show.[138]

In Mankato, Minnesota, on December 26, 1862, the U.S. Army carried out the largest mass execution in U.S. history following the Dakota War of 1862. Thirty-eight Dakota Native Americans were hanged in Mankato for their parts in the Dakota uprising. In the *Mankato Daily Free Press* on June 16, 1920, the newspaper's front-page headline reported on the Duluth lynchings: "Three Black Hawks Swung from Poles." The Mankato press relayed that even after the remaining black prisoners were finally secured by the Minnesota National Guard, several carloads of Duluth lynchers drove to Virginia, Minnesota, the day following the lynchings to get their hands on the remaining black circus workers who were imprisoned at the Virginia jail.

The Mankato newspaper reported Duluth's reaction to the lynchings: "Negresses employed as ushers in several Duluth theatres have been replaced by white girls and negro shoe shiners by whites." Acting Chief of Police Louis Osborne of Superior, Wisconsin, stated, "We are going to run all idle Negroes out of Superior and they're going to stay out." African Americans who were working at the carnival in Superior at the time of the Duluth lynchings were immediately discharged and told to get out of the city. The area's response to the murder of three innocent young men was to punish any African American who lived or worked in the general area.

An editorial was written in the *Mankato Daily Free* Press on June 18, 1920, telling the people of Duluth that there should be less indignation over the lynching of the African Americans and more outrage over what occurred to Irene Tusken. The newspaper told the city of Duluth that their city was not disgraced and that in a few years, "People will have forgotten the incident." The main concern in Duluth should have been the unfortunate girl, whose fate was far worse than what occurred to those young men, according to the Mankato press. "Mad dogs are shot dead without ceremony," and this happening was preferable to the poor victim being subjected to humiliating questions. The "frail" young woman in this abhorrent attack, Irene Tusken, lived to the ripe age of ninety-four.

The first newspaper report of the Ku Klux Klan in Mankato was front-page news in July 1923. Dr. W.S. Harper came to speak there, and the *Mankato Daily Free Press* stated that Harper's presentation "Spoke for Klan Talks Very Mild." Principles that the Klan advocated, according to the Mankato press, were the tenants of Christian religion, white supremacy, protection of pure womanhood and the upholding of the Constitution of the United States, and the outstanding feature of the Ku Klux Klan organization was better Americanism, with obedience to the laws of the United States. That same month, the Klan in Mankato was out in the open and organizing, with Klan organizers meeting at the end of Hickory Street. An editorial in the *Mankato Daily Free Press* noted that if it wasn't for men who believed in socialism, attempts would not be made "to stir the negro to open revolt against the United States." Below this Mankato editorial was a news report of an African American farm hand who was burned alive at a stake in the middle of a swamp for an attack on the wife of a merchant in Mississippi.

In August 1923, fiery crosses were reported being burned in the Mankato area. Klan crosses were burned on top of Pigeon Hill, located on Lake Crystal road; one witness said that he saw a crowd gathered around the cross estimated at about at two hundred. Moonshiners and bootleggers were being arrested in increasing numbers in the Mankato area. John Rumpel, a missionary of the South Baptist Church, pointed out how bad the conditions were in Mankato. Rumpel went on to tell his audience that the moral conditions in Mankato were some of the worse Rumpel had ever seen and that the Ku Klux Klan needed to remedy the situation there. It was not just morals that were an issue in Mankato, but immigration as well. Reverend E.C. Clemans from Owatonna, had a speech of his make the front page of the Mankato newspaper, proclaiming that the American Legion desired that those who teach in public elementary schools should be American citizens.

On June 16, 1920, the *Faribault Daily News* reported that Company H of the Sixth Regiment of Faribault was ordered to Duluth for guard duty due to the

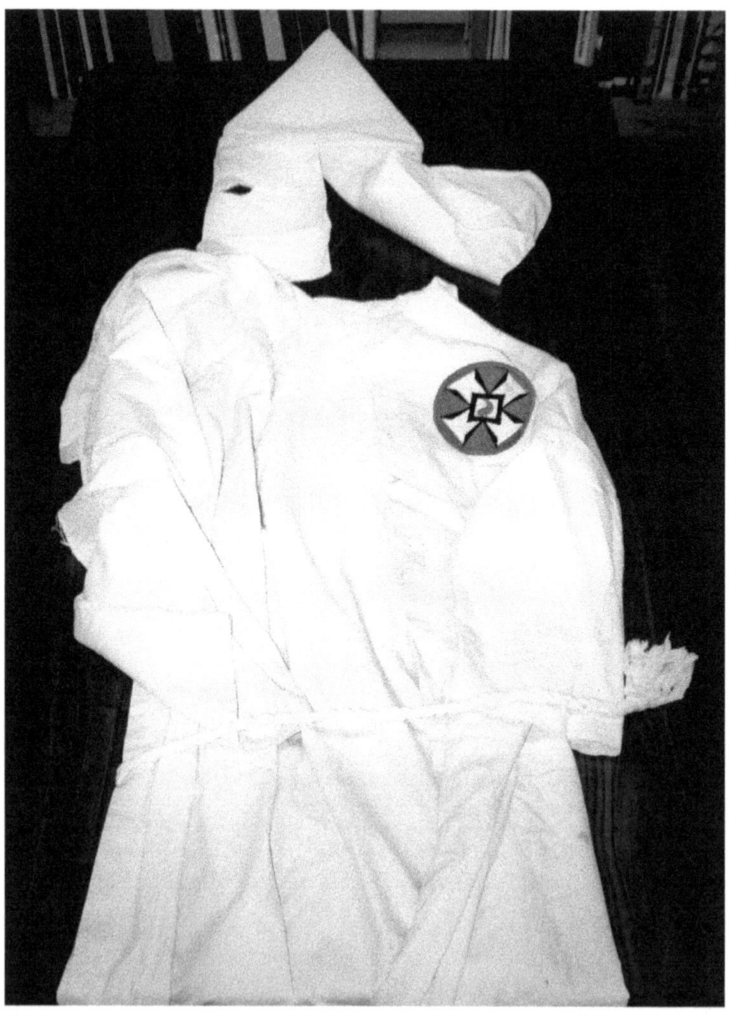

Albert Lea Klan regalia. *Courtesy of Freeborn County Historical Society.*

lynchings. A particular fact that the Clayton, Jackson, McGhie Memorial Committee had not heard about was included in the Faribault newspaper reports of the lynchings. The three young men who were lynched that awful night saved three other young African American men, also jailed, from being strung up. A mock trial was held in the jail before Clayton, Jackson and McGhie were taken out and killed. During this "trial" that night, Clayton, Jackson and McGhie said that the three other young men also being held were not responsible. The Faribault paper's description of what occurred in the jail that night was quite detailed.

The *Faribault Daily News* gave front-page coverage of the Ku Klux Klan meeting in Cannon Falls on June 26, 1923. On September, 17, 1923, the paper reported that it was now confirmed that Faribault had a Klan chapter of its own. This was verified when it was reported that a number of Klansmen from Faribault attended the initiation of four hundred candidates in Austin, Minnesota, the week previous. There had been rumors that Faribault had a Klan chapter, but the reported appearance and participation of the Faribault Klan chapter in Austin had now confirmed its existence, according to the Faribault newspaper. The *Faribault Journal* reported on August 20, 1924, on the Klan parade and meeting in Faribault, with the typical Klan parade's 8:30 p.m. start, with a large number of white-robed Klan members marching in absolute silence through the streets, followed by heading out to the fairgrounds for the Klan program of fireworks and initiations later that evening.

In Faribault, Minnesota, Mrs. Helen Simes wrote a personal letter to Stanford King "apologizing" for the current mess she was in. Mrs. Helen Simes was the Rice County District Court clerk; her husband, Robert, was the district court clerk up until his death, whereupon his wife took over the position. Robert was a World War I veteran, member of the Episcopal church in Faribault and a Mason. In 1929, the "trouble" she referred to in her letter to King was that she filed an appeal to the county board disputing how her opponent (a German Catholic) acted in the election and noting how he publicly stated that Mrs. Simes was overpaid compared to other district court clerks in Minnesota. In her letter to King, Simes wrote, "My Faribault friends did not want me to send you a check so that the story would ever get out around here." Why did a widow in Faribault need to send Stafford King money? The widow Simes told King that her Catholic brother opened her mail.[139]

Near Faribault, the headline of the *Cannon Falls Beacon* of October 2, 1925, noted, "Ku Klux Klan to Parade Here Saturday Evening." On October 13, numerous visitors were expected in Cannon Falls, invited by the local

Klan chapter. Hundreds of participants, men and women of the Ku Klux Klan of southern Minnesota, were expected. It was to be one of the largest gatherings of members of the white-robed order ever held in southern Minnesota, if not the state. The gathering was planned for the fairgrounds, with the typical Klan program. In the evening, there was a parade through the city of Cannon Falls, on Fourth Street. The imperial representative, the head of the men's organization in the state, was to be there, as was the state leader of the women's KKK organization.

The last Klan activities for Faribault were reported in November 1928 when a large fiery Klan cross was located on the bluff of the Straight River near the girls' school section of St. Mary's Hall, accompanied by two sharp charges of dynamite at about 10:30 p.m. This occurrence may have been in response to Catholic Al Smith's defeat at the hands of Herbert Hoover in the presidential election. The *Faribault Daily News* gave quite a bit of coverage to the presidential election between Smith and Hoover, with the paper noting how Smith denounced the Ku Klux Klan and the Anti-Saloon league, connecting those two organizations with the Republicans' vicious campaign against him. The burning cross set that night was most likely the Faribault Klan celebrating Herbert Hoover's 1928 presidential win over Smith.

CHAPTER 9

The End of the Klan in Minnesota

The Midwest's last Ku Klux Klan grand dragon was the mayor of St. James, Minnesota, Clyde E. McNaught, a World War I veteran and a Mason. In 1923, Dr. McNaught opened a twelve-bed hospital with an operating room at his home in St. James. McNaught served two terms as mayor of St. James. Typically, there is a lack of editorials found in rural Minnesota newspapers concerning the Klan, whose existence was too financially precarious to be risked though vitriolic newspaper crusades. This is what makes Herman Haislet and his St. James newspaper stand out to such a degree. His statements against the Klan were not vague or without substance. There is a letter between the Haislet, editor of the *St. James Independent*, and Stafford King, referring to an article that appeared in the paper about a Klan organizer visiting Haislet.[140]

The name of the organizer who came to town was H.A. Tuttle from Albert Lea, and the interview Haislet had with Tuttle was printed in Haislet's newspaper. Tuttle and Haislet "discussed" the Klan. Shortly after this interview, there was correspondence between Haislet and King that seems to be like a cat and mouse game between the two men discussing the Klan. Considering Haislet's coverage of the KKK in his area, he may have just been feeling King out to see if rumors he may have heard about King were true or not. Stafford King knew other people in St. James. There was a letter sent to Stafford King from Louis Rabe, marked "personal." Rabe, a World War I veteran, was an employee at a St. James Catholic-owned car dealership; his wedding announcement shows that Rabe was not a Catholic, though. Rabe pointed out how he was a 40 & 8 member, writing to King that they need to help their friend George Higgins, district court clerk of the county of Watonwan.[141]

Editor Haislet made a particular point of covering Clyde E. McNaught's activities in his newspaper. There were seventy-eight newspaper KKK articles from the *St. James Independent* dating from 1922 to 1925; that's an awful lot of coverage. The St. James Klan leader also performed abortions for extra cash, and in February 1926, McNaught was out on bond after being arrested upon complaint of the county attorney—a young woman was confined at the local hospital due to an infection after having signed an affidavit giving a detailed account of an abortion. Haislet also had a running battle with the *St. James Plaindealer*'s editor, making a strong implication in his newspaper articles that the editor, Will Curtis, was a Klan member. Curtis was the editor from 1908 until his death in 1926. McNaught's loudest opponent, Haislet, sold the *St. James Independent* in 1926. James McNaught ran to be St. James's mayor in 1928 and won.

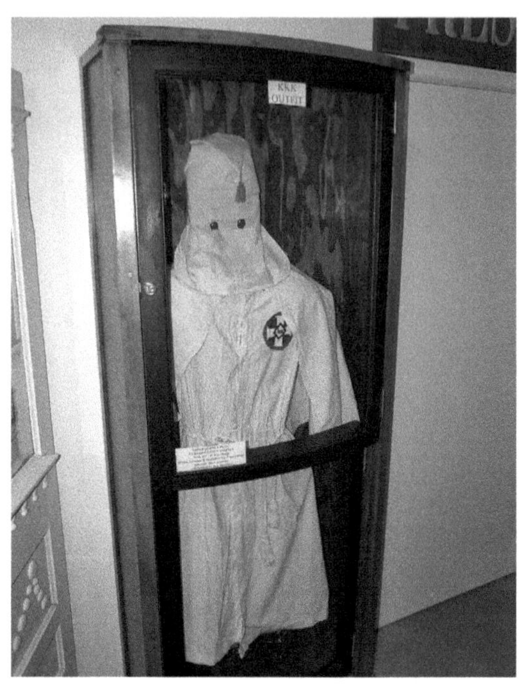

St. James Klan regalia. *Courtesy of St. James Historical Society.*

Mr. Haislet continued to live in his St. James home until his death on February 3, 1942, with a front-row seat seeing McNaught's rise to political power in St. James, with his old newspaper now an ardent supporter of McNaught. The local newspaper now stated that McNaught had many friends in the city, and McNaught's Klan connections were no longer mentioned. McNaught later went on to become the KKK grand dragon for the Dakotas, Minnesota and Wisconsin in 1930. As Klan strength declined, the North and South Dakota organizations were merged with the Minnesota Realm. The Tri-State Klan Realm was perpetuated for a time, but by the middle of the 1930s, the north-central Klan was dead, and McNaught had moved to St. Paul, Minnesota. Minnesota was one of the last states in the Midwest to give up on the Ku Klux Klan.

Mabel Willebrandt received on August 29, 1921, her appointment as assistant attorney general of the United States from Warren Harding, assigned to prohibition enforcement. The Catholic Al Smith blasted the Ku Klux Klan, the Republican Party and Mabel Willebrandt for turning his Catholic faith into a political issue in his bid for the presidency against Herbert Hoover in 1928. No speaker before church groups was as much in demand as Willebrandt, and she stirred up religious prejudices with her direct appeal to Protestant churches to align Protestant forces against Smith, who replied to these attacks by saying, "The world knows no greater mockery than the use of the blazing cross, the cross upon which Christ died, as a symbol to instill into the hearts of men a hatred of their brethren, while Christ preached and died for the love and brotherhood of man." Representative Walter H. Newton, native Minnesotan, head of the Speakers' Bureau of the Republican National Committee, admitted that Willebrandt's popularity topped all others and that her services were in great demand in "every part of the Middle West."

In Willebrandt's book, she wrote about the killing of a Minnesotan from International Falls on June 8, 1929, during which prohibition officers "had to do only, what they had to do," according to her. If Henry Wirkkula had been mistakenly killed by a policeman for a possible burglary, there would not had been such an outcry, according to Willebrandt, but because "Virkula" (as the papers named him) was mistakenly shot by a prohibition officer, that made it overemphasized in the press.[142] Henry "Virkula's" real name was Gus Henry Wirkkula. His death certificate notes, "Gun shot wounds from a 12 gauge Remington riot shotgun, held in the hands of one Emmett White instantaneous."[143] Emmett J. White had shot at Wirkkula's car several inches too high, killing the father of two little girls. White was indicted by the State of Minnesota for second-degree murder, but the federal government had the case transferred to its own courts. Emmett J. White used what was then called a "riot rifle," which was in reality a sawed-off shotgun. Mrs. Wirkkula stated that her husband was shot while slowing his car down to obey the command to stop. No liquor was found in the Wirkkula car.

Wirkkula was a Big Fork restaurant owner and the father of two little girls, nine years old and seven years old. The newspaper in International Falls described the feelings during the trial of the prohibition officer as being extremely tense. N.A. Linderberg, assistant collector of customs, said that White was justified in firing on the Wirkkula car when it failed to stop immediately. National protests were heard from across the county reacting to the Minnesota case, noting that prohibition laws were not paramount to the protection of the average citizen. Duluth congressman William Alvin Pittenger said, "If prohibition can only be enforced by use of sawed-off shotguns in the hands of irresponsible government agents then indeed we have reached the high tide of fanaticism and bigotry in this matter." Reverend Edward Malmquist, pastor of the Methodist church in International Falls, supported the shooting, saying, "If the city had better behaving and more law abiding citizens, patrolmen would not be necessary in the area." President Hoover deplored the "dry deaths" taking place at the hands of prohibition agents and limited the type of firearms to be used by border custom agents to revolvers after Wirkkula's death.

Stafford King was born in Fairhaven, Minnesota, in 1893 and was a civilian aide to the secretary of war, an American Legion national vice-commander, a state commander and department adjutant and a grand chef of the 40 & 8/Voitures. King was also a member of the Freemasons of St. Paul and Osman Temple and a member of the Royal Order of Jesters. He died in 1970, and his personal papers were restricted and closed until 1987. The duties of the Minnesota state auditor, which King was for several decades, meant that he had oversight responsibility for all units of local government, including counties, cities, townships, school districts, fire relief association pension funds and housing and redevelopment authorities. King was in a perfect position to monitor Minnesota's political pulse and its voters.

Stafford King tried to weld together a motley assortment for his own political gain during a confused time in Minnesota politics in which three political parties were vying for power. Through his "bookkeeping" technique of belonging to as many organizations as he did, King developed a following that kept him in the public eye for more than thirty years in Minnesota. His numerous scrapbooks testify to his varying memberships, with scores of cards to different organizations, including his Klan membership card. King followed up careful calculations with action: a complimentary letter here, a mild disengagement there, a letter of recommendation to this man, an appearance at one strategic meeting and a meaningful absence from another. No one knew better than King which types of votes each Minnesota county commanded or the strength of any local political, religious or ethnic opposition with which he might have to deal.

King described himself as a "faithful" Methodist and probably thought that enough time had passed with his election to the state auditor's office in 1931, combined with his American Legion accomplishments, to make him a viable candidate for governor. King was lulled into a false sense of security, though, as the Klan charges against him had not died and gone away. In the *St. Paul Press*, an editorial was written titled, "That Stafford King Smear." At a political rally for King, a shirt (or perhaps a Klan robe or hood) was "waved before the Negro voters just prior to the campaign." The editorial went on to say that the paper did not know whether Stafford King ever "flirted" with the Ku Klux Klan. In 1938, the Levine Printing Company had printed for Al Erickson a large poster bringing up again the *Midway News* articles suggesting that Stafford King had belonged to the Klan. As Mr. Erickson trumped in his ad, "This Challenge still stands and it has never been properly refuted."[144]

King couldn't let his dreams of being governor die and decided to run against Youngdahl for the Republican nomination in 1947. When asked by one reporter, King neither denied nor affirmed the charge that he was once a member of the Ku Klux Klan. The 1920s *Midway News* articles came to public attention again. Even though the editor of the *Midway News*, the late James H. Burns, posted a surety bond of any sum for King to disapprove Burns's report, and with members of the American Legion offering King the services of attorneys to bring charges against the editor, King never did. The *Midway News* also noted that King wouldn't start any court action fighting this charge in St. Paul because it would result in bringing "prominent business men who are members of the Klan into court under subpoena." King could not respond any better in the 1940s than he did in the 1920s as to why he did not take the editor of the *Midway News* to court for libel.[145]

King made another try for governor in 1952. He ran against Elmer Anderson for the Republican nomination. In Anderson's biography, *A Man's Reach*, there is absolutely no mention at all made of Stafford King. Neither man got the 1952 nomination, although in Anderson's next try to be governor, he was elected. King's repeated attempts at governor seem desperate. Claude Efnor, the publisher and editor of the *Northwest Industrial News*, wrote to King telling him that it was time for King to "strike out at your enemies. They never hesitated to try to assassinate your character and career." Just going out to shake hands was not enough—King couldn't shake enough hands to win, Efnor said. King was referred to as a "perennial candidate" who always wanted to be governor.

Mower County News reported on September 26, 1926, "William Allen White, who tried to banish the Ku Klux Klan from Kansas, is on another campaign now. He wants to junk the county form of government in Kansas." The Kansas county government system was similar to that in Minnesota.

White proposed to have county commissioners be elected at large for county government instead of elected by geographical units. "Herman Roe of the *Northfield News* has advanced an idea along the same line." Control of county governments by Klan members typically meant stricter enforcement of the vice laws. Having county commissions elected at large would eliminate county governments being loaded up with local Klan members. Minnesota had counties in which offices were held by Klan members. Roe must have recognized that this is exactly what was happening in his county government, where there was a strong Klan presence in the Northfield area.

When Stafford King made his attempt to run for the Republican nomination for governor in 1948, Herman Roe did not support him, but his brother, Ludwig Roe, did. Ludwig became state chairman of the King volunteer committee, supporting King for the nomination against Governor Youngdahl. Herman had come out condemning the Ku Klux Klan starting in 1924, stating that the Klan exerted its influence on Northfield elections. "There is danger to every community in playing with fire like the Klux Klan, to permit the injection into a peaceful and self-respecting atmosphere any influence so through contrary to what all must recognize as primary precepts of fair play." Ludwig had supported King when all the Ku Klux Klan claims were being made against King in 1924. Herman Roe's feelings on King running for governor are clear in his editorial: "It is unfortunate that he chose to file."[146]

Edward J. Thye, from Northfield, Minnesota, was the state's twenty-sixth governor and a World War I veteran. In a letter from October 15, 1946, between Governor Edward J. Thye and Rabbi Irving Miller of the American Jewish Congress, Thye noted, "In reply to your letter of October 7 in which you ask that Ku Klux Klan activities in this state be searched out and investigated, with appropriate court proceedings to revoke any charters or license granted by state officials to this organization or its counties, I am glad to be able to say that an inspection of the official records of the state has failed to reveal any license or charter granted by the State of Minnesota to the Ku Klux Klan." Actually, Thye did not do this or even look into Rabbi Miller's request. Minnesota Ku Klux Klan chapters stayed on the Minnesota corporation books until 1996.

By setting up nonprofits, it was possible for the Klan not to pay any taxes, and having a state-incorporated charter kept the Klan leaders from being sued personally for damages. In Kansas in 1925, the "Charter Board rejected the Klan's applications there, because there were no provisions in Kansas statutes for 'mystic' corporations." Republican Mike Holm was Minnesota

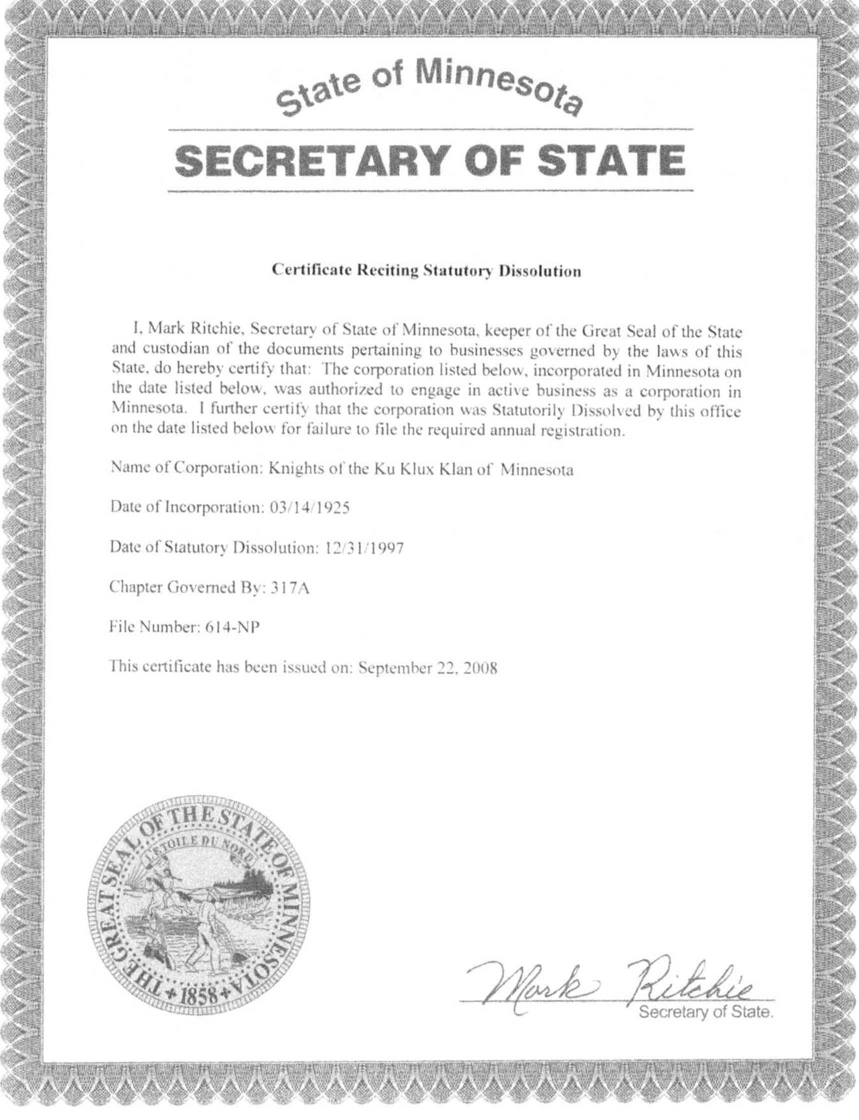
State of Minnesota

SECRETARY OF STATE

Certificate Reciting Statutory Dissolution

I, Mark Ritchie, Secretary of State of Minnesota, keeper of the Great Seal of the State and custodian of the documents pertaining to businesses governed by the laws of this State, do hereby certify that: The corporation listed below, incorporated in Minnesota on the date listed below, was authorized to engage in active business as a corporation in Minnesota. I further certify that the corporation was Statutorily Dissolved by this office on the date listed below for failure to file the required annual registration.

Name of Corporation: Knights of the Ku Klux Klan of Minnesota

Date of Incorporation: 03/14/1925

Date of Statutory Dissolution: 12/31/1997

Chapter Governed By: 317A

File Number: 614-NP

This certificate has been issued on: September 22, 2008

Mark Ritchie
Secretary of State.

This page and next: Klan dissolutions of 1997. *Courtesy of Minnesota Secretary of State's Office.*

secretary of state from 1921 to 1952. Kansas did not allow the KKK to even incorporate in the state in the 1920s. Wisconsin didn't stop Klan chapters from incorporating like Kansas had, but it did make a public and conscious effort to remove its incorporated Klan chapters from its books in the 1940s. Unlike Kansas, Minnesota did not prevent Klan chapters from incorporating

State of Minnesota

SECRETARY OF STATE

Certificate Reciting Statutory Dissolution

I, Mark Ritchie, Secretary of State of Minnesota, keeper of the Great Seal of the State and custodian of the documents pertaining to businesses governed by the laws of this State, do hereby certify that: The corporation listed below, incorporated in Minnesota on the date listed below, was authorized to engage in active business as a corporation in Minnesota. I further certify that the corporation was Statutorily Dissolved by this office on the date listed below for failure to file the required annual registration.

Name of Corporation: Holding Company of the Ku Klux Klan of Steele County, Minnesota

Date of Incorporation: 03/03/1927

Date of Statutory Dissolution: 12/31/1997

Chapter Governed By: 317A

File Number: 892-NP

This certificate has been issued on: September 22, 2008

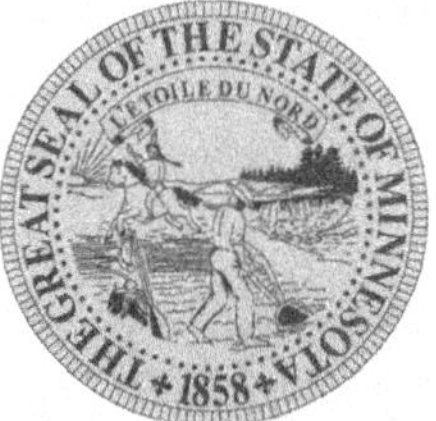

Mark Ritchie
Secretary of State.

in this state and, unlike Wisconsin, did not remove Klan nonprofits from the state corporate files until the late 1990s.[147]

Minnesota had a direct connection to the Silver Shirts (active in the 1920s and 1930s), established by William Dudley Pelley, son of a Methodist minister. The Silver Shirts group was a political vehicle established to promote anti-Semitic beliefs. Sylvester P. Ehr, born in 1903 in Moose Lake, Minnesota, moved with his family to Portland, Oregon, in 1924. His father, John Her, was a hardware and lumberyard owner in Moose Lake. John had come into conflict

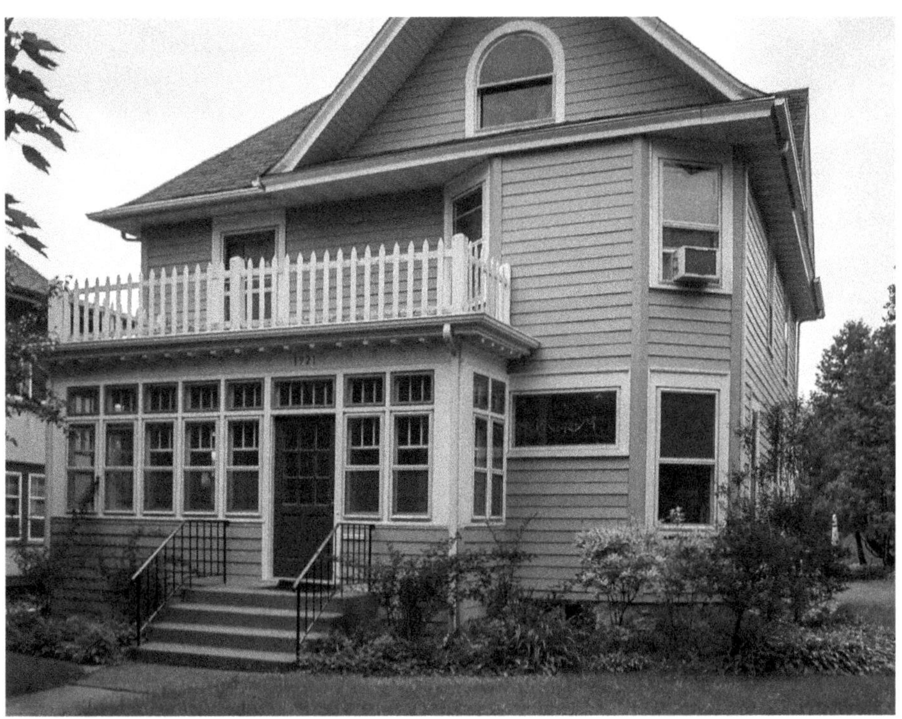

Reverend Ambrose's parsonage house, St. Paul, Minnesota. *Courtesy of Kevin B. Hatle.*

with his business partner Frank Bloomquist and was described as a man who was "always more or less nervous" and often "blew his top." Sylvester Ehr was later active in the Sheriff's Posse Comitatus in Oregon in the 1970s. Ehr, a sign painter, displaced Henry Lamont Beach as a leader of the Multnomah County Posse in Oregon.[148]

In 1923, Presbyterian reverend F. Halsey Ambrose spoke to the North Dakota legislature to block the passage of an anti-masking law. Ambrose, the Grand Forks North Dakota Ku Klux Klan leader, appeared regularly at Moorhead Klan events. In 1926, Reverend Ambrose was considered one of the great orators of the Midwest, according to the *Moorhead Country Press*, and brought in thousands to hear his lectures, such as "The Unadulterated American," "Why the Klan" and "The Word Beneath the Bark." Ambrose moved to Minnesota in 1930 and became minster of Merriam Park Presbyterian Church in St. Paul from 1932 to 1934, leaving for Clinton, Iowa, in 1935. Clinton is where the American Protective Association (APA), an extremist anti-Catholic organization, was founded. The APA was seen as the link between the Klan and Know-Nothingism; accounts of the methods of the APA might easily be mistaken for accounts of the Klan.[149]

The lawsuit brought against Charles Babcock in 1935 by John Regan had the latter accusing the former that an arbitrary set of rules was set for the highway department enabling a few contractors to monopolize the highway construction in Minnesota. The building of the highway system back in the 1920s had federal, state and local money pouring into states. Indiana's KKK grand dragon David Stephenson made it one of his main priorities to politically restructure the highway commission in Indiana so that he would be in a position to sell patronage and have influence in that state's expanding road-building program. After the lengthy Babcock lawsuit, contractors were compelled to return nearly $400,000 to the state through court action. When Floyd B. Olson took office as governor, he contacted Highway Commissioner Babcock to set forth future regulations to govern the assigning of highway contracts.

Alleging price fixing, in collusion with construction companies, was the charge brought against the Minnesota Highway Department. This lawsuit, long in the making, was among many lawsuits filed against Babcock, but the Regan lawsuit made it to the Minnesota Supreme Court. The construction companies involved in the suit were those favored by Babcock. It was uncovered in the lawsuit that closed meetings were held by the Minnesota Highway Department to decide who was going to bid the lowest, but the work wasn't actually done at the lowest bid. Regan pointed out how there were no public mentions made in the newspapers about whom highway contracts were awarded to. Later in his first term as governor, Olson released Babcock as head of the highway department. In Babcock's *Minneapolis Journal* obituary, it is reported that those who received the contracts from Babcock were receiving 21 percent over what the actual jobs should have cost.[150]

Ray Chase went though a brutal process to be the Republican nominee for governor in 1930. Chase ran on "law and order" as his campaign platform, charging that Floyd Olson had failed to push vigorous criminal investigations and had allowed lawbreakers to escape prosecution. Chase pulled out all the stops in an attempt to personally smear the reputation of the popular Olson. Chase reached out to Stafford King for help (calling him "Staff") during the governor campaign. Chase was upset about receiving a letter from a prominent man in Minnesota and told King that there was a "situation" in Winnebago with which he needed help. Chase was told that leading members of the American Legion in Winnebago were opposed to him being elected governor. Chase asked King to "take care of it for him." Chase lost the governor race and served as a Republican U.S. congressman from 1933 to 1934.

Chase voted to repeal prohibition, but in the 1930s, when he came into contact with those who did not want prohibition repealed, he was willing to use "dry" votes against the Democrats. Chase wrote to a Mr. Kerman telling him that he did not want to "inject the prohibition question" into the campaign, but there was then and always would be temperance enthusiasts whom the Minnesota Republican Party could exploit. Chase pointed out how the Republicans in the state could place responsibility for the repeal of prohibition on the Democrats, "utilizing channels reaching to the Drys and not to the Wets." In 1932, Chase received a letter from the ministers of the Evangelical Lutheran Augustana Synod arguing that the Eighteenth Amendment should be retained, and a lawyer wrote to Chase about his record as a "dry" (both political and personal). Chase put all the blame on the Farmer-Labor Party for the repeal of the Eighteenth amendment, even though Chase himself voted to repeal the Volstead Act.[151]

Another political causality involving Minnesota Klan connections is Earle Brown, who ran for governor of Minnesota against Olson in the 1930s. Brown's campaign manager issued a speech noting that "[f]antastic means devised to tear down Mr. Brown's character and popularity include charging him with membership in the Ku Klux Klan." Brown's work was deliberately distorted and maliciously publicized, but the Brown's campaign never did categorically deny that he was a Klan member. There is correspondence in Floyd Olsen's campaign manager's files noting that during Brown's run against Olson for governor, some ethnic communities pointed out Earle Brown's KKK activities to the Olson campaign. The *St. Paul Pioneer Press* reported on October 7, 1932, that Brown had publicly admitted that he joined hands with the Ku Klux Klan when he was sheriff to "spy" on the organization. "It remained for Floyd B. Olson, then county attorney of Hennepin county, without the assistance of Mr. Brown, to accomplish the only prosecution and conviction in the United States of this infamous organization."[152]

Brown was a member of the Sons of the American Revolution and had a second home on the East Coast, where instead of playing "farmer" as he did in Minnesota, he played country squire. In 1935, the Browns bought the historic Jonathan Elkin's Tavern in Peacham, Vermont, as their summer home. Brown restored the home to its Revolutionary War period styling. Stafford King tried to find a Son of the American Revolution connection for himself, and in September 3, 1929, he wrote, "Frankly I am not a genealogy bug, but I do realize that we come from probably one of the purest lines of Americans in the county and I would like to know more about them." H.H. Pratt, using

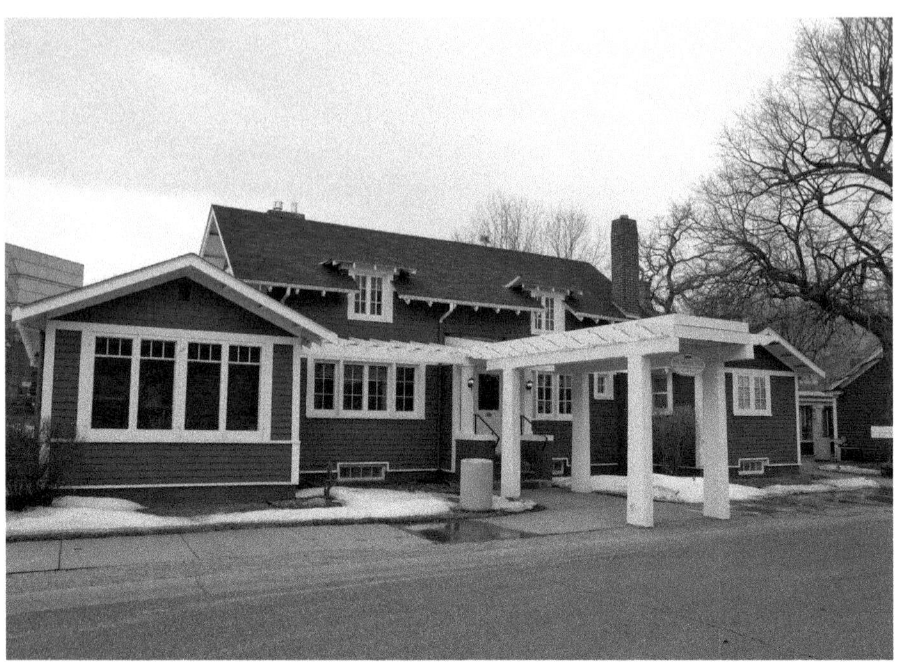

Earle Brown's farmhouse. *Courtesy of Kevin B. Hatle.*

information that King's mother had, pointed out to King that there was no mention made of Revolutionary War service in his family line. Stafford King was unsuccessful joining the Sons of the American Revolution.[153]

Charles Babcock was looking to establish a Minnesota Highway Patrol Department and wanted Earle Brown to be put in charge of it. When the highway patrol was established and Brown placed in charge, he later used the patrol to "help" break the farmers' strike. Barbara Cyrus worked at Sears in St. Paul in the mid-1930s and recalled when a group of men came into Sears on Harley Davidson motorcycles. Barbara remembered what type of motorcycles they were because she went out into the parking lot not wanting to wait on the men and saw a group of all the same type of motorcycles—the kind that Earle Brown had purchased for the Minnesota Highway Patrol to use. The men who came into Sears the Saturday before Easter Sunday were all wearing black leather jackets with large white "KKK" letters on the back of each jacket. Who else may have had a motorcycle "gang" back then, all riding the same type of motorcycles, except for the Minnesota Highway Patrol?[154]

Barbara Cyrus enrolled at the University of Minnesota in 1937, commuting to school from her home because there wasn't any housing for African

American college students at the University of Minnesota. Barbara's father was a waiter at the Curtis Hotel, and she said that after her family bought a home, the real estate agent "directed" her father to certain Minneapolis neighborhoods where it would be better to buy. Neighbors circulated a petition in an attempt to force Barbara's family to move out, people threw burning rags onto their porch and chased Barbara and her siblings home from school. In the 1920s, the National Association of Real Estate Board helped launch a series of textbooks on real estate that became the bibles of the profession, and these books noted that "certain racial types...diminish the value of other property in the section."

After Earle Brown retired from public life, childless, he spent his remaining years negotiating with the University of Minnesota about donating his large estate to the university. Brown was emphatic in not wanting his estate used for scholarships, according to W.L. Nunn, director of University Relations. Brown said, "There are too many people going to college anyway," calling certain parts of the educational program at the university that led to liberal arts degrees "academic rubbish." Also involved in these negotiations was Mahlon Babcock, who was Brown's lawyer and the executor of his estate. Mahlon, son of Charles Babcock, was also Earle Brown's office manager from 1944 until Brown's death in 1963. Mahlon is referred to facetiously by University of Minnesota officials as "Mahlon Babcock, the son of the 'father of the Minnesota Highway System.'" John Regan had accused Charles Babcock of having a nepotism-based relationship with Earle Brown, whose position in the department as chief of the highway patrol was held open for him to take back (and this he did after losing the governor's race). Brown went back to work for Charles Babcock, and his son, Mahlon, went to work for Brown.

Another "problem" when deciding what to do with the Earle Brown "farm" involved Mrs. Philip Van Blom and Mrs. William E. Cratic. During most of 1954 and 1955, Van Blom and Cratic were, according to Mahlon Babcock, making "first class nuisances" of themselves trying to get the regents to issue a public proclamation that no part of the Earle Brown gift would be sold to anybody other than an open occupancy developer. Mrs. Van Blom even involved the Mayor's Council on Human Relations, the Minnesota Jewish Council, the Minneapolis Urban League, the Anti-Defamation League of B'nai B'rith and the NAACP. Did Brown request restrictions to keep African Americans or immigrants (and likely Jewish residents as well) from building homes on his farm after he died?[155]

David Stephenson was the Ku Klux Klan grand dragon of Indiana and at one time a rising star in the organization. Before this, Stephenson was a salesman for a manufacturing company that made and sold typesetting machines and printing equipment. Stephenson joined the Klan primarily to organize a political power base, and his first connection with the Klan stemmed from his efforts to make a niche for himself in local politics. He was appointed by Hiram Evans in 1923 as grand dragon of Indiana. Earlier, Evans had appointed Stephenson king kleagle of Kentucky, Maine, Michigan, Minnesota, New Jersey, Ohio and Wisconsin. The future Indiana Ku Klux Klan grand dragon was stationed at Fort Snelling during World War I. Also stationed there with Stephenson at the same time was Stafford King.[156]

Stephenson's arrest for rape and sentencing to prison in 1925 precipitated a decline in the Ku Klux Klan's national popularity, but not in Minnesota. Minnesota continued Klan activities and chapters beyond 1930. The Stephenson arrest in the rape and later death of a female acquaintance did not break the back of local klaverns in Minnesota. The state was even Stephenson's chosen location to flee to after he was released from prison. Investigators found Stephenson there, working in a print shop in Robbinsdale, Minnesota. He was arrested on November 15, 1950, for parole violation. The Minnesota Supreme Court ordered Stephenson sent back to Indiana to be returned to prison.[157]

One disturbing thing learned when interviewing Chris Milow was that G. Fred Anderson never left the Fairmont area. Anderson, Klan representative for Martin County, was still in Fairmont in 1932 and running for political office in the county. There is a political cartoon in the *Fairmont Daily Sentinel* captioned, "Strange Bedfellows Again" on the front page of the local paper. The cartoon shows G. Fred Anderson and Leo A. Milow in bed together. Strange bedfellows indeed, as both men were running for political office at the same time. As author David Chalmers stated in his book, this was proof that the Klan movement was still strong in Minnesota in 1930 and maybe beyond. It also explained Governor Olson regularly visiting Martin County and Leo Milow for political insight into the rural Minnesota Klan during his governor campaigns.

In 1934, Andrew Volstead wrote a letter to the author of a biography of Wayne Wheeler in which Wheeler received most of the credit for prohibition going into effect. Volstead very bluntly asked the author if the reason for sending him his book about Wheeler was to get Volstead's approval or denial of the question of who authored the National Prohibition Act. Volstead said that he took sections out of Mr. Wheeler's bill to use, but Volstead's bill also "contained many radical changes." Volstead said that what Wheeler attempted to do was to weld a number of statutes against alcohol from different states into a bill; instead, Volstead "devised a scheme" that would fit into federal law and federal conditions and be air-tight. According to Volstead, no one who knew the facts would hesitate to ascribe to Volstead authorship of the prohibition bill. Volstead ended his four-page letter to Wheeler's biographer with, "This is not for publication."[158]

After Thomas Schall was elected, Arthur Jacobs was thrown to the wolves and put in state court, facing Magnus Johnson on libel charges. Convicting Jacobs made the trail clear for Schall being seated as a senator because everything that Magnus Johnson said Schall was guilty of could instead be put onto Jacobs. Jacobs was Jewish, and his parents were Russian immigrants. Jacobs continued working in Minnesota politics, but no longer for the Republicans. Jacobs grew to have a considerable reputation as a lobbyist, and in the 1937 session, Jacobs became secretary to Democratic Speaker Barker. In 1939, Jacobs died of cancer of the spine. It was a who's who of the Democratic Party that attended Jacobs's funeral, and one obituary called Jacobs a "Political Storm Figure," referring to his book *The Tinhorn*, a "thinly disguised expose of Minnesota politics."

Schall's right-hand man, Laughlin, personally went to Olson in 1930 to tell him that Schall had evidence linking Olson to certain unsavory elements in Minneapolis during his tenure as prosecutor and that if Olson did not stop speaking publicly for Senator Schall's rival, Einar Hoidale, this evidence would be turned over to the news media. Laughlin admitted later that there was very little hard evidence, but he had suggested to Olson that some could be "manufactured with little difficulty." At first, it looked as if Hoidale had won the Senate race, but at the last minute, the final tabulations from St. Louis County came in. This gave the election to Schall, and Laughlin commented that he had the impression that Schall knew more about what was going on in St. Louis County than anyone else in the organization. Still, Laughlin had absolutely no evidence to substantiate his suspicion. Like Magnus Johnson, Einar Hoidale filed a complaint with the Senate Committee against Schall.

When I interviewed Professor George Daniel Harden, who knew James Laughlin personally, he said that Laughlin had told Harden that Schall was very calm that election night. Laughlin said that this was not typical behavior for Schall when waiting for elections results—almost as if Schall knew that those needed votes were coming from St. Louis County and would win him the race. Laughlin said that Schall did not keep his staff completely in the loop with everything he was doing out there. Harden did not think that it would be strange if Schall had worked with Klan chapters in the state to gather votes. Votes were votes as far as Schall was concerned, Harden

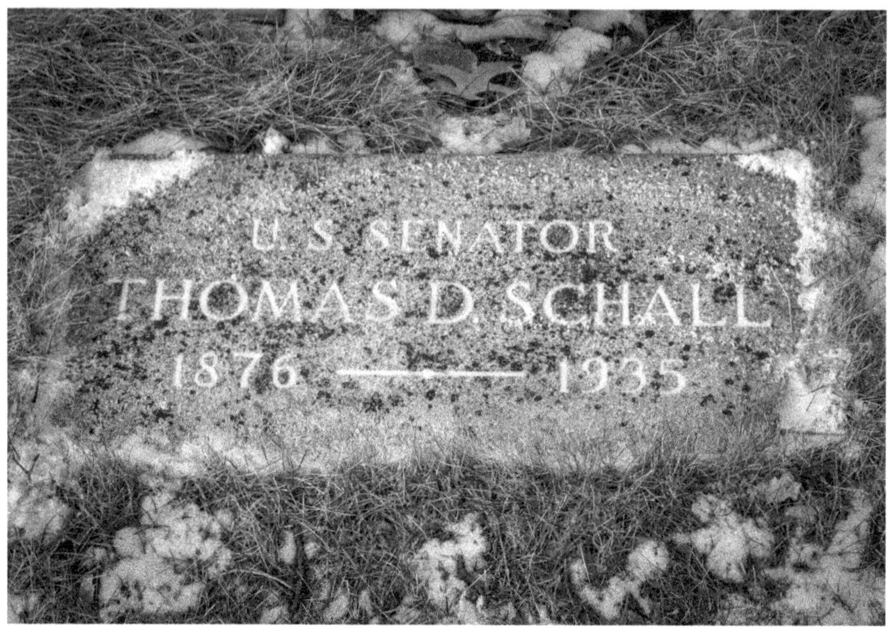

Thomas Schall's grave site, Lakewood Cemetery, Minnesota. *Courtesy of Kevin B. Hatle.*

said, and Schall didn't care where they came from. Laughlin told Harden that they didn't have "a damn thing on Olson." But Olson never stood at a podium or was seen with Hoidale in public again. Laughlin told Harden that Hoidale never could figure out what happened.[159]

Jacobs would not be the last reporter whom Republican senator Thomas Schall would use for nefarious political purposes. Journalist Walter Liggett became another pawn. Thomas Schall personally paid for Liggett's apartment, likely in exchange for numerous negative articles that Liggett wrote about Olson. Liggett was later found shot to death in an alley; his murderer was never found.[160] Jacobs at least got out alive, though not professionally unscathed, from his association with Schall. Schall was hit by a car in December 1935, dying at the age of fifty-eight. W.I. Norton and Andrew Rahn attended his funeral. Margaret Schall did not choose to be by her husband's side in death at Lakewood Cemetery; she moved with her oldest son, Thomas Schall Jr., to New Mexico, where she died in 1955 and is buried.

Periods of social turbulence are often accompanied by the emergence of hate groups. History is full of politicians who scapegoat minority groups, particularly religious sects and the economically disadvantaged, setting up

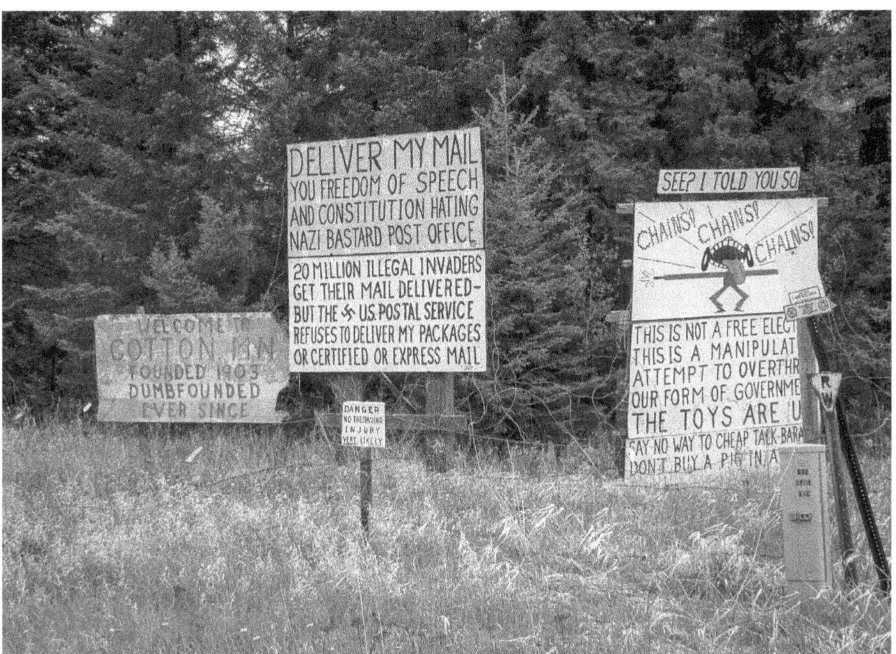

Hate billboards, northern Minnesota, 2012. *Courtesy of Kevin B. Hatle.*

a siege mentality to gain political power. The second wave of the Ku Klux Klan based its platform on stereotypes—if you weren't a true American, you were anti-American. The burning Klan cross terrorized generations and haunted the American consciousness for more than a century. Communities as well as individuals can be afflicted with irrational behavior, and this is what the Ku Klux Klan appealed to and used as a lever for recruitment.

The Klan recognized that prejudice could be a powerful force in American politics. Klan members or Klan-minded individuals said that they were defending the Constitution and the American way of life by belonging to or supporting the KKK. The Klan used hectoring, innuendo and dirty tricks, taking a bully's delight in the ruin of people. The Southern Poverty Law Center in 2012 listed twelve hate groups in Minnesota, and the state ranked higher in number of hate groups than Wisconsin, Iowa, Kansas, Nebraska, North Dakota and South Dakota. More sophisticated versions of some Klan methods are often used by some political groups today. A truthful history about our historical differences is needed. As Minnesota poet Bill Holm wrote, "Only the dead are pure—and then, only in memory, never in fact."[161]

APPENDIX

Minnesota Klan Chapters

1. Aitkin County Klan
Noted by William Durham in an e-mail, November 24, 2011, Brainerd, Minnesota.

2. Albert Lea Klan
Noted by the *Red Wing Republican*, September 21, 1923.

3. Austin Klan
Noted by the *Minneapolis Journal*, September 1923.

4. Becker County Klan
Noted by the *Masonic Observer*, June 7, 1924.

5. Blackduck County Klan
Noted by William Durham in an e-mail, November 24, 2011, Brainerd, Minnesota.

6. Boyd Ku Klux Klan
Noted by Fred Eckardt, who remembered that his father belonged to the Boyd KKK chapter in Lac qui Parle County.

7. Brainerd County Klan
Noted by William Durham in an e-mail, November 24, 2011, Brainerd, Minnesota.

8. Canby Klan
Noted by the *Faribault Daily News*, September 17, 1923.

9. Cannon Falls Klan
Noted by the *Cannon Falls Beacon*, October 2, 1925.

10. Chapter of the Ku Klux Klan organized at the University of Minnesota
Noted by the *Winona Republican*, January 16, 1923, and the *Grand Forks Herald*, January 14, 1923.

11. Clay County Klan
Noted by the *Clay County Historical Newsletter*, March/April 2006.

12. Cook County
Noted by the *Duluth Rip-Saw*, June 7, 1924.

13. Cottonwood County Klan
Noted by the *Citizen*, April 22, 1925.

14. Dakota County Knights of the Ku Klux Klan
Identified by Minnesota grand dragon Kettering in a letter to Governor Christianson, August 27, 1925.

15. Dickinson County Klan
Noted by the *Jackson Republic*, July 18, 1924, "Pres. Church Visited by Ku Klux Klan" ("At the close of the sermon, representatives of the Ku Klux Klan of Clay, Emmet and Dickinson counties…").

16. Dodge Center Ku Klux Klan
Noted by the *National Observer*, November 11, 1924, "Charters Given to Five Klan Bodies on Tuesday"; the *Owatonna Journal-Chronicle*, October 1, 1926; and the *Minneapolis Journal*, October 1, 1926. Five Ku Klux Klan chapters in this section of Minnesota received their charters at a Klan session held at the Firemen's Hall on a Tuesday evening that was attended by eight hundred people, according to local Klan leaders. These included the units of Steele County, Waseca, Kenyon, Dodge Center and Rochester. And if Owatonna and Northfield had a Women's KKK (WKKK) chapter, why wouldn't these other identified Minnesota KKK chapters not also have WKKK chapters. That could possibly double the number of Minnesota KKK members.

Maggie Lee from Northfield said that her father was a Klan member, and her mother was asked to join the WKKK in that city.

17. Douglas County Klan
Noted by the *Masonic Observer*, June 7, 1924.

18. Duluth Klan
Due to Virginia and Hibbing being in the same county, they were hotbeds of Klan activity and had their own Klan chapters. They each had separate floats for their cities in the Owatonna KKK parade, as noted in photos at the Minnesota Historical Society, St. Paul, Minnesota, in a graphic by Ouradnick Studio of a Steele County demonstration in 1925.

19. Ellendale vicinity Ku Klux Klan
Noted by the *Ellendale Eagle*, January 8, 1926, "Klan Holds Meeting Here" ("Members of the Ku Klux Klan of the Ellendale vicinity…").

20. Emmet County Klan
Noted by the *Jackson Republic*, July 18, 1924.

21. Fergus Falls Klan
Noted by the *Masonic Observer*, June 7, 1924.

22. Grant County Klan
Noted by the *Masonic Observer*, June 7, 1924.

23. Itasca Klan
Noted by the *Call of the North*, October 1923.

24. Kenyon Ku Klux Klan

25. Lakefield Klan
Noted by the *Lakefield Standard*, July 3, 1924.

26. Martin County Klan
Noted by the *Fairmont Sentinel*, February 24, 1929.

27. Montevideo Klan
Noted by the *Faribault Daily News*, September 17, 1923.

28. Northfield Klan of Rice County
Noted by the *Northfield Independent*, September 9, 1926, and the *Northfield News*, May 30, 1924.

29. North Star Klan No. 2 of Minneapolis
Noted by the *Winona Republican*, May 29, 1923. Additionally, Nos. 1, 3, 4, 5, 6, 7, 8, 9 and 10 of Minneapolis and the suburban Klans of Excelsior, Hopkins, Wayzata, St. Louis Park and Robbinsdale, as noted in *Voices of the Knights of the Ku Klux Klan*, published on April, 10, 1923.

30. Otisco Klan-Waseca County
Noted by the *New Richland Star*, October 1926; December 23, 1927; January 13, 1928.

31. Otter Tail County Klan
Noted by William Durham in an e-mail, November 24, 2011, Brainerd, Minnesota, plus the *Masonic Observer*, June 7, 1924.

32. Paynesville Ku Klux Klan
Indicated by a seal/stamper held by the Paynesville Historical Society No. 51. Paynesville is still in Stearns County, so it had its own chapter as well. So there were two chapters in Stearns, one named after the county, and the other after town in the county.

33. Pine River County Klan
Noted by William Durham in an e-mail, November 24, 2011, Brainerd, Minnesota, and the *Pine River Journal*, October 29, 1926.

34. Pipestone Klan
Noted by the *Faribault Daily News*, September 17, 1923, and the *Call of the North*, October 15, 1923.

35. Preston Klan
Noted by the *Faribault Daily News*, September 17, 1923.

36. Rochester Ku Klux Klan

37. Rushford Klan
Noted by the *Faribault Daily News*, September 17, 1923.

38. Spring Lake Klan
Noted by the *Faribault Daily News*, September 17, 1923.

39. Stearns County Klan No. 7
Noted by the *St. Cloud Journal Press*, January 18, 1923.

40. Steele Ku Klux Klan Chapter No. 11
Indicated by an Owatonna Women's Chapter of the KKK No. 12 banner.

41. St. Paul Klan
Noted by the *Midway News*, February 26, 1927.

42. Todd County Klan
Noted by the *Masonic Observer*, June 7, 1924.

43. Virginia Klan
Noted by the *Duluth Rip-Saw*, June 7, 1924.

44. Wadena County Klan
Noted by the *Masonic Observer*, June 7, 1924.

45. Waseca Ku Klux Klan

46. Watonwan County Knights of the Ku Klux Klan
Noted by the *St. James Independent*, May 13, 1926.

47. Wilkin County Klan
Noted by the *Masonic Observer*, June 7, 1924.

48. Worthington/Nobles County Klan
Noted by the *Nobles County Times*, August 21, 1924.

49. Zumbrota Klan
Noted by the *Faribault Daily News*, September 17, 1923.

Notes

Chapter 1

1. *Glencoe Enterprise*, July 19, 1917, 1.
2. *Lester Prairie News*, December 6, 1917, 1, 8.
3. Muller and Hofmann, *William Pfaender*.
4. *Princeton Union*, March, 25, 1920, 1.
5. Hubert, *Voices from the Past*, 20.
6. *Lamberton Star*, October 21, 1920, 1.
7. *Northern Legionnaire* 2, no.1 (November 1921): front page.
8. *Duluth Herald*, August 19, 1922, front page; *Redwood Gazette*, August 23, 1922, front page.
9. Chrislock, *Watchdog of Loyalty*, 317–18.
10. Ibid.
11. Chase Papers, Box 37, 1918–19 file.
12. Dean, "Did Townley Have a Fair Trial?"
13. *Lamberton Star*, March 24, 1921, front page.
14. *Redwood Gazette*, September 13, 1922, front page.
15. *Redwood Gazette*, June 8, 1921, front page; *Redwood Gazette*, September 6, 1922.
16. *Lamberton Star*, August 26, 1920; September 2, 1920; April 13, 1921; April 28, 1922, front page.
17. *Lamberton Star*, October 7, 1920, front page.
18. *Northfield Independent*, September 6, 1926, front page.
19. *Northfield News*, December 21, 1928, 6.

20. *On the Square* corporate records, 1917–18, March–April 1918 file; Smelker, *Putting Up Loyalty*; Teigan Collection, exposé of Fred Carpenter and Andrew Rahn.
21. Gimmestad, *Legion 50*, 56.
22. Pritchett, *History of the American Legion*, 58.
23. Millikan, *Union Against Unions*, 201.

CHAPTER 2

24. *Indianapolis News*, February 4, 1949, 21; *Indianapolis News*, "Son's Defense of a Klansman," April 13, 1965, 12; *Indiana Biography Series*, vol. 34.
25. *Masonic Observer*, August 11, 1923, 3; April 5, 1924, 3; June 21, 1924, 3; August 16, 1924, 3; September, 13, 1924, 5.
26. King Papers, Box 2, 1924 file, letters written by Z.L. Begin and B.D. Grogan.
27. Bessler, *Legacy of Violence*, 188.
28. Carl Hammerberg died shortly after being released at the age of twenty-one in 1924; cause was noted as "accidental means asphyxiation by gas."
29. Interview with Warren Read, May 31, 2011.
30. Duluth lynchings of 1920, selected materials, 1920–76, Subject Prisoners, Minnesota Historical Society.
31. *Duluth Herald*, July 1, 1922, front page; 1925 and 1926 rosters of the Duluth Ku Klux Klan, Welch Papers.
32. Taylor, "John Quincy Adams."
33. State of Minnesota, County of Ramsey, *In the Matter of the Inquisition*.
34. *St. Paul Pioneer Press*, February 5, 1931, 1; *St. Paul Dispatch*, February 5, 1931, 1; *St. Paul Pioneer Press*, February 12, 1931, 1; *St. Paul Dispatch*, February 13, 1931, 3.
35. St. Paul Telephone Book, 1922.
36. See Christenson, *Christian Center Inc.*
37. *Waseca Herald*, September 10, 1924, front page; *Waseca Herald*, September 17, 1924; *Waseca Herald*, June 11, 1925.
38. *Waseca Journal*, September 19, 1923, front page.
39. Furlow Papers, Prohibition file.
40. *Northfield Independent*, September 9, 1926, front page; Christianson Papers, Box 114 and Box 118, Prohibition files.
41. Christianson Papers, Box 117, Prohibition file, 1928.
42. Ku Klux Klan ceremonial sword found by and donated by Mrs. Ralph Plaisted from Wright County in March 1969, available at Minnesota Historical Society.
43. Booth, *Mad Mullah of America*, 130; Dowling Papers, NCWC, General Education Papers, Box 2, letter from Ryan to Dowling telling him his bishop has released him to work for Dowling, January 13, 1921.

44. Dowling Papers, NCWC, General Education Papers, Box 2, Bills-Swift-Shepherd Towner Bill (letter handwritten by Archbishop Dowling); Dowling Papers, NCWC, General Education Papers, Box 2.
45. Dowling Papers, NCWC, General Education Papers, James Ryan, 1919–23, Box 3, letter October 29, 1923.
46. Dowling Papers, NCWC, May 17, 1923, Archbishop, General J-K-L file, Box 3, and NCWC, General Education Papers, James Ryan, 1919–23, Box 3.
47. Dowling Papers, NCWC, General Education Papers, Box 2, letter dated May 28, 1924. The Oregon Law 2012 banned teachers from wearing any religious dress. When the law was passed in the 1920s, it was a clear jab at Roman Catholic priests or nuns teaching in public schools. Teachers who violate this rule can be suspended or have their teaching licenses revoked.
48. Krey, *History and Other Social Studies*.
49. Dowling Papers, NCWC, General Education Papers, James Ryan, 1919–23, Box 3, date of letter November 11, 1922.
50. Whelan, *Sisters' Story*.
51. *Masonic Observer*, May 20, 1922, 5.

CHAPTER 3

52. *Masonic Observer*, September 17, 1921, front page.
53. *Masonic Observer*, October 1, 1921, front page; *Masonic Observer*, November 12, 1921.
54. *Masonic Observer*, "Ku Klux Klan Initiation," July 21, 1923, front page.
55. 1925 and 1926 rosters of the Duluth Ku Klux Klan, Welch Papers.
56. *Forum of Fargo-Moorhead*, March 7, 2009.
57. Minnesota Senate Journal, 1927, 337; Minnesota House Journal, 1927, 485, H.F. No. 837.
58. Minnesota Senate Journal, 1927, 1,383, bills of the Senate, S.F. No. 103 A.
59. *Mower County News*, January 13, 1927, 2.
60. Riley, "Bryan the Great Commoner and Christian."
61. Russell, "William Bell Riley."
62. Riley, "Anti-Evolution Bill."
63. Haycraft Papers, *Minnesota Daily*, November 19, 1926, Letter to Howard Haycraft from Riley, April 3, 1927.
64. *Mower County News*, September 23, 1927, front page.
65. Clemans, *Methodist Episcopal Church Annual Reports*, Minnesota Annual Conference Archives. Clemans was appointed Methodist presiding elder in the Duluth district in 1903 and superintendent of the Duluth District Anti-Saloon League on October 4, 1909.

66. King papers, Box 8, January 1929 file.
67. *Carleton College News Bulletin*, December, 1923, 3; *Mower County News*, May 6, 1926; *Carleton College News Bulletin*, December 1923, 3.
68. Hoob Han!, "Klan at 'Karleton.'"
69. *Moorhead County Press*, March 26, 1926, 1; *Masonic Observer*, October 11, 1924, front page.
70. *Ellendale Eagle*, February 11, 1925, front page.

CHAPTER 4

71. Interview with Randy Mills, March 19, 2010.
72. *Lakefield Standard*, "Ku Klux Klan Invaded Heron Lake—Burn Cross," September 4, 1924.
73. Thorbus, *Ku Klux Klan*, 8; interview with Earl Williams, May 24, 1954.
74. Interview with Phyllis Kahn, February 1, 2011, and February 3, 2011; interview with Arvonne Fraser, March 25, 2011.
75. North Star Klan No. 2, *Voices of the Knights*, 3.
76. *Winona Republican-Herald*, April 5, 1923, 3; Minnesota legislature, "Act Prohibiting the Public Wearing Under Certain Conditions of Masks," 181.
77. Minnesota legislature, "Act to Prevent Lynching."
78. *Northwestern Bulletin*, September 14, 1922; September 23, 1922; September 30, 1922, front page; June 16, 1923, 2; January 17, 1923; March 24, 1923; April 21, 1923, front page.
79. Christianson Papers, Box 116, NAACP file, letter from May 2, 1925, from St. Paul, Minnesota.
80. Dight, *History of the Early Stages*.
81. *Midway News*, August 23, 1924, front page.
82. Booth, *Mad Mullah of America*, chapters 14–16.
83. King Papers, Box 23, Miscellaneous file, January–April 1927, and Box 35, Miscellaneous file, 1923, 1938.
84. *St. Paul Pioneer Press*, September 13, 1932, front page; State of Minnesota Death Certificate No. 24718, cause of death was noted as "one shot wound of heart"; Ramsey County Bar Association, "Memorial to William J. Quinn"; *Winona Republican-Herald*, "Mrs. Hodge Will Sue for $300, 000," April 23, 1926, front page.
85. Chase Papers, Box 4, Harold Birkeland file.
86. Chase Papers, Box 4, Otto Diercks file; *Anoka Herald*, August 14, 21, 28, 1928; September 4, 1928, front page.

CHAPTER 5

87. Sageng Papers, Box 4, location P2645.
88. King Papers, Box 23, Miscellaneous file, July–December 1930.
89. Marlin Sigstad interview.
90. Harden, "Career of Thomas D. Schall," 67.
91. *Windom Reporter*, May 9, 1924, front page; August 13, 1924, front page.
92. Brown Papers, four boxes.
93. *Anoka Herald*, April 9, 1918, 4.
94. Chase Papers, Box 20, J.A.O. Preus file; King Papers, Box 2, 1922 file.
95. Howard, *Leaders of the Nonpartisan League*; Sageng Papers, Box 4, 1872–1963, the Agricultural Credits Act of 1923, Rural Credit System, State of Minnesota, 1926.
96. Dunn Papers, Box 1, Dunn Political and Leg file and 1934 file, general.
97. Minneapolis City Council Minutes, January 12, 1923, 768. Minneapolis Public Library, downtown Minneapolis.
98. *Masonic Observer*, April 21, 1923, 3; May 19, 1923, front page; June 9, 1923, front page.
99. *Masonic Observer*, September 22, 1923, front page.
100. Minneapolis City Council Meeting, Official Proceedings, January 12, 1923, 768; State of Minnesota, County of Hennepin, *State of Minnesota, Plaintiff v. R.N. Miner*; State of Minnesota Warrant of Commitment—Workhouse, No. 21037, Shurley J. Reichert, 1925; Governor J.A.O Preus Papers, Box No. 102, file no. 694, Ku Klux Klan, letter from Minneapolis Klan to Governor Preus, April 11, 1921; State of Minnesota Death Certificate No. 18258, Donald Grant Hughes; Stafford King Papers, Box 7, Mayor Leach file, Minnesota Reports, Cases Argued and Determined in the Supreme Court of Minnesota, April 17–June 19, 1925, such as *State v. R.M. Miner* and others, No. 23,866; Stafford King Papers, Box 15, American Legion file, 1928, Stone correspondence; *Masonic Observer*, "Brother George J. Silk of Hopkins Passes," August 30, 1924, 3.

CHAPTER 6

101. Harden, "Career of Thomas D. Schall," 35.
102. King Papers, Box 2, 1924 file; Chase Papers, Box 16, Arthur Jacobs file, and Box 3, Correspondence file, May 1925.
103. King Papers, Box 2 and Box 4, 1924–25 files; MacNider Papers, Hon. Stafford King file.
104. King Papers, Box 18, Miscellaneous Committee file, 1928.
105. King Papers, Box 15, August 15, 1928.

106. King Papers, Box 18, Legislative file, 1925.
107. Millikan, *Union Against Unions*, 336–37; Sevareid, "Reporter Tells the Truth."
108. Stafford King Papers, Box 2, December 1923 and August 1924 files.
109. MacNider Papers, Republican Service League, Iowa state file, 1924, letter to Cozad; Stafford King's KKK membership cards, No. 1233, Box 21, American Legion Speaker file, Personal file, 1924 (there are two 1924 files; the card is in the second 1924 file). Also, King was identified by the *Midway News* as belonging to the Ku Klux Klan by the identified Klan No. 1233. Clarke University has a collection of KKK membership cards identical in appearance to Stafford King's KKK membership card; *Minnesota Fiery Cross*, "Mason City Klansmen Attend Funeral Following National Emblem and Bible," April 14, 1924, 1.
110. Anonymous, *Senator from Iowa Report.*
111. Luke Boyce–Northland Information Bureau, American Legion file, October–November 1925, American Legion file, December 1925–April 1926.
112. King Papers, Boxes 2, 6 and 7.
113. "Military Justice During the War," "Baker to Reply to Charges of Army Severity," February 19, 1919, 4.
114. Hughes, *World War I Diary of James Hughes*. He was in the Fifty-fourth Pioneer Infantry, which was composed of only black soldiers.
115. Interview/e-mail exchange with Al Zdon, April 22, 2011.
116. Christianson Papers, Box 103, 1925, A–M Folders, and Box 112, 1925, A–Z Folders.

CHAPTER 7

117. Interview with Glenn Donnay, October 22, 2012.
118. Paynesville Historical Society. *Paynesville: Year 125*, 69.
119. Oral interview with Mary Bisenius, Stearns County Historical Society; *Belgrade Tribune*, January 18, 1923, front page.
120. *St. Cloud Daily Journal*, September 12, 1928, front page.
121. Interview with Fred Eckhardt, October 23, 2010.
122. Letter dated May 6, 1925, Clay County Historical Society.
123. *Minneapolis Star Tribune*, August 12, 2012.
124. Interview with Chuck Lucas, July 3, 2013. His mother, Mary Ellen Lucas, at the age of ten years old, was taken in 1926 by her father, Guy Sill, to a Klan parade in Fairmont in 1926. To his daughter, Guy Sill identified William Carver, the county sheriff, as the leader of the Martin County Klan chapter.
125. Babcock Papers, September 11, 1929; King Papers, Box 20, American Legion file, July 27, 1923; King Papers, Box 20, American Legion file, Personal file,

1922–23; July 7, 1923; July 26, 1923; King Papers, Box 9, Correspondence file, September 10, 1930.

126. King Papers, Box 29, Political Files file, 1924–27, Minnesota Republican Directory, 1924.

127. King Papers, Box 31, Political Files file, November 1930; King Papers, Box 9, Correspondence file, November 1929; King Papers, Box 29, Political Files file, February 1930.

CHAPTER 8

128. *Jackson Republic*, October 16, 1925, front page; Deed Record No. 116, "Lots 1, 2 and the South Half of Lot 3 all in Block One of Wards Addition to the Village of Fairmont, to G.F. Anderson, Trustee, September 26, 1926," Parcel ID 232810020, available at the Martin County Assessor's Office in Fairmont, Minnesota.

129. Minnesota Republican Directory, 1924.

130. *Waseca Herald*, December 13, 1934, 4; interview with Chris Milow, September 17, 2011.

131. Copy of postcard sent to Leo Milow, courtesy of Chris Milow, September 3, 1923.

132. Christianson Papers, Box 105, 1926 file, H-R, December 11, 1926.

133. Interview with Don Gorrie, October 7, 2011.

134. Janet Roeglin Bauman account, *Waseca History Notes*, April 2010; *New Richland Star*, December 23, 1927, 1; January 13, 1928, 4.

135. Wallace with Bishop, *And Justice for None.*

136. Christianson Papers, Box 113, Miscellaneous Correspondence file, 1926–30.

137. *Northfield News*, June 27, 1924, 6; interview with Maggie Lee, May 2010.

138. *Call of the North*, "Pipestone Klan Issues a Monthly," October 15, 1923, front page.

139. King Papers, Box 23, Miscellaneous file, July–December 1930; Alfred Thonet obituary, "Long-Time Member of the Knights of Columbus," *Faribault Daily News*, March 29, 1992.

CHAPTER 9

140. The *St. James Independent* newspaper is not on microfilm and can only be found at the Madelia Historical Society. *St. James Independent*, vol. 8, no. 50, November 8, 1923, 1–2; Knudson, *History of Watonwan County*; King Papers, Box 20, American Legion file, Personal file, November 23, 1923.

141. King Papers, Box 8, Personal file, October 1929; October 15, 1929; *St. James Plaindealer*, October 18, 1923, front page; King Papers, Box 31, Political Files

file, July 1930. Both Dr. C.E. McNaught's and Louis Rabe's names are on a letter of support for Stafford King and George Higgins.

142. Willebrandt, *Inside of Prohibition*, 130.

143. State of Minnesota Death Certificate No. 6895.

144. King Papers, Box 47, June 1939–42 file, volume 16; King Papers, Box 32, Political Files file, form letters, 1934.

145. *Minneapolis Spokesman*, September 10, 1948.

146. *St. Paul Pioneer Press*, "Roes Split on Politics," August 28, 1948; *Northfield News*, March 21, 1924, 18.

147. Jones, "Ku Klux Klan in Eastern Kansas"; *Winona Republican-Herald*, March 14, 1925, 8; Certificate of Involuntary Dissolution Holding Company of the Ku Klux Klan of Owatonna, No. 9813458; Certificate of Involuntary Dissolution Knights of the Ku Klux Klan of Minnesota, No. 9813222. Both dissolved on December 31, 1997, certificates available at the Minnesota secretary of state's office in St. Paul. See also Jewish Community Relations Council of Minnesota Papers, letter to Rabbi Irving Miller, American Jewish Congress, from Governor Edward J. Thye, October 15, 1946.

148. Toy, "Posse Comitatus"; Anderson, David, *Moose Lake History*.

149. St. Paul City Directory, 1932, 1933, 1934; *Merriam Park Presbyterian Church, Golden Anniversary*.

150. State of Minnesota Supreme Court, *John J. Regan et al. v. Charles M. Babcock*; *Minneapolis Journal*, November 24, 1936; Regan Papers, Robert Regan interviewed by Bruce L. Larson and Karin Theim, August 1, 1977.

151. Chase Papers, Box 20, Prohibition file, 1932–36; December 19, 1932; June 4, 1934; May 22, 1936.

152. Chase Papers, Box 5, Brown for Governor Club file, 1932; McGovern Papers, Earle Brown file, 1918–77.

153. King Papers, Box 8, September 1929 file.

154. Brown Papers, Box 1, "Gentleman Cops Take to Highways," May 25, 1930; interview with Barbara Cyrus, June 2010.

155. Brown Papers, Box 1.

156. *Complete Directory of Fort Snelling Training Camp*, Thirty-sixth Company D Infantry.

157. *Winona Republican-Herald*, November 15, 1950, 1.

158. Volstead Papers, Box 3, Folder March 1922 to 1954, letter dated February 10, 1934.

159. Interview with Professor G. Daniel Harden, April 25, 2012.

160. State of Minnesota, Death Certificate No. 22652. Cause of death noted as "homicide—gunshot wounds of chest and abdomen."

161. *Minneapolis Star Tribune*, 'Trying to Track Hate, in Minnesota and Around the Country," August 13, 2012, B1.

Bibliography

Allen J. Furlow Papers, 1925–29. Available at Minnesota Historical Society, St. Paul, Minnesota.

American Legion. *Committee Reports, Resolutions, Adopted at the First National Convention of the American Legion in Minneapolis, November 10, 11 and 14, 1919.* Available at Minnesota Historical Society, St. Paul, Minnesota.

———. *Constitution and Resolutions Adopted at Second Annual Convention Duluth, August 16, 17 and 18, 1920.* Available at Minnesota Historical Society, St. Paul, Minnesota.

Anderson, David. *Moose Lake History.* Vol. 1. Moose Lake, MN: Moose Lake Area Historical Society, 1965.

Andrew Volstead Papers. Available at Minnesota Historical Society, St. Paul, Minnesota.

Anonymous. *Senator from Iowa Report of the Committee on Privileges and Elections, 1926, Regarding the Contest of Daniel F. Steck, Smith W. Brookhart for the Seat in the United Sates Senate from the State of Iowa, Senator from Iowa Report Authorizing the Investigation of Alleged Unlawful Practices in the Election of a Senator from Iowa.* The Making of Modern Law Collection, New York City Bar. Washington, D.C.: Government Printing Office, 1926.

Asher, Howard. *The Leaders of the Nonpartisan League; Their Aims, Purposes and Records Reproduced from Original Letters and Documents; with a Letter to the Public by Senator Ole O. Sageng, J.E. Haycraft and Frank E. Reed.* Minneapolis, MN: A. Howard, 1920. Available at Minnesota Historical Society, St. Paul, Minnesota.

Bessler, John D. *Legacy of Violence: Lynch Mobs and Executions in Minnesota.* Minneapolis: University of Minnesota Press, 2003. Available at Minnesota Historical Society, St. Paul, Minnesota.

Bishop Austin Dowling Papers. St. Paul Diocese, St. Paul, Minnesota.

Bishop Thomas Welch Papers. Catholic Diocese of Duluth.

Booth, Edgar Allen. *The Mad Mullah of America.* Indianapolis, IN: Wayne Associates Publishing, 1927.

Carleton College News Bulletin, 1923–24. Available at Minnesota Historical Society, St. Paul, Minnesota.

Charles Babcock Papers. Available at Minnesota Historical Society, St. Paul, Minnesota.

Chrislock, Carl H. *Watchdog of Loyalty: The Minnesota Commission of Public Safety During World War I.* St. Paul: Minnesota Historical Society Press, 1991.

Christenson, Nellie Grant. *The Christian Center Inc., for Religious Training and Character Building Education, Founded and Directed by Joseph Walter Harris, Pastor, Memorial Baptist Church, St. Paul, Minnesota.* St. Paul, MN: Christian Center Inc., 1931. Available at Minnesota Historical Society, St. Paul, Minnesota.

Clemans, E.C. *The Methodist Episcopal Church Annual Reports, Published in the Annual Journals.* Minnesota Annual Conference Archives, United Methodist Church, Minneapolis, Minnesota.

Complete Directory of Fort Snelling Training Camp, September 11, 1917. Available at Minnesota Historical Society, St. Paul, Minnesota.

David's Sling (March 1923–25). David Wisted Post No. 28, American Legion, Duluth, Minnesota. Available at Minnesota Historical Society, St. Paul, Minnesota.

Dean, Ezra C. "Did Townley Have a Fair Trial? A Straight Forward Statement Worth Considering." Available at Minnesota Historical Society, St. Paul, Minnesota.

Dight, Charles Fremont. *History of the Early Stages of Organized Eugenics Movement of Human Betterment in Minnesota.* Minneapolis: Minnesota Eugenics Society, 1935. Available at Minnesota Historical Society, St. Paul, Minnesota.

Duluth Legion Monthly (October 1920–March 1921).

Earle Brown Papers, 1920–49. Elmer L. Anderson Library, University of Minnesota, Minneapolis/St. Paul, Minnesota.

Gimmestad, Ben. *Legion 50.* Minneapolis, MN: Ross & Haines Inc., 1970.

Governor J.A.A. Burnquist Papers. Letter from Walter White, assistant secretary of the New York NAACP, July 23, 1920, regarding the Duluth lynchings. Box 83, file no. 648C. Available at Minnesota Historical Society, St. Paul, Minnesota.

Governor J.A.O. Preus Papers, 1921–36 (bulk 1921–24). Available at Minnesota Historical Society, St. Paul, Minnesota.

Governor Theodore Christianson Papers, 1925–30. Available at Minnesota Historical Society, St. Paul, Minnesota.

Graham, Billy. *Just as I Am: The Autobiography of Billy Graham.* New York: Harper Collins Publishers, 1984.

Hanford MacNider Papers. Herbert Hoover Library.

Harden, Dr. George Daniel. "The Career of Thomas D. Schall." Master's thesis. Winona State University, 1968.

Hennepin County Legionnaire (1920–21). American Legion Posts.

Henry G. Teigan Papers, some undated and some dated 1916–41. Correspondence and other material collected by Teigan as a participant in the Farmer-Labor movement and as secretary of the National Nonpartisan League (1919–23). Available at Minnesota Historical Society, St. Paul, Minnesota.

Historical Documents Relating to the Tragic Events of June 15, 1920. An in-depth and scholarly resource of primary source materials related to the lynchings in Duluth, Minnesota, of three young black men on June 15, 1920. Available at Minnesota Historical Society, St. Paul, Minnesota.

Hoob Han! "The Klan at 'Karleton.'" December 2, 2012. www.hoobhan.com/tag/ku-klux-klan.

Hormel, James, and Erin Martin. *Fit to Serve: Reflections on a Secret Life, Private Struggle, and Public Battle to Become American's First Openly Gay U.S. Ambassador.* New York: Skyhorse Publishing Books, 2011.

Howard Haycraft Papers. Walter Anderson Library, University of Minnesota.

Hubert, Colleen. *Voices from the Past: A History of the Lamberton, Minnesota Community, 1872–97.* Redwood Falls, MN: Redwood County Historical Society, n.d.

Hughes, James Thomas. *World War I Diary of James Hughes, Prepared by Elizabeth J. Hughes, 1894–1977.* Available at Minnesota Historical Society, St. Paul, Minnesota.

Indiana Biography Series. Vol. 34. Available at Indiana State Library, Indianapolis, Indiana.

Jacobs, Arthur N. *The Tinhorn.* Minneapolis, MN: Sexton Press, 1927.

Jewish Community Relations Council of Minnesota Papers. Letter to Rabbi Irving Miller, American Jewish Congress, from Governor Edward J. Thye, October 15, 1946, Klan file. Minnesota Historical Society.

John Regan Papers. Mankato State University.

Jones, Lila Lee. "The Ku Klux Klan in Eastern Kansas during the 1920s." *Emporia State Research Studies* 23, no. 3 (Winter 1975).

Jones, Richard Seelye. *A History of the American Legion*. New York: Bobbs-Merrill Company, 1946.

Knudson, Shirley R. *A History of Watonwan County, Minnesota.* N.p.: Curtis Media Inc., 1995. Available at Watonwan Historical Society.

Krey, A.C., et al. *History and Other Social Studies in the Schools*. Report of a committee submitted to the Council of the American Historical Association, December 1926. Available at Minnesota Historical Society, St. Paul, Minnesota.

Liggett, Walter. *The Truth About Floyd B. Olson*. Pamphlet available at Minnesota Historical Society, St. Paul, Minnesota.

Luke Boyce–Northern Information Bureau. Organization records, 1909–33. Available at Minnesota Historical Society, St. Paul, Minnesota.

Mathias Koll Papers. Available at Minnesota Historical Society, St. Paul, Minnesota.

McDaniel, George William. *Smith Wildman Brookhart, Iowa's Renegade Republican.* Ames: Iowa State University Press, 1995.

Merriam Park Presbyterian Church, Golden Anniversary. St. Paul, MN: self-published, 1884–1934.

"Military Justice During the War, a Letter from the Judge Advocate General of the Army to the Secretary of War." In reply to a Request for Information. Washington, D.C.: Government Printing Office, 1919.

Millikan, William. *A Union Against Unions.* St. Paul: Minnesota Historical Society Press, 2001.

Minneapolis City Council Minutes. Minneapolis Public Library, downtown Minneapolis, Minnesota.

Minnesota House Journal, 1927. Available at Minnesota Historical Society, St. Paul, Minnesota.

Minnesota legislature. "An Act Prohibiting the Public Wearing Under Certain Conditions of Masks of Other Means of Concealment of the Identity of Persons and Prescribing Penalties for Violations Thereof." Chapter 160, H.F. No. 138, 1923. Journal of the House, State of Minnesota, 1923. Available at Minnesota Historical Society, St. Paul, Minnesota.

———. "An Act to Prevent Lynching; to Fix Indemnity for the Dependents of Any Person Lynched and to Provide for the Removal from Office of the Sheriff and Deputy Sheriff's Having Charge of Any Person Lynched." Chapter 401, H.F. No. 785, 1921.

Minnesota Senate Journals, 1927. Available at Minnesota Historical Society, St. Paul, Minnesota.

Minnesota Supreme Court. *John Regan, A.E. Morrison and Albert E. Floan, Plaintiffs, v. Charles M. Babcock.* Records available at Minnesota Historical Society, St. Paul, Minnesota.

Muller, Hans, and Annette R. Hofmann. *William Pfaender and the German American Experience.* Roseville, MN: Edinborough Press, 2009.

Nall, T. Otto, Bishop. *Forever Beginning: A History of the United Methodist Church and Her Antecedents in Minnesota to 1969.* Commission on Archives and History, Minnesota Conference of the United Methodist Church in Minnesota. Nashville, TN: Parthenon Press, 1973.

Negro Year Book (Tuskegee University). N.p.: Negro Year Book Publishing Company, 1914–46. Available at Minnesota Historical Society, St. Paul, Minnesota.

North Star Klan No. 2. *Voices of the Knights of the Ku Klux Klan* 1, no. 1–2 (February 8–April 10, 1923). Available on microfilm at Minnesota Historical Society, St. Paul, Minnesota.

Old Settlers Benefit Association of Duluth, Minnesota. Available at Minnesota Historical Society, St. Paul, Minnesota.

Ole O. Sageng Papers, 1872–1963. Available at Minnesota Historical Society, St. Paul, Minnesota.

On the Square Publishing Company corporate records. 1 box. Correspondence, legal and financial documents and reports of the publisher of *On the Square* magazine, a vehicle for a group of Minnesota businessmen to denounce socialism and the national Nonpartisan League. Available at Minnesota Historical Society, St. Paul, Minnesota.

Paynesville Historical Society. *Paynesville: Year 125, 1758–1883.* Paynesville, MN: self-published, n.d.

Pritchett, John. *History of the American Legion in Hennepin County.* St. Paul, MN: Macalester College, 1919.

Ramsey County Bar Association. "Memorial to William J. Quinn (1899–1932)." N.p.: self-published, April 15, 1933.

Ray Chase Papers. Available at Minnesota Historical Society, St. Paul, Minnesota.

Riley, Dr. William B. "The Anti-Evolution Bill Speech, March 9, 1927." Berntsen Library, Northwestern College, St. Paul, Minnesota.

———. "Bryan the Great Commoner and Christian." Sermon at First Baptist Church, August 2, 1925. Berntsen Library, Northwestern College, St. Paul, Minnesota.

Roy Dunn Papers, 1927–66. Box 1, Pelican Rapids, Otter Tail County, Minnesota. Available at Minnesota Historical Society, St. Paul, Minnesota.

Rumer, Thomas A. *The American Legion: An Official History, 1919–49.* New York: M. Evans and Company Inc., 1990.

Russell, C. Allyn. "William Bell Riley: Architect of Fundamentalism." *Minnesota History* (Spring 1972). Available at Minnesota Historical Society, St. Paul, Minnesota.

Sevareid, Eric. "A Reporter Tells the Truth about the Silver Shirts: An Exposé of Un-American Activities in Minneapolis." N.p., n.d. Available at Minnesota Historical Society, St. Paul, Minnesota.

Sigstad, Marlin. Interview on tape by Roger Benson interviewer, June 1985. Cottonwood Historical Society.

Sletterdahl, P.J. ("Twilight Orn"). *The Nightshirt in Politics: Americanism Abused.* Minneapolis, MN: Ajax Publishing Company, 1926.

Smelker, R.C. *Putting Up Loyalty: The Patriotism of the People Exploited by Political Profiteers, Documents Furnish Proof.* Pamphlet, includes telegram and letter by Andrew Rahn to F.H. Carpenter, St. Paul, Minnesota, 1918. Available at Minnesota Historical Society, St. Paul, Minnesota.

Stafford King Papers. Available at Minnesota Historical Society, St. Paul, Minnesota.

State of Minnesota, County of Hennepin. *State of Minnesota, Plaintiff s. R.N. Miner, Gladys Kennedy, Shurley Reichert, Thomas Sullivan and George Silk, Defendants, Appeal 1925.*

State of Minnesota, County of Ramsey. *In the Matter of the Inquisition on the Body of John Quincy Adams, Foreman J.E. McElligett, Coroner C.A. Ingerson, Assistant County Attorney Allen McGill.* St. Paul, MN: Ramsey County Corner's Office, September 9, 1922.

St. James Independent. Not on microfilm and can only be found at the Madelia Historical Society in Madelia, Minnesota.

St. Louis County Club and Farm Bureau Association Records. Available at Minnesota Historical Society, St. Paul, Minnesota.

St. Paul Telephone Book, 1922. Available at Ramsey County Historical Society in downtown St. Paul, Minnesota.

Sylvester McGovern Papers, 1918–77. Available at Minnesota Historical Society, St. Paul, Minnesota.

Taylor, David Vassar. "John Quincy Adams: St. Paul Editor and Black Leader." *Minnesota History* (1973).

Thorbus, Richard W. *Ku Klux Klan.* River Falls: Wisconsin State University, 1969. Minnesota County Historical Society, St. Paul, Minnesota.

Toy, Eckard. "Posse Comitatus." Oregon Encyclopedia. http://www.oregonencyclopedia.org/entry/view/posse_comitatus.

Wallace, Evelyn Fesenmaier, and Greta Bishop. *And Justice for None.* Milwaukee, WI: In Your Hands Books Publishing, 2002.
Waseca County Historical Society. *Waseca History Notes*. Monthly newsletter.
Wheat, George Seay. *The Story of the American Legion*. New York: G.P. Putnam's Sons, 1919. Available at Minnesota Historical Society, St. Paul, Minnesota.
Whelan, Sister Ellen, OSF. *The Sisters' Story: Saint Mary's Hospital/Mayo Clinic, 1889–1939.* Rochester, MN: Mayo Foundation for Medical Education and Research Publishing, 2002.
Willebrandt, Mabel Walker. *The Inside of Prohibition.* Indianapolis, IN: Current News Feature Inc., Bobbs-Merrill Company, 1929.
Wisconsin Superior Court. "Constitution, Bylaws, and Member Lists, 1922." Available at Minnesota Historical Society, St. Paul, Minnesota.

INTERVIEWS

Cyrus, Barbara. Personal interview, June 2010. Barbara died on September 23, 2011.
Donnay, Glenn. Personal interview, October 22, 2012.
Eckhardt, Fred. Personal interview, October 23, 2010.
Fraser, Arvonne. Personal interview, March 25, 2011.
Gorrie, Don. Personal interview, October 7, 2011.
Harden, G. Daniel, Professor. Personal interview, April 25, 2012.
Kahn, Phyllis. Personal interview, February 1, 2011, and February 3, 2011.
Lee, Maggie. Personal interview, May 2010, Northfield News office.
Lucas, Chuck. Personal interview, July 3, 2013.
Mills, Randy. Personal interview, March 19, 2010.
Milow, Chris. Personal interview, September 17, 2011.
Read, Warren. Personal interview, May 31, 2011.
Zdon, Al. Personal interview/e-mail exchange April 22, 2011.

Index

U

V

W

Y

Z

About the Author

Elizabeth Dorsey Hatle is a high school history teacher working in the Minneapolis school district. She is married to Kevin B. Hatle and is the mother of two sons, Andrew Dorsey Hatle and Matthew Dorsey Hatle. She is a graduate of the University of Minnesota. After an article about the Minnesota Ku Klux Klan appeared in *Minnesota History* magazine, a flood of information came to Elizabeth with even more information on this subject (people were more "comfortable" now about the skeletons in their family closets, providing additional information on this subject). There are applicable lessons from this era in Minnesota's history that can still be learned from today.

Visit us at
www.historypress.net

....

This title is also available as an e-book

www.ingramcontent.com/pod-product-compliance
Lightning Source LLC
LaVergne TN
LVHW052337100826
845147LV00020B/1089